Advanced Introduction to International Trade Law

Elgar Advanced Introductions are stimulating and thoughtful introductions to major fields in the social sciences and law, expertly written by the world's leading scholars. Designed to be accessible yet rigorous, they offer concise and lucid surveys of the substantive and policy issues associated with discrete subject areas.

The aims of the series are two-fold: to pinpoint essential principles of a particular field, and to offer insights that stimulate critical thinking. By distilling the vast and often technical corpus of information on the subject into a concise and meaningful form, the books serve as accessible introductions for undergraduate and graduate students coming to the subject for the first time. Importantly, they also develop well-informed, nuanced critiques of the field that will challenge and extend the understanding of advanced students, scholars and policy-makers.

Titles in the series include:

International Political Economy
Benjamin J. Cohen

International Conflict and Security Law
Nigel D. White

The Austrian School of Economics
Randall G. Holcombe

Comparative Constitutional Law
Mark Tushnet

Cultural Economics
Ruth Towse

International Human Rights Law
Dinah L. Shelton

Law and Development
Michael J. Trebilcock and Mariana Mota Prado

Entrepreneurship
Robert D. Hisrich

International Humanitarian Law
Robert Kolb

International Trade Law
Michael J. Trebilcock

Advanced Introduction to

International Trade Law

MICHAEL J. TREBILCOCK

Professor of Law and Economics, Faculty of Law, University of Toronto, Canada

Elgar Advanced Introductions

Cheltenham, UK • Northampton, MA, USA

Published by
Edward Elgar Publishing Limited
The Lypiatts
15 Lansdown Road
Cheltenham
Glos GL50 2JA
UK

Edward Elgar Publishing, Inc.
William Pratt House
9 Dewey Court
Northampton
Massachusetts 01060
USA

A catalogue record for this book
is available from the British Library

Library of Congress Control Number: 2014950766

ISBN 978 1 78347 159 1 (cased)
ISBN 978 1 78347 160 7 (paperback)
ISBN 978 1 78347 161 4 (eBook)

Typeset by Servis Filmsetting Ltd, Stockport, Cheshire
Printed and bound in Great Britain by T.J. International Ltd, Padstow

Contents

Preface

This revised edition of *Understanding Trade Law* (2011) is an introductory book on international trade law (principally GATT/WTO law) and builds on a 25-year-long involvement in the field. Over this period I have taught an introductory trade law course at the University of Toronto Faculty of Law and as a visitor at New York University Law School, Yale Law School, the University of Virginia Law School, and Tsinghua Law School (Beijing) – sometimes with co-teachers including my former student, former colleague and co-author Robert Howse (now at NYU Law School), Donald Macdonald, former Minister of Finance for Canada and Dr. Sylvia Ostry, former Senior Trade Negotiator for Canada. I have also authored or co-authored numerous scholarly articles on issues in international trade law and a major treatise, with Robert Howse and Antonia Eliason, *The Regulation of International Trade* (London: Routledge, 4th edition, 2013). My experience as a teacher, author, occasional policy advisor or expert witness, and media commentator in the international trade field has underscored to me the need for a short, straightforward account of the basic structure and principles of international trade law that is widely accessible to beginning students and non-specialist scholars and policy advisors. Our treatise (which now runs to 900 pages) presupposes a need or desire to invest in acquiring a sophisticated understanding of the field that is beyond what this broader readership requires. My hope in writing this book is that this broader readership, with a limited investment of time and intellectual effort, can acquire a basic understanding of the field, while recognizing that acquiring a more sophisticated understanding of the complexities of the field will require much larger investments of time and effort. In my view, the basic elements of international trade law are no more arcane or inaccessible than any other area of law.

Throughout the book, I have kept citations to relevant case law and scholarly literature to a minimum, while nevertheless providing references to basic sources that readers can pursue if they wish.

In writing this book, I have had the benefit of helpful comments on earlier drafts from anonymous reviewers and my colleague, Andrew Green, who specializes in the field, which have substantially improved the final version and for which I am greatly indebted. I am also indebted to legions of students who have challenged me constantly to render the field of international trade law both accessible and interesting to them. I am extremely grateful to my research assistant, Kristen Pue, for her help in preparing this new edition and to my assistant, Nadia Gulezko, for her endless patience and meticulousness in correcting numerous drafts of the manuscript.

1   Setting the context

1.1   Classical free trade theory

Members of different societies have traded with each other since the beginning of recorded history.[1] However, one of the first efforts to articulate a rigorous intellectual basis for the economic benefits of facilitating trade between members of different societies was made by Adam Smith. In *The Wealth of Nations*, published in 1776, Adam Smith argued that the gains that could be realized from specialization in domestic economic activity could readily be extended to international economic activity.[2]

> The tailor does not attempt to make his own shoes, but buys them off the shoemaker. The shoemaker does not attempt to make his own clothes, but employs a tailor. . . What is prudence in the conduct of every private family can scarcely be folly in that of a great kingdom. If a foreign country can supply us with a commodity cheaper than we ourselves can make it, better buy it off them with some part of the produce of our own industry, employed in a way in which we have some advantage.[3]

Smith's Theory of Absolute Advantage essentially stated that countries should export those products which they can produce more efficiently than other countries and import those products which they cannot. For example, if countries with tropical climates can produce bananas or pineapples more cheaply than countries with temperate climates,

---

1 See William J. Bernstein, *A Splendid Exchange: How Trade Shaped the World* (New York: Atlantic Monthly Press, 2008); Nayan Chanda, *Bound Together: How Traders, Preachers, Adventurers and Warriors Shaped Globalization* (Yale University Press, 2007).

2 For a comprehensive account of the intellectual history of free trade theory, see Douglas A. Irwin, *Against the Tide: An Intellectual History of Free Trade* (Princeton, NJ: Princeton University Press, 1996); Elhanan Helpman, *Understanding Global Trade* (Cambridge, MA: Belknap Press of Harvard University Press, 2011).

3 Adam Smith, *The Wealth of Nations* (1776) (reprinted New York: Modern Library Edition, 1937) at 424.

the latter should purchase these products from the former. Conversely, if countries with industrialized economies can produce hydro-electric plants or communications systems more efficiently than countries that enjoy a cost advantage in producing tropical fruit, the latter should buy these products from the former. In Smith's view, international trade is merely a means by which to broaden the division of labour by expanding the size of the market. It is important to note that, according to Smith's theory, unilateral trade liberalization would be an advantageous policy for a country to pursue. Even if other countries did not liberalize their trade policy, a country which did liberalize its trade policy could realize economic gains by importing products made more efficiently by foreigners.

It is equally easy to appreciate the force of this argument for free trade within nation states. For example, in a large federal state like the USA, Michigan specializes in producing automobiles (*inter alia*), Florida citrus fruits and tourism, Texas oil and beef, and California wine and high-technology products. If each state of the USA were to have attempted to become self-sufficient in these and all its other needs, the USA would today be immeasurably poorer.

A key question raised by Smith's Theory of Absolute Advantage is what relevance international trade has to a country that has no absolute advantage, that is, a country which cannot produce any product more efficiently than its trading partners. This question was addressed by David Ricardo's Theory of Comparative Advantage, set out in his book *The Principles of Political Economy*, published in 1817. Ricardo famously postulated the following scenario: Portugal can produce a given quantity of wine with 80 units of labour, and a given quantity of cloth with 90 units of labour. England can produce the same quantity of wine with 120 units of labour, and the same quantity of cloth with 100 units of labour. Thus, Portugal enjoys an absolute advantage over England in both wine and cloth. Ricardo argued that trade between the two countries was still mutually advantageous. England is able to export cloth which took 100 units of labour to produce in exchange for wine which it would have required 120 units of labour to produce. Similarly, Portugal, by exporting wine which it took 80 units of labour to produce, gains cloth which would have taken 90 units of labour to produce. Both countries are rendered better off through trade. Another way of understanding the same intuition is to imagine the following simple domestic example.[4] Suppose

---

4 Adapted from P. Samuelson and A. Scott, *Economics* (Toronto: McGraw-Hill, 1980) at 807.

a lawyer is not only more efficient in the provision of legal services than her secretary, but is also a more efficient secretary. It takes her secretary twice as long to type a document as it would if the lawyer typed it herself. Suppose, more specifically, that it takes the lawyer's secretary two hours to type a document that the lawyer could type in one hour, and that the secretary's hourly wage is $20, and that the lawyer's hourly rate to clients is $200. It would pay the lawyer to hire the secretary and pay her $40 to type the document in two hours while the lawyer is able to sell for $200 the hour of her time that would otherwise have been committed to typing the document. In other words, both the lawyer and the secretary gain from this exchange.

Ricardo's insight was that the crucial question is the relative or comparative advantage of one country vis-à-vis another in producing a product. In other words, the issue is not whether Portugal can produce both wine and cloth more efficiently than Britain, but rather Portugal's relative efficiency in producing cloth versus producing wine compared to Britain's relative efficiency in producing the same goods. In an international trade context, this generalizes to the proposition that a country should specialize in producing and exporting goods in which its comparative advantage is greatest, or comparative disadvantage is smallest, and should import goods in which its comparative disadvantage is greatest.

Although Ricardo's theory still constitutes the basis of conventional international trade theory, it has been refined by subsequent analysis. One deficiency in Ricardo's theory is that it assumes that countries will specialize completely in those products in which they have a comparative advantage, without taking into account the possibility of decreasing returns to scale. Hecksher and Ohlin's Factor Proportions Hypothesis recognized that most products were a function of multiple factors of production (in the case of wine, land and labour), and that combining factors of production at ever-increasing levels of output did not necessarily lead to increasing production in constant proportions. For example, bringing more land into the production of wine may result in utilizing less productive land, which requires more intensive use of labour. In recognition of these considerations, the Factor Proportions Hypothesis states that countries will tend to specialize in producing goods that use their abundant factors of production more intensively, and will import goods that use their scarce factors more intensively.

The Factor Proportions Hypothesis does not, however, provide an adequate explanation of manufacturing activities in advanced industrialized economies. Casual observation suggests that firms in different countries often specialize in different segments of the same or closely related product markets, simultaneously importing and exporting products in these sectors. The Product Cycle Theory, developed by Raymond Vernon, incorporates the idea that products undergo a variety of stages in their life cycle, and firms in different countries will specialize in their manufacture depending upon the particular stage the product is in.[5] Highly developed economies will tend to specialize in the manufacture of products in the early stages of development, where financial capital, specialized human capital and innovation are at a premium. In the later stages of the product cycle, as production technology becomes standardized, it is adopted by producers in other countries, typically countries with lower labour costs. At this point in the product cycle, comparative advantage shifts to these countries. Moreover, as is evident in the increasingly globalized production chains for many products (for example, automobiles, computers), different countries may have a comparative advantage in different stages of the production process for given products. More generally, classical theories of international trade are relatively static in nature, and did not centrally focus on dynamic factors that might shift a country's comparative advantage through time (for example, England moving beyond cloth manufacturing; Portugal moving beyond wine production) or the role that government policy may play in promoting new sources of comparative advantage – through, for example, investments in infrastructure, education, research and development, selective subsidies or trade protection – which, in turn, may intensify tensions with the countries who perceive some of these policies as a source of unfair trade.[6]

---

5 See Raymond Vernon, "International Investment and International Trade in the Product Cycle", (1966) 80:2 *Quarterly Journal of Economics* 190.

6 For a masterful review of the evolution of modern trade theory, see Elhanan Helpman, *Understanding Global Trade* (Harvard University Press, 2011). See also Justin Lin, *The Quest for Prosperity* (Princeton: Princeton University Press, 2012) and Dani Rodrik, *One Economics, Many Recipes: Globalization, Institutions, and Economic Growth* (Princeton: Princeton University Press, 2007) on dynamic conceptions of comparative advantage.

1.2   Qualifications to the case for free trade

1.2.1   Reciprocity

The development of the current international trade regime has been animated by the classical theory set out above. However, a great deal of the debate in international trade law today centers around the extent to which international trade law should permit deviations from classical theory.

A major qualification to the case for free trade is the concept of reciprocity. Recall that classical trade theory views unilateral trade liberalization as advantageous for the liberalizing country. From this perspective, the emphasis placed on reciprocity in trade liberalization commitments in the General Agreement on Tariffs and Trade (GATT) may seem anomalous.[7] However, it is clearly better for the liberalizing country if its trading partners also liberalize, since the first country will realize benefits on the export side in addition to the benefits on the import side. One strategy might be for the first country to refuse to remove any of its existing trade restrictions on imports unless its trading partners agree to do the same. This may result in a classic Prisoner's Dilemma game, whereby trading partners who recognize that it is in the first country's interests to liberalize no matter what the trading partners do will withhold concessions in the hopes of gaining the benefits of the first country's liberalization for free. The dominant strategy becomes protectionism, and such individually rational action leads to an inefficient collective outcome of restrictive trade policies.[8] Trade agreements incorporating reciprocal tariff reductions thus offer governments a means of escape from a Prisoner's Dilemma.[9]

Reciprocity is also important from a political economy stand-point. Certain domestic producer interests may oppose any governmental effort to liberalize trade policy on the import side if they are likely to be uncompetitive with foreign producers in the absence of tariffs. If it is to be politically tenable for a government to engage in such liberalization, it will likely need concessions from its trading partners on the export

7 Kyle Bagwell and Robert W. Staiger, *The Economics of the World Trading System* (Cambridge, MA: MIT Press, 2002) at 7.
8 Bernard M. Hoekman and Michel M. Kostecki, *The Political Economy of the World Trading System: The WTO and Beyond* (New York: Oxford University Press, 2001, 2nd edn) at 109.
9 Bagwell and Staiger, supra note 7 at 3.

side in order to enlist the countervailing political support of export-oriented producer interests. According to Bagwell and Staiger, one of the main functions of trade agreements is that they represent credible commitments by governments that they will not protect certain industries.[10] In summary, while the concept of reciprocity plays a marginal role in classical trade theory, it is nonetheless crucial to an understanding of the institutional arrangements that govern international trade.

1.2.2   The Optimal Tariff

A second qualification to the case for free trade is the concept of the so-called Optimal Tariff. On this theory, countries that account for a large proportion of international demand for a particular good may exercise monopsony power by imposing a tariff which effectively forces exporters from other countries to reduce the price of their products and absorb the tariff. Consumers pay the same price for the good as before, and the government gains revenue from the tariff. While arguably maximizing national welfare, these policies are likely to reduce global welfare and, if replicated by foreign countries, are also likely to reduce national welfare. Bagwell and Staiger argue that the centrality of principles of reciprocity and non-discrimination in the GATT can in part be explained as an attempt by countries (particularly larger countries) to escape from a terms-of-trade driven (non-cooperative) Prisoner's Dilemma where each country, acting unilaterally, has incentives to adopt trade policies (for example, tariffs on imports, taxes on exports) that externalize a high proportion of the costs of its trade policies onto foreigners. "Beggar-thy-neighbour" trade policies adopted by many countries during the Great Depression are often viewed as exemplifying this danger.

1.2.3   Infant industries

A third qualification relates to infant industries.[11] In the early stages of a country's economic development, a case may be made that import restrictions are justified in order to permit domestic industry to develop by selling to a protected domestic market. Ideally, such protection is temporary and the infant industry eventually develops the scale and

---

10 Bagwell and Staiger, supra note 7 at 4; see also Douglas A. Irwin, Petros C. Mavroidis, and Alan O. Sykes, *The Genesis of the GATT* (New York: Cambridge University Press, 2008), chapter 3, for a discussion of economic and political rationales for trade agreements.
11 See Irwin, supra note 2, chapter 8.

sophistication required to compete not only in a liberalized domestic market but also in international export markets. A major case in point is the "special and differential status" accorded to less-developed countries (LDCs) under the GATT, which permits them to protect domestic industries and engage in import substitution trade policies to some extent. A variant of the infant industry argument is Strategic Trade Theory, which argues that governments can assist domestic firms in establishing strategically dominant pre-emptive positions in industries where economies of scale imply that there is room for only a limited number of firms in international markets (for example, large jet airplane manufacturers), in part by maintaining entry barriers to potential foreign competitors or subsidizing domestic firms.[12]

However, the case for government-led protection and/or promotion of domestic industries may be critiqued on a number of grounds, chiefly: (i) private capital markets may be better equipped than governments to identify the long-term growth potential, if any, for an infant industry, and should thus be relied on rather than government to "pick winners"; and (ii) the vulnerability of governments to capture by rent-seeking special interests with regard to the decision to promote and sustain an infant industry through trade-restrictive policies.[13] Nevertheless, according to some commentators, a number of the high-performing East Asian economies have deployed infant-industry protection policies or strategic trade theory successfully; other developing countries much less successfully. It is also true that many currently developed countries early in their development adopted extensive infant-industry protection policies (for example, the USA, Canada, Germany).

1.2.4 Revenue raising

A fourth qualification to the case for free trade relates to the revenue-raising potential of customs duties. In industrialized countries, income, consumption, and business taxes constitute the vast majority of government revenue. However, in less developed countries with weak internal taxation systems, import and export duties are often an important source of government revenue and may be difficult to replace in the short term.

---

12 See Paul R. Krugman (ed.), *Strategic Trade Policy and the New International Economics* (Cambridge, MA: MIT Press, 1986).

13 See Robert E. Baldwin, "The Case Against Infant Industry Protection", (1969) 77:3 *Journal of Political Economy*, 295–305.

1.2.5   National security

A fifth qualification to the case for free trade relates to national security considerations. These may arise on both the import and the export sides. With respect to imports, it is often argued that there may sometimes be a case for trade restrictions in order to protect domestic industries which, even though not internationally competitive, may be required in the event of war or other international disruptions (for example, domestic steel or coastal shipping industries). On the export side, national security considerations have sometimes been invoked to restrict exports of strategically sensitive products or military material to "unfriendly" foreign countries. More generally, trade agreements are often designed to serve broader foreign policy objectives, for example greater economic integration may enhance global or regional peace and reduce the potential for military conflicts by raising the costs of such conflicts. This was clearly a major rationale for the emergence of the European Community and also seems to have been part of the motivation for the GATT.

1.2.6   Adjustment costs

A further qualification to the case for free trade relates to the adjustment costs that firms, workers, and communities may face with abrupt forms of trade liberalization and argues for gradual implementation of such policies.[14]

1.2.7   Health, safety and environmental concerns

Finally, where imports threaten the health, safety and environmental conditions of citizens in importing countries, trade restrictions may be justified to minimize these risks.

1.3   Objections to free trade

In the last decade or so, public perturbations leading up to and surrounding meetings of the World Trade Organization and other international financial institutions, in particular the World Bank and the IMF, in Seattle, Washington, Quebec City and Genoa, supported by

---

14 See Michael Trebilcock, *Dealing with Losers: The Political Economy of Policy Transitions* (Oxford: Oxford University Press, 2015), chapter 5.

a burgeoning anti-globalization literature,[15] have raised fundamental objections to free trade and economic liberalization. These objections take various forms:

a) Globalization is leading to a global mono-culture.
b) Trade liberalization exacerbates inequalities of wealth between and within countries and threatens the welfare state.
c) Trade liberalization trumps environmental, health and safety, labour standards, and human rights concerns.
d) Trade liberalization undermines economic self-sufficiency in food production and other staples, creating dangerous dependencies on foreigners.
e) The WTO is an undemocratic and unaccountable form of global government that improperly constrains domestic political sovereignty and democratic politics.

There are convincing refutations of most of these objections.[16] In particular, it needs to be emphasized that trade liberalization is likely to increase the total economic pie and average per capita incomes by increasing economic productivity but says nothing about what policies nation states should adopt to increase the productivity of citizens threatened by trade liberalization or to reduce income inequality more generally. Arguably, the capacity of states to underwrite such policies, if their citizens are so-minded, is enhanced rather than diminished by the greater wealth generated by trade liberalization. Nevertheless, popular and scholarly debates over the virtues and vices of economic globalization ensure that international trade policy has forever forsaken the quiet and obscure corners of trade diplomacy that it once occupied, and become a matter of "high politics".

---

15 See for example, Naomi Klein, *No Logo: Taking Aim at the Brand Bullies* (Toronto: Vintage Canada, 2000) and *The Shock Doctrine: The Rise of Disaster Capitalism* (Toronto: Vintage Canada, 2008); see also John Gray, *False Dawn: The Delusions of Global Capitalism* (London: Granta Books, 2002); Joseph E. Stiglitz, *Making Globalization Work* (New York: W.W. Norton & Co., 2006); Dani Rodrik, *The Globalization Paradox* (New York: W.W. Norton, 2011).

16 See Jagdish N. Bhagwati, *In Defense of Globalization* (Oxford: Oxford University Press, 2004); Philippe Legrain, *Open World: The Truth About Globalization* (London: Abacus, 2002); Martin Wolf, *Why Globalization Works* (New Haven: Yale University Press, 2004); Michael Trebilcock, "Critiquing the Critics of Economic Globalization", (2005) 1 *Journal of International Law and International Relations* 213.

1.4   Institutional history of international trade policy

While international trade policy is commonly viewed as a post-World War II phenomenon, it has in fact a much longer genesis. During the latter half of the nineteenth century, nations such as France, Germany, and Britain negotiated bilateral trade treaties amongst themselves and with other European nations. In particular, Britain's resolute commitment to the principle of free trade was reflected in its unilateral removal or reduction of hundreds of tariffs on imported goods, beginning in the mid-nineteenth century with the repeal of the Corn Laws and lasting until the early years of the twentieth century. However, a severe recession in Europe in the 1870s resulted in many countries retreating from liberalized trade. The onset of World War I and the attendant disruption in trade relations, followed by the collapse of the world economy in the Great Depression beginning in the late 1920s, prompted many countries to adopt policies of extreme protectionism. The most dramatic example of such policies was the enactment of the Smoot-Hawley Tariff by the United States Congress in 1930, which raised average duties to 60 per cent on imported goods and provoked retaliatory measures by most of the USA's trading partners. As a result of these "beggar-thy-neighbour" policies, international trade ground to a virtual standstill. Although the US Congress signaled a shift in policy by passing the Reciprocal Trade Agreements Act in 1934, which gave the President authority to negotiate bilateral trade agreements, the outbreak of World War II shattered any hope of renewed international trade. As World War II wound down, post-war planners set their minds to the task of reconstructing the world economy after the war. As part of the Bretton Woods Agreement in 1944, they proposed the formation of the International Trade Organization (ITO) to oversee a new multilateral system of liberalized international trade (along with the IMF to stabilize international exchange rates and the World Bank to provide development assistance). However, the ITO never came into existence due to strong opposition to it from the US Congress, which feared that the ITO would encroach excessively on domestic sovereignty. Instead, a provisional agreement negotiated in 1947 amongst 23 major trading countries as a prelude to the ITO, the General Agreement on Tariffs and Trade (GATT), became by default the permanent institutional basis for today's world trade regime, now comprising of about 160 nations.[17]

---

17 See Irwin, Mavroidis, and Sykes, supra note 10.

Under the GATT, nine "rounds" of negotiations have now been undertaken. The first six of these rounds, up to and including the Kennedy Round which concluded in 1967, focused mainly on reciprocal reductions in tariffs on manufactured goods.[18] More recent rounds, including the Tokyo Round ending in 1979 and the Uruguay Round ending in 1993, have increasingly focused on non-tariff barriers to trade, such as government procurement policies, subsidy policies, customs valuations policies, health and safety and technical standards. From an institutional perspective, the Uruguay Round was particularly important in that it resulted in the creation of the World Trade Organization (WTO), the overarching governing body that had been missing from the world trade regime since the failure to create the ITO.

Recent developments in the GATT/WTO system have seen increasing strains being placed upon the world trade regime by a multitude of factors, including the dramatic increase in the number of members in very different states of development. In addition, the inclusion of several new issues in trade negotiations that had previously been considered outside the ambit of the GATT, such as foreign investment, intellectual property, and trade in services, has entailed a greater focus on domestic policy divergences as potential distortions of international trade, and thus raised concerns about the degree to which GATT/WTO commitments on these issues may excessively constrain domestic sovereignty. Contentious issues such as trade in agricultural products, which had previously largely escaped GATT discipline, are now also being addressed. As well, developing countries have shown an increased willingness to form coalitions in order to advance their collective interests during negotiations, as exemplified by the formation of the "Group of 20" voting block of developing countries at the 2003 Cancun Ministerial meetings of the current Doha Round (launched in 2001).

1.5   Governance and dispute settlement in the WTO

The governance structure of the WTO system comprises the Ministerial Conference that meets every two years, a General Council comprised of delegates of all member countries and its various committees, the Secretariat headed by the Director-General who is

---

18 The success of these rounds is reflected in the fact that average world tariffs on manufactured goods have dropped from more than 40 per cent in 1947 to about 5 per cent today.

appointed by consensus of the member states, and the quasi-judicial dispute settlement body.

The Agreement Establishing the World Trade Organization ("WTO Agreement") sets out various provisions for adjusting GATT commitments over time.[19] Article X:1 of the WTO Agreement requires that any proposal to amend a WTO Agreement must be tabled for a minimum of 90 days before the agreement can be amended. Amendments to WTO agreements are voted on by the Ministerial Conference of the WTO. Article X:2 sets out specific provisions of WTO Agreements that can only be amended by unanimous agreement of all members. All other provisions can be amended by a two-thirds majority of the Ministerial Conference; however, such amendments are only binding on the members who have voted in favour of the amendment (Article X:3). This feature of the WTO Agreement is subject to Article X:5, which stipulates that the Ministerial Conference may decide by a three-fourths majority that an amendment is of such a nature that any member which has not accepted it within a period specified by the Ministerial Conference in each case shall be free to withdraw from the WTO or to remain a member with the consent of the Ministerial Conference. Article IX:2 grants exclusive authority to the Ministerial Conference and the General Council to adopt authoritative, binding interpretations of the various WTO Agreements, provided that the proposed interpretation receives the support of three-fourths of the members. Finally, Article IX:3 of the WTO Agreement provides that in exceptional circumstances, the Ministerial Conference may decide to waive a WTO obligation of a member, provided that any such decision shall be taken by three-fourths of the members. Despite these formal voting rules, the convention has developed by most decisions being taken by "consensus" (meaning the absence of explicit objections).

With respect to specific disputes between members (which it must be emphasized are governments, not private parties), Article XXII of the GATT imposes an obligation on members to accord sympathetic

19 For recent reviews of institutional challenges facing the WTO, see Report of the Consultative Board to the Director-General of the WTO (2004), *The Future of the WTO: Addressing Institutional Challenges in the New Millennium*; Debra P. Steger, "The Future of the WTO: The Case for Institutional Reform", (2009) 12 *Journal of International Economic Law* 803; more generally, Debra P. Steger (ed.), *Redesigning the World Trade Organization for the Twenty-first Century* (Ontario: Wilfrid Laurier University Press, 2010); Tomer Broude, *International Governance in the WTO: Judicial Boundaries and Political Capitulation* (London: Cameron May, 2004).

consideration to complaints of other parties and adequate opportunity for consultation with such parties. If the members cannot resolve a dispute through mutual negotiations, perhaps assisted by mediation of a third party, including the Director-General of the GATT or his or her staff, the dispute must then be addressed within the framework of Article XXIII, now substantially elaborated on in the Uruguay Round Understanding on Rules and Procedures Governing the Settlement of Disputes. Under this Article, if a member considers that any benefit accruing to it directly or indirectly under the GATT is being "nullified or impaired" by a policy or practice of another member, the complaining member can refer its complaint to the members as a group (the General Council of the WTO acting as the dispute-settlement body), which will appoint a panel to investigate the complaint and make recommendations to the Council for resolution of the dispute. Panels typically comprise three individuals acting in their personal capacities, drawn from countries other than the disputing parties, who meet privately with the disputing parties to ascertain the facts and the precise nature of the allegations, and if possible to resolve the dispute informally. If this is not possible, the Panel will make recommendations to the Council as to the resolution of the matter. The Council makes decisions on Panel recommendations on a negative consensus basis, requiring consensus in favour of rejection of the Panel's recommendations (which would require the support of the prevailing country before the Panel, which means in practice that adoption of Panel decisions is automatic). Under the Dispute Settlement Understanding, Panel decisions may now be appealed on matters of law to a standing Appellate Body of seven members (sitting in panels of three), whose decisions are subject to a similar negative consensus adoption rule in the WTO Council. If the Council adopts the recommendations of the Panel or the Appellate Body, then a member is required to modify or withdraw its policy or practice to bring itself into conformity with the Council's decision. If it fails to do so, the Council may authorize retaliatory action by the aggrieved member in the form of suspension of trade concessions or other obligations of equivalent value, the level of which is subject to arbitration in the event of disputes over the equivalence of proposed retaliatory measures. The dispute settlement regime under the GATT has evolved significantly since the genesis of the GATT in 1947, from relatively informal diplomatic forms of conciliation toward much more formal and binding forms of quasi-judicial adjudication. This has led to vigorous contemporary debates over whether the quasi-judicial arms of the GATT (now the WTO) have become too powerful relative to the political organs of the WTO and whether various forms of institutional rebalancing are warranted.[20]

1.6   Preferential trade agreements

Running parallel with the evolution of the multilateral trading system under the GATT in the post-war period has been another institutional development of considerable significance – the rise of preferential trading blocks. Approximately 300 preferential trade agreements were in force as of 2010, an increase from the 70 that came into force between 1948 and 1990.[21] The most important of these arrangements is the European Union, which began in 1957 under the Treaty of Rome with six initial members and has now expanded to twenty-eight members (with other countries negotiating accession). Another such arrangement of considerable significance is the North American Free Trade Agreement (NAFTA) between the USA, Canada and Mexico, which was entered into in 1992. Other regional trading blocks have emerged in Latin America (MERCOSUR), the Caribbean (CARICOM), Asia (ASEAN) and Eastern and Southern Africa (COMESA), and others are currently under negotiation. Such arrangements are permitted under Article XXIV of the GATT provided that they meet two conditions: a) trade restrictions are eliminated with respect to most trade between the member countries; and b) customs duties shall not be higher thereafter than the duties prevailing on average throughout the constituent territories prior to the formation of the regional trading agreement. Article XXIV contemplates two different kinds of regional trading agreements: a free trade agreement, which leaves the contracting parties free to adopt their own trade and tariff policies with respect to the rest of the world, and a customs union, which involves not only liberalization of trade between the member countries but also requires that these countries adopt a common external tariff with regard to other countries. In these terms, the EU is a customs union while NAFTA is a free trade area.

In considering institutional arrangements to promote regional economic integration, it is useful to think of an integration continuum.

20 See Joost Pauwelyn, "The Transformation of World Trade", (2005) 104:1 *Michigan Law Review* 1; Steger, supra note 19.

21 Michael Trebilcock, Robert Howse, and Antonia Eliason, *The Regulation of International Trade*, 4th edn (London: Routledge, 2013), 83.

First, there are free trade areas (like NAFTA), where two or more countries agree to remove border restrictions on goods amongst themselves, but each reserves the right to maintain whatever external trade policy it wishes with respect to non-member countries. A particular problem raised by this kind of arrangement is importation of goods through low tariff member countries and trans-shipment to higher tariff member countries, which can only be resolved with complex rules of origin that typically specify the extent of the product transformation or value-added required to have been undertaken in a country in order for a product to qualify as having originated in that country. Second, there are customs unions where, in addition to removing border restrictions on trade and goods among member countries, member countries also agree to harmonize their external trade policies vis-à-vis non-member countries. Third, there are common markets or economic unions, like the European Union, where – in addition to removing border restrictions on trade in goods among member countries and harmonizing external trade policy – free movement of services, capital and people, as well as perhaps a common monetary policy and currency, might be contemplated. Fourth, there are federalist structures, like the USA, Canada, Australia, and Germany, where economic units form a single state, with the central government being vested with dominant jurisdiction over economic functions, but with some agreed division of economic powers between the central and sub-national levels of government, with constitutional or other arrangements designed to guarantee internal free movement of goods, services, capital, and people, and minimization of internal barriers to trade. Finally, there are unitary states where, over a given geographic region, one government, to all intents and purposes – with some exceptions for local governments – possesses exclusive jurisdiction over all significant economic functions, so that problems of inter-governmental coordination of economic policies within the geographic area are eliminated.

While some analysts believe that preferential trading blocks and the multilateral system can be viewed as complementary and mutually reinforcing, other analysts consider them as inherently discriminatory and a major threat to the future stability and integrity of the multilateral system.[22]

---

22 See for example, Jagdish Bhagwati, *Termites in the Trading System* (New York: Oxford University Press, 2008); Razeen Sally, *New Frontiers in Free Trade: Globalization's Future and Asia's Rising Role* (Washington, D.C.: Cato Institute, 2008), chapter 5.

1.7   Overview of the substantive provisions of the GATT/WTO

1.7.1   Tariffs

Under Article XXVIII bis of the GATT, members commit themselves to entering into periodic negotiations on a reciprocal and mutually advantageous basis, directed to the substantial reduction in the general level of tariffs. Once tariff concessions are agreed to in a particular set of negotiations, these become "tariff bindings", which are set out in particular members' tariff schedules that constitute an Annex to the GATT. By virtue of Article II of the GATT, all members must adhere to these tariff bindings by not imposing customs duties in excess of those set forth in each country's schedule. Article XXVIII of the GATT permits members to renegotiate their GATT tariff commitments periodically. Every three years, members may enter into negotiations with other concerned members to modify or withdraw tariff concessions previously made (Article XXVIII:1). Such negotiations must include provisions for compensating concessions to affected parties and must seek to maintain a general level of reciprocal and mutually advantageous concessions not less favourable to trade than that existing prior to such negotiations (Article XXVIII:2).

In terms of the domestic administration of tariffs (or customs duties), Article VII of the GATT requires that the value for customs purposes of imported merchandise should be based on its "actual value", a definition that has been elaborated on subsequently in a special Customs Valuation Code. Similarly, most members have agreed to harmonize their systems of customs classifications to reduce room for ambiguity or debate as to the proper tariff classification of a particular good. Finally, Article VIII of the GATT restricts the imposition of fees or charges related to the administrative processing of inbound goods to the approximate cost of services rendered.

1.7.2   Quantitative restrictions

Article XI prohibits the use of quotas or import or export restrictions on the importation or exportation of goods into or out of any member state, reflecting the theory that if barriers to trade were expressed solely in the form of tariffs, the relative transparency of tariffs relative to quotas and other forms of quantitative restrictions would make possible their reduction over time through periodic negotiating rounds. However, there are a number of important exceptions to Article XI. First, Article XI itself contains important exceptions pertaining to restrictions on agricultural trade. Second, Articles XII and XVIII permit members to impose quotas if they are experiencing balance of payment problems, and in the case of Article XVIII, if a developing country wishes to protect an infant industry. Third, since the 1980s there have been a number of bilateral "Voluntary" Export Restraint Agreements (VEAs) negotiated in clear violation of Article XI and usually under threat of unilateral action by the importing country. However, the Agreement on Safeguards negotiated during the Uruguay Round now largely prohibits the use of VEAs. A prime example of such a voluntary export agreement is the Multi-fibre Arrangement (MFA) governing trade in clothing and textiles. The Uruguay Round Agreement on Textiles and Clothing provides for the gradual removal of the quantitative restrictions provided for under the MFA.

1.7.3   Non-discrimination

The principle of non-discrimination – often viewed as the cornerstone of the GATT – is referred to in the Preamble to the Agreement and is amplified in two key provisions: Article I, adopting the Most Favoured Nation (MFN) Principle; and Article III, adopting the National Treatment Principle. Under Article I of the GATT (MFN), with respect to customs duties or charges of any kind imposed by any country on any other member country, any advantage, favour, privilege, or immunity granted by such country to any product originating in any other country shall be accorded immediately and unconditionally to a like-product originating in the territories of all other members. Thus, notwithstanding that tariff concessions may be principally negotiated between country A and country B, which may be the principal suppliers and purchasers of the products in question respectively, if either country A or country B makes a binding tariff concession to the other, it must extend exactly the same concession to all other members of the GATT/WTO, without being able to demand quid pro quos as a condition of the extension of this concession, at least if these were not part of the initial negotiations. The MFN Principle is designed to constrain discrimination by members amongst different foreign exporters, that is, playing favourites among foreigners.

The National Treatment Principle, set out in Article III of the GATT, addresses another form of discrimination, namely where a member adopts internal or domestic fiscal or regulatory policies designed to favour its domestic producers vis-à-vis foreign producers of like products, even though the latter may all be treated in a uniform way. The National Treatment Principle requires that once border duties have been paid by foreign exporters, as provided for in a country's tariff schedules, no additional burdens may be imposed through internal taxes or regulations on foreign exporters where domestic producers of the like product do not bear the same burden.

With respect to both the Most Favoured Nation Principle and the National Treatment Principle, the issue of what constitutes "like products" has been the subject of a number of high profile GATT/WTO trade disputes.

1.7.4   State trading enterprises

Under Article XVII of the GATT, each member undertakes that its state trading enterprises (state-owned enterprises or private enterprises operating under state-conferred monopolies or privileges) shall, with respect to purchases or sales involving either imports or exports, act in a non-discriminatory manner and make such purchases or sales solely in accordance with commercial considerations. This provision does not apply to imports of products for immediate or ultimate consumption in governmental use and not otherwise for resale.

1.7.5   Subsidies

Government subsidies that affect international trade by artificially reducing the price of products have proven an intractable problem for the multilateral trading system. It is helpful to keep in mind a basic taxonomy of subsidy scenarios. The first scenario is where country A subsidizes its exports into country B's market. This is the scenario which has classically attracted the potential for countervailing duties under Article VI of the GATT and complementary domestic trade remedy laws. The second scenario is where country A subsidizes its exports to country C, and in so doing displaces country B's exports from country C's market. In this scenario the subsidized goods are not moving from country A to country B and thus cannot be countervailed by country B, so that country B is remitted to a complaint under the Uruguay Round Subsidies and Countervailing Measures Agreement (SCM Agreement) for resolution under the multilateral dispute resolution process. The third subsidy scenario is the case where country A is subsidizing its domestic producers to service principally country A's own domestic market, and in so doing displaces country B's exports to country A's market. Again, as in scenario two, the subsidized goods are not moving from country A to country B so as to attract possible countervailing duties in country B, so that country B is again remitted to the multilateral dispute resolution process under the SCM Agreement. This Agreement sets out detailed rules governing prohibited and actionable subsidies.

1.7.6   Government procurement

The GATT initially exempted government procurement policies from the National Treatment Principle under paragraph 8(a) of Article III. However, under the Tokyo Round Code on Government Procurement and the Uruguay Round Government Procurement Agreement the National Treatment Principle applies to government procurement practices albeit with many exceptions and qualifications for state-owned enterprises and sub-national levels of government, as well as financial thresholds for contracts to which these principles apply. Moreover, the Government Procurement Agreement is a plurilateral not multilateral agreement to which all members of the WTO are committed, and has only 28 signatories.

1.7.7   Trade remedies

Article VI of the GATT recognizes the right of members to take unilateral action under domestic trade remedy laws where domestic industries are being materially injured because of unfair foreign trading practices, specifically either subsidization (discussed above) or dumping. Dumping occurs in its most typical form where foreign producers are selling goods into another country's market at prices below those which they would normally charge in their home market. Where this pricing practice is causing material injury (or a threat thereof) to domestic producers of like products, antidumping duties in the amount of the difference between the export market price and the home market price may be imposed on the imported goods. Article VI is amplified by an antidumping code initially negotiated during the Kennedy Round and revised in the course of the Tokyo and Uruguay Rounds.

Where foreign government subsidization of exports is causing material injury to a domestic industry producing like products in the importing country, domestic trade remedy laws may permit the unilateral imposition of countervailing duties on the subsidized imports so as to offset or neutralize these foreign subsidies. Again, the rules governing countervailing duty actions are now subject to a special code on subsidies initially negotiated during the Tokyo Round and extensively revised during the Uruguay Round (the SCM Agreement).

Unilateral trade measures may also be invoked as "safeguards". Under Article XIX (commonly referred to as the safeguards or escape clause) if, as a result of unforeseen developments and of the effect of prior obligations incurred by a member under the GATT (including tariff concessions), any product is being imported into the territory of that member in such increased quantities or under such conditions as to cause or threaten serious injury to domestic producers of like or directly competitive products in that territory, a member is entitled to suspend or modify obligations or concessions on a temporary basis in order to alleviate the injury. Unlike dumping and subsidization, the use of unilateral measures in this context is not seen as a response to "unfair" trade but to unexpected changes in circumstances. The rules governing safeguard actions have now been substantially refined and elaborated in the Uruguay Round Agreement on Safeguards.

1.7.8   Developing countries

"Special and differential status" is accorded to developing countries under the GATT/WTO, both with respect to actions which they are permitted to take relating to imports and with respect to actions that developed countries are expected to take towards them with respect to their exports. Under Article XVIII, developing countries are given broader latitude to impose restrictions on imports, typically through quantitative restrictions such as quotas and licenses, for balance of payment reasons or in order to foster infant industries. Under Part IV of the GATT, added in 1966, Article XXXVI:A provides that developed countries do not expect reciprocity for commitments made by them in trade negotiations to reduce or remove tariffs and other barriers to the trade of less-developed members. Article XXXVII, in turn, provides that developed countries commit themselves to according high priority to the non-reciprocal reduction and elimination of barriers to trade in products currently or potentially of export interest to less developed members. These latter provisions led to the introduction of the Generalized System of Preferences (GSP) in the early 1970s and the unilateral adoption of special preferences by many developed countries with respect to some exports of LDCs, initially under a waiver granted by GATT members and then subsequently a permanent Enabling Clause adopted in 1979 permitting exceptions to the MFN principle.

1.7.9   Exceptions to GATT obligations

Under Article XXI of the GATT, various national security exceptions are provided for that permit a member to take any action which it considers necessary for the protection of its essential security interests or which reflects the exigencies of war or other emergency in international relations.

International trade commitments entered into by federal states, such as the USA, Canada, Australia and Germany, pose problems in international trade law to the extent that commitments made by national levels of government do not constitutionally bind sub-national levels of government, who are not direct signatories of the GATT and hence are not bound by GATT/WTO commitments entered into by their national governments. Unitary states see this as resulting in an unfair form of asymmetry in reciprocal commitments. Article XXIV(12) of the GATT provides that each member shall take such reasonable measures as may be available to it to ensure observance of the provisions of this Agreement by regional and local governments within its territories and has been interpreted strictly by GATT panels, thus limiting the extent to which national governments can avoid the consequences of non-compliance with GATT obligations by sub-national levels of government.

However, by far the most important set of exceptions to GATT obligations in practice are contained in Article XX of the GATT, which provides for a number of exceptions from GATT obligations with respect to the adoption or enforcement by members of measures, for example: necessary to protect public morals; necessary to protect human or animal health or life; necessary to secure compliance with laws or regulations which are not inconsistent with the GATT; imposed for the protection of national treasures; or relating to the conservation of exhaustible natural resources, provided that none of these measures are applied so as to constitute an arbitrary or unjustifiable form of discrimination between countries where the same conditions prevail or a disguised restriction on international trade. The exceptions provided for in Article XX and the conditions limiting these exceptions set out in the Preamble or Chapeau of Article XX have been the subject of a number of high-profile GATT/WTO trade disputes.

1.7.10   Specialized Uruguay Round Agreements

Pursuant to the Uruguay Round negotiations that culminated in 1993, specialized agreements were entered into on agricultural trade liberalization (the Agreement on Agriculture); international trade in textiles and clothing (the Agreement on Textiles and Clothing); trade-related intellectual property rights (the TRIPS Agreement); trade-related investment measures (the TRIMS Agreement); international trade in services (the General Agreement on Trade in Services (GATS)); health measures (the Sanitary and Phyto-sanitary Measures (SPS) Agreement); and technical barriers to trade (the Technical Barriers to Trade (TBT) Agreement). These agreements will be described in subsequent chapters.

1.8   The Doha Round

The Doha Round of multilateral negotiations, launched in November 2001, initially embraced a very ambitious negotiating agenda, including "new" issues such as trade and investment and trade and competition policy, but the agenda has become more modest over time (with investment and competition policy abandoned). Negotiations – which have been stalled since 2008 over key issues regarding non-agricultural market access, agricultural trade liberalization, trade in services, and rules regarding antidumping, subsidies, countervailing duties, and regional trade agreements – achieved a small success at the ninth Ministerial Conference in Bali December 2013 when member states agreed to the "Bali Package", which consists of ten separate decisions pertaining to trade facilitation, agriculture, cotton, and development and least developed country issues. Notably, the Bali Package included the first multilateral trade agreement (the Trade Facilitation Agreement) since the WTO was established in 1995. Some have expressed hope that negotiators will build from the momentum of the ninth Ministerial Conference as the Doha Development Round addresses remaining issues, but the outcome is likely to be much less ambitious than originally envisioned in 2001.[23] Moreover, India has withdrawn its support for the Trade Facilitation Agreement unless rules relating to food subsidies are relaxed.

23 See Paul Blustein, *Misadventures of the Most Favored Nations: Clashing Egos, Inflated Ambitions, and the Great Shambles of the World Trading System* (New York: PublicAffairs, 2009); World Trade Organization Ministerial Conference Ninth Session. "Ministerial Declaration and Decisions", (3–6 December 2013). Online: http://wto.org/english/thewto_e/minist_e/mc9_e/ bali_texts_combined_e.pdf. Accessed 11 July 2014; Georg Koopman and Stephan Wittig, "Whither WTO – The Multilateral Trading System After Bali", (2014) 49:1 *Intereconomics* 2; Bernard Hoekman and David Vines, "Multilateral Trade Cooperation: What Next?", (2007) 23:3 *Oxford Review of Economic Policy*, 311–34.

2   Dispute settlement under the WTO

2.1   History

In initial negotiations after World War II for the creation of a multilateral trading system, negotiating countries failed to adopt the Havana Charter, which would have led to the creation of the International Trade Organization (ITO). The GATT, as a provisional agreement, by default became a permanent framework for the multilateral trading system. It established an anaemic institutional structure that member countries, by consensus, elaborated over time. Initial disputes were referred to the Chairman of the Contracting Parties for rulings on the legality of disputed measures – a process for which there was no provision in the GATT – and then evolved into the creation of five member Working Parties, comprising representatives of the two parties in dispute (member countries) and representatives of three other countries. These Working Parties were conceived as largely serving a diplomatic or conciliatory function where attempts were made to work out compromises acceptable to both disputing parties. In turn, by the mid-1950s Working Parties had evolved into something similar to the current Panels, typically comprising five individuals in their personal capacities and excluding representatives of the countries in dispute. These Panels would hear confidential written and oral submissions from the parties and make recommendations to the General Council of the GATT, which, by convention, required a positive consensus (including the acquiescence of the losing party) for their adoption. In the event of adoption, the Contracting Parties would recommend remedial measures to the party found in violation of its GATT obligations and in the event of failure to adopt such measures could authorize the aggrieved party to impose retaliatory sanctions against the party in violation, typically in the form of tariffs or quotas on imports from the latter. This process found its legal authority, such as it was, in Article XXII of the GATT, prescribing initial consultations with a view to mutually acceptable resolutions of disputes, and in Article XXIII of the GATT, authorizing the Contracting Parties to investigate complaints of "nullification or impairment" of benefits expected under the Agreement in the event of failure of consultations, to recommend resolutions of disputes, and to authorize retaliatory sanctions in the event of failure to adopt such measures (although neither Article XXII nor Article XXIII in fact mention Panels).

Despite this rather fragile and ad hoc basis for resolving complaints, almost 300 complaints were filed with the GATT (many of them referred to Panels) between 1948 and 1989. A study of these cases by Robert Hudec et al.[1] found that it took about two years to resolve a dispute from the time a complaint was filed to the implementation of remedial measures. They also found a perhaps surprisingly high compliance rate for successful complaints of 88 per cent, with some decline in the compliance record in the 1980s to 81 per cent, a decade which witnessed an explosion of complaints. For the entire 42-year period studied, 73 per cent of all complaints were filed by the USA, the EU and its members, Canada, and Australia. The USA, the EU and its member countries, Canada and Japan accounted for 83 per cent of all appearances as defendants. Of all complaints, 92 per cent involved either the USA or the EU (or its members) as a party. For the entire period, 52 per cent of all complaints related to non-tariff barriers (NTBs), 21 per cent to tariffs, 16 per cent to subsidies, and 10 per cent to antidumping/countervailing duty (AD/CVD) measures. Over time, NTBs and AD/CVDs increased as a percentage of complaints while tariffs sharply declined; in the 1950s, only 23 per cent of all complaints involved agricultural trade, while for the period 1960 to 1984, one half of the complaints involved agricultural trade measures, many relating to the EU's Common Agricultural Policy.

However, despite, in many ways, the relative effectiveness of this dispute settlement regime, a number of countries (especially the USA) became dissatisfied with the functioning of the dispute-settlement system. In particular, these countries were critical of the ability of parties to engage in strategic foot-dragging in the appointment of panels, settlement of their terms of reference, and adoption of their findings, given the ability of a party seeking to resist formal dispute settlement in effect to exercise veto rights at any of these critical decision junctures through the operation of the positive consensus rule. Hence, during the Uruguay Round (1986 to 1993), a concerted effort was made

---

1 Robert E. Hudec, Daniel L.M. Kennedy and Mark Sgarbossa, "A Statistical Profile of GATT Dispute Settlement Cases, 1948 to 1989", (1993) 2 *Minnesota Journal of Global Trade* 1.

to strengthen the dispute-settlement system, resulting in the Dispute Settlement Understanding (DSU) that came into force in 1995 with the creation of the World Trade Organization. The principal modifications to the dispute-settlement system made by the DSU fall into three broad categories: a) strict deadlines on various stages in the consultation and dispute-settlement process; b) replacement of the positive consensus rule with a negative consensus rule, meaning that Panel and Appellate Body decisions were deemed to be adopted by the General Council of the WTO in the absence of a consensus favouring rejection, which would entail the prevailing party acquiescing in the rejection of a decision in its favour. This has meant that Panel (and Appellate Body) decisions are now adopted automatically by the WTO General Council; c) the creation of a standing Appellate Body of seven members, which sits in panels of three and has jurisdiction to hear appeals on matters of law from ad hoc Panel decisions.

2.2   The contemporary complaints process[2]

The contemporary complaints process typically follows the following sequence:

1.   The complaining party must initially engage in consultations with the party whose measures are in dispute. If the parties fail to settle a dispute (with the assistance of mediation if requested) within 60 days of the request for consultations, then the complaining member can request the establishment of a Panel.
2.   A Panel must be established at the meeting of the Dispute Settlement Body (the General Council of the WTO) following the meeting at which the request for a Panel first appears on the Dispute Settlement Body agenda.
3.   Standard terms of reference are typically adopted for Panels unless the disputing parties agree otherwise within 20 days from the establishment of a Panel.
4.   Panel members are typically drawn from a roster maintained by the Dispute Settlement Body with the consensus of member countries. If disputing parties cannot agree on panelists within 20 days of the establishment of a Panel, the Director-General

---

2 See generally, Henrik Horn and Petros Mavroidis, "International Trade: Dispute Settlement", in Andrew T. Guzman and Alan O. Sykes (eds), *Research Handbook in International Economic Law* (Cheltenham, UK: Edward Elgar, 2007).

of the WTO shall appoint panelists who may not be citizens of countries involved in the dispute. Other countries with a substantial interest in the matter can participate as Third Parties in Panel proceedings.

5. Under Article 11 of the DSU, a Panel's functions are to make an objective assessment of the facts and the applicability of relevant agreements to the facts and to present their findings and recommendations to the Dispute Settlement Body.

6. In Panel proceedings, the complaining party files its written submissions first, followed by written submissions from the responding party. Typically there is then one oral meeting with the Panel, then written rebuttal submissions are submitted, followed by a second oral meeting with the Panel. The Panel will then present to the parties a summary of their arguments and the factual description of the issues in contention for their comments. This is then typically followed by the presentation to the parties of an interim report by the Panel for the parties' comments. Following receipt of their comments, the Panel typically then prepares a final report. Proceedings before Panels are not normally to take longer than six months from the striking of a Panel to the issuance of a final report to the parties.

7. Panel reports are to be adopted by the Dispute Settlement Body within 60 days of circulation of the report to members, unless there is a negative consensus favouring rejection of the report, or the Panel's decision is appealed to the Appellate Body.

8. The parties may appeal panel decisions to the Appellate Body on matters of law and the Appellate Body is required to report within 60 days from notification of an appeal. The Appellate Body's report is to be adopted by the Dispute Settlement Body within 30 days of circulation to members, unless there is a negative consensus favouring rejection.

9. Members have a reasonable period to comply with Panel or Appellate Body rulings, once adopted by the Dispute Settlement Body, but this period is not normally to exceed 15 months and is to be determined by arbitration failing agreement of the parties.

10. Where there is disagreement as to whether measures taken to comply with rulings in fact constitute compliance, the matter can be remitted to the original Panel (and potentially the Appellate Body on appeal) under Article 21.5 of the DSU.

11. If non-compliance persists, the Dispute Settlement Body may authorize retaliatory trade sanctions which typically involve

the withdrawal of equivalent trade concessions, the issue of equivalence being subject to arbitration under Article 22.4.

2.3   Utilization of the new dispute-settlement process

Kara Leitner and Simon Lester have for a number of years prepared an annual cumulative analysis of WTO dispute-settlement proceedings since the institution of the new dispute-settlement process in 1995. Their latest analysis[3] reports the following basic statistics on utilization of the new dispute-settlement system.

As of 1 January 2014 there have been 474 WTO complaints filed under the DSU since 1995, involving a total of 348 matters. The leading complaining parties have been the USA (with 106 complaints), the EU (with 90 complaints), Canada (with 33 complaints), Brazil (with 26 complaints), Mexico (with 23 complaints), and China (with 21 complaints). In terms of responding parties, the USA has been the principal respondent in 122 disputes and the EU, the second most frequent respondent, in 77 disputes. That is to say that the USA or the EU has been the complaining party in 41 per cent of total complaints and the responding party in 43 per cent of total complaints. However, increasingly other countries have become significant participants in the dispute-settlement system, including developing countries. Between 1995 and 2013, 285 complaints were filed by high-income countries, 107 by upper-middle-income countries, 70 by lower-middle-income countries, and 28 by low-income countries. Numbers for respondents are roughly comparable. However, there are enduring concerns that many developing countries lack the capacity to participate effectively in the increasingly complex dispute-settlement system and even where they prevail may lack effective retaliatory sanctions against much larger countries.[4] In terms of issues that are most frequently disputed, general GATT provisions account for the overwhelming number of issues in dispute at 379, followed by antidumping duties at 102, subsidies and countervailing measures issues at 99, and agricultural trade issues at 71.

---

3 Kara Leitner and Simon Lester, "WTO Dispute Settlement 1995–2013 – A Statistical Analysis", (2014) 17:1 *Journal of International Economic Law* 192.

4 See Chad P. Bown, *Self-enforcing Trade: Developing Countries and WTO Dispute Settlement* (Washington, D.C.: Brookings Institution, 2009).

Since the institution of the new dispute-settlement system in 1995, 153 Panel reports and 92 Appellate Body reports have been issued. The percentage of Panel reports appealed to date to the Appellate Body is 68 per cent.

2.4   Critical issues in evaluating the dispute-settlement system in world trade law

In many respects, the GATT/WTO dispute-settlement system is the envy of many other international legal regimes that lack any or effective enforcement regimes. A critical threshold question is why the GATT/ WTO dispute-settlement system has worked relatively well over the course of the history of the GATT/WTO, despite some highly idiosyncratic features of the system, at least compared to domestic judicial dispute-settlement processes, especially prior to the 1995 reforms when the positive consensus rule applied. Even under the new system, why do parties mostly comply with adverse rulings, despite the absence of a supra-national Leviathan that can forcibly compel compliance? A related question is whether the evolution of the GATT/WTO dispute-settlement system from a diplomatically-oriented conciliation process to a much more formal, adversarial, quasi-judicial process is in every respect desirable?[5]

Reform proposals tend to fall into two broad categories – those that seek to strengthen the existing dispute-settlement system, and those that seek to retrench it relative to the political decision-making organs of the WTO, each of which needs to be carefully analyzed and debated. Proponents of strengthening the dispute-settlement system advance various reform proposals:

a)   Greater transparency in dispute-settlement proceedings by making written submissions of the parties available to the public when filed and making oral proceedings before Panels and the Appellate Body (subject to confidentiality protections) open to the public;

b)   Expanding the opportunities for participation by non-state interveners through the filing of amicus curiae briefs and perhaps participation in oral hearings before Panels and the Appellate Body;

---

5 See Joost Pauwelyn, "The Transformation of World Trade", (2005) 104:1 *Michigan Law Review* 1; Tomer Broude, *International Governance in the World Trade Organization: Judicial Boundaries and Political Capitulation* (London: Cameron May, 2004).

c) Permitting private parties to initiate complaints under the WTO dispute settlement regime, which it must be emphasized has hitherto been exclusively the preserve of state-to-state complaints;

d) Providing that GATT/WTO rules have "direct effect" in the domestic legal systems of member states (as with the EU constitution), where private parties can assert those rules in domestic legal proceedings, presumably subject to some kind of appeal process to the WTO dispute-settlement system (akin to appeals to the European Court of Justice in the EU) so that the GATT/WTO becomes a kind of global constitution;

e) Strengthening remedies for non-compliance with dispute-settlement rulings by, for example:

    i)   providing for monetary compensation for past losses (including legal costs, at least in the case of developing countries) and perhaps future losses in the event of continuing non-compliance, as an alternative to retaliation, which may be of limited efficacy for small countries that prevail in disputes against much larger countries;[6]

    ii) disproportionate or non-equivalent retaliation as a form of punishment or punitive damages to deter violations, as opposed to equivalent retaliation that might be thought to facilitate some violations, which some commentators view as efficient breaches if the benefits of breach exceed the costs to other parties;[7]

    iii) tradeable retaliation rights that small countries could trade to larger countries who may be able more effectively to exercise these rights;

    iv) collective retaliation rights/obligations, where all member countries are obliged or entitled to adopt retaliatory sanctions against another member's violation, whether they are directly affected or not.

Proponents of retrenching the dispute-settlement system on the grounds that it has grown too powerful relative to the political decision-making organs of the WTO and reflects excessive judicial activism or law-making argue that Panel or Appellate Body decisions should

---

6 For a critique, see Alan O. Sykes, "Chapter 16: Optimal Sanctions in the WTO The Case for Decoupling (and the Uneasy Case for the Status Quo)", in Chad Brown and Joost Pauwelyn (eds) Retaliation in WTO Dispute Settlement (Geneva: Cambridge University Press, 2010), 339–54.

7 For a critique, see Warren F. Schwartz and Alan O. Sykes, "The Economic Structure of Renegotiation and Dispute Resolution in the World Trade Organization", (2002) 31:1 *Journal of Legal Studies* 179.

not be adopted if some significant minority, for example, one-third, of member countries object to a decision. Complementary proposals are sometimes advanced for facilitating or streamlining decision-making by the political organs of the WTO. For example, there have been proposals to move away from a consensus rule of decision-making to more formal majority or supra-majority voting, with voting rights perhaps weighted by trade volumes (somewhat akin to weighted voting rights in the EU), and perhaps the appointment or election of a representative Executive Committee of the WTO to make a broad range of decisions without requiring the direct participation or endorsement of all 160 members (a form of delegated decision-making).

3 Tariffs and the Most Favoured Nation Principle

3.1 The economic (welfare) effects of a tariff

In the case of a prohibitive tariff, where imports are completely priced out of an importing country's market, domestic producers are likely to price up to the tariff, consumers in these countries who remain in the market will pay more for the domestically produced goods than they otherwise would without the tariff, and some consumers will be priced out of the market (often referred to as a dead-weight social cost). Consumers in importing countries lose more than producers in these countries gain (by virtue of this dead-weight social cost), thus reducing domestic welfare. Adverse impacts on foreign exporters of these goods also make the tariff globally welfare-reducing. In the case of a non-prohibitive tariff, governments in the importing country collect some revenue from the tariff, but this is almost never sufficient to offset the negative impact of the tariff on domestic consumers or to produce a net welfare improvement in the importing country. Further, foreign exporters are adversely affected through changing the terms of trade.

The welfare effects of a tariff need to be considered relative to other protectionist instruments – in particular, quantitative restrictions and subsidies. In the case of quantitative restrictions, depending on how import quotas are allocated, domestic recipients of these quotas may realize scarcity rents from the quotas, or if the quotas are allocated to foreign exporters the latter are likely to realize scarcity rents from the quotas. However, as in the case of a non-prohibitive tariff, these benefits are highly unlikely to offset the negative impacts on domestic consumers from higher prices, and may exacerbate them relative to a non-prohibitive tariff that permits more efficient foreign exporters to surmount the tariff. Quantitative restrictions are banned under Article XI of the GATT, with numerous exceptions which must be applied on a non-discriminatory basis under Article XIII. With respect to domestic production subsidies that render domestically produced products artificially competitive with lower-priced imports, consumers will not face distorted prices relative to the prevailing world price for the product, but the subsidies will attract excessive resources into the domestic industry. In the case of both tariffs and quantitative restrictions, these distort both consumption and production decisions in importing countries.

3.2   International tariff negotiations

The preamble to the GATT commits members to enter into reciprocal and mutually advantageous arrangements directed to the substantial reduction of tariffs and other barriers to trade and to the elimination of discriminatory treatment in international commerce. Article XXVIII bis further provides that "members recognize that customs duties often constitute serious obstacles to trade and that negotiations on a reciprocal and mutually advantageous basis, directed to the substantial reduction of the general level of tariffs are of great importance to the expansion of international trade". Pursuant to these provisions, eight rounds of multilateral negotiations have been concluded to date, with a ninth round – the Doha Round – nearing completion. Over the course of these rounds, tariffs on industrial goods have been reduced worldwide on average from over 40 per cent in 1947 to less than 5 per cent today. There are significant remaining tariffs on industrial goods from country to country on particular classes of goods, and extremely high tariffs on particular agricultural products that often run, in the case of many countries, to several hundred per cent. Negotiations over tariff reductions have adopted different negotiating principles over time. The first five negotiating rounds adopted product-by-product negotiations, which were extremely transaction-cost intensive. Later rounds adopted some combination of linear cuts and exceptions which were negotiated on a product-by-product basis, typically with further agreement that in the case of linear cuts, countries with high tariffs should cut by deeper percentages than countries with already lower tariffs. The reduction of tariffs on industrial goods worldwide has been perhaps the most important achievement of the GATT over the course of its history.

Once tariff negotiations have been concluded, these become tariff bindings which are set out in particular members' tariff schedules that constitute an Annex to the GATT. By virtue of Article II of the GATT, all parties must adhere to these tariff bindings by not imposing custom duties in excess of those set forth in each country's tariff binding schedule. This is subject to an exception provided for in Article XXVIII, where at scheduled triennial intervals, any member that has made previous tariff concessions can reopen these concessions with other members who have a substantial interest in the concession, with a view to modifying or withdrawing the concession. The member reopening tariff concessions must offer other concessions so that a general level of reciprocal, mutually advantageous concessions not less favourable to trade than those existing between the parties prior to such reopening is maintained.

3.3   Domestic administration of tariffs

Five issues are required to be addressed in the domestic administration of tariffs.

3.3.1   Valuation of imported goods

Most tariffs today are *ad valorem* tariffs, requiring the importer to pay a certain percentage of the good's value in duty. Thus, valuation of the imported goods is an important determinant of the ultimate import duty. Article VII of the GATT requires parties to the Agreement to base value for customs purposes of imported merchandise on the actual value of the imported merchandise and not on the value of merchandise of national origin or on arbitrary or fictitious values. During the Tokyo and Uruguay Rounds a Customs Valuation Agreement was negotiated that seeks to elaborate a detailed set of valuation rules, establishing as the primary standard of valuation "transaction value", which is the price paid or payable for the goods when sold for export to the country of importation, plus certain additions such as the cost of packaging and the value of various items provided to the buyer free of charge in connection with the sale of the goods. Alternative methods of valuation are provided where transaction value is inappropriate, such as sales between related parties.

3.3.2   Classification

Because there is a wide variation in the level of tariffs from product to product, goods must be located in the correct product category in a country's tariffs schedule to receive appropriate tariff treatment. A detailed harmonized classification system has now evolved that attempts to reduce both ambiguity and opportunism in the classification of imported goods.

3.3.3   Rules of origin

Because tariff rates often vary depending on from where the goods originate, rules of origin are often required in order to determine the country of origin. For example, Canada has five major tariff treatments, depending on where goods originate: the general tariff on nonmembers of the GATT/WTO; the MFN rate under the GATT; the NAFTA rate for imports from the other two NAFTA members; the GSP rate for imports from developing countries to whom preferences have been extended; and a small residual category for preferences, such as preferences to other British Commonwealth countries, prevailing at the inception of the GATT. In the contemporary global economy, where goods or components thereof are often produced in many different countries, rules of origin are often exceptionally complex and somewhat arbitrary. Little progress has been made towards harmonizing these rules both within countries in different trade policy contexts, and between or among countries.

3.3.4   Customs fees and administration

Article VIII of the GATT restricts the imposition of fees or charges related to the administrative processing of inbound goods to the approximate cost of services rendered, which must not represent an indirect protection to domestic producers or a taxation of imports for fiscal purposes.

3.3.5   Trade facilitation

In December 2013 at the WTO's ninth Ministerial Conference in Bali, the most recent phase of Doha trade talks, member states agreed to the Trade Facilitation Agreement (TFA), the first new WTO multilateral agreement since it was established in 1995.[1]

As goods transit internationally, they must pass through border offices and comply with rules regarding border fees and paperwork,

---

1 Antonia Eliason, "The Trade Facilitation Agreement – Episode IV: A New Hope for the World Trade Organization", (6 March 2014) SSRN Working Paper. Online: http://dx.doi.org/10.2139/ssrn.2405640. Accessed 12 May 2014.

as well as other requirements on goods in transit such as terminal handling charges. Clearing customs can be costly and time consuming (sometimes leading perishable items to spoil before reaching market), impacting the volume of trade that takes place. The costs of transiting goods are often heightened due to redundant requirements for information and differences in technological levels between states. Trade facilitation aims to cut red tape in customs and border procedures through increased speed, efficiency, and transparency, and through improved trade-related infrastructure. It comprises policies dealing with the entry of goods into a country, as well as the provision of measures and information to do with the entry of goods. The TFA could reduce the cost of cross-border trading, currently estimated at more than $2 trillion per year, by as much as $1 trillion. However, India has withdrawn its support for the TFA, unless rules on food subsidies are relaxed, casting doubt on the future of the Agreement.

3.4 The Most Favoured Nation Principle

Once tariff commitments have been agreed to in tariff negotiations and become tariff bindings under Article II of the GATT, these must be extended to all members of the GATT/WTO system under the Most Favoured Nation Principle set out in Article I, which is why the MFN Principle is often viewed as the cornerstone of the multilateral trading system (in contrast to a system of bilateral deals). Article I provides:

> With respect to customs duties and charges of any kind imposed on or in connection with importation or exportation or imposed on the international transfer of payments for imports or exports, and with respect to the method of levying such duties and charges, and with respect to all rules and formalities in connection with importation and exportation, and with respect to all matters referred to in paragraphs 2 and 4 of Article III, any advantage, favour, privilege or immunity granted by any Contracting Party to any product originating in or destined for any other country shall be accorded immediately and unconditionally to the like product originating in or destined for the territories of all other Contracting Parties.

This principle is subject to a number of exceptions, the most important of which relate to preferential trading agreements, and GSP preferences for developing countries, which are discussed in later chapters. I first explore the theoretical rationales for the MFN Principle, and then a number of important interpretive issues that have arisen in its application and have engaged the dispute-settlement system under the GATT/WTO.

3.4.1   Theoretical rationales for the MFN principle

A political justification for the MFN principle relates to the reduction of factionalism by constraining countries from engaging in playing favourites amongst foreigners for foreign policy or national security reasons, which were thought to have severely exacerbated international tensions leading up to World War II. However, in a contemporary setting, the principal rationales for the MFN Principle relate to the economic or welfare properties of the principle, and in this respect three such properties have been identified in the theoretical literature.[2]

3.4.1.1   *Constraining bilateral opportunism in sequenced concessions favouring participating third parties*

Here the scenario involves A and B trading tariff concessions, and B subsequently making more favourable concessions to C. Under the MFN Principle the more favourable concessions that B grants to C must also be extended to A. In the absence of the MFN Principle, A would have to contemplate the risk of B making more favourable concessions subsequently to C, and might then make less substantial concessions to B in the first round of negotiations, or withhold concessions altogether, preventing the conclusion of a mutually beneficial agreement. This kind of concern was very much in evidence in successive negotiations over the Canada–US Free Trade Agreement in the late 1980s, which was then largely superseded by NAFTA between Canada, the USA and Mexico in the early 1990s. If Canada had declined to participate in the subsequent negotiations over NAFTA, it risked losing the benefits of preferential access to the US markets negotiated under the Canada–US Free Trade Agreement if the USA and Mexico were to negotiate more favourable concessions with each other with respect to access to each other's markets, hence largely forcing Canada's hand in participating in the subsequent negotiations.

---

2 See Warren F. Schwartz and Alan O. Sykes, "Towards a Positive Theory of the Most Favoured Nation Obligation and its Exceptions in the WTO/GATT System", (1996) 16 *International Review of Law and Economics* 27; and Kyle Bagwell and Robert W. Staiger, *The Economics of the World Trading System* (Cambridge, MA: MIT Press, 2002) at 5.

3.4.1.2   *Constraining bilateral opportunism disadvantaging non-participating third parties*

Here the concern is that when two parties (A and B) negotiate tariff or related concessions with one another, while liberalizing trade between themselves (trade creation), this may disadvantage non-participating third parties (for example, C) with respect to access to either A or B's markets (trade diversion). Trade may be diverted away from C to either A or B who are parties to this arrangement. More extremely, A and B may negotiate a bilateral agreement between themselves which takes the form of a customs union, which enables them to raise common duties vis-à-vis non-participating third parties and change the terms of trade vis-à-vis these parties in effect by exercising monopsony power against them. Article XXIV of the GATT, in dealing with free trade agreements and customs unions, attempts to constrain these effects by requiring that countries party to such arrangements: a) substantially eliminate restrictions on all trade between or among themselves (the internal condition); and b) do not raise average duties subsequent to entering into such a bilateral arrangement vis-à-vis third parties relative to the average duties that prevailed prior to the negotiation of such an arrangement (the external condition).

3.4.1.3   *The free rider problem*

Where A and B negotiate tariffs or related concessions between themselves, under the MFN Principle, C is not required to provide any quid pro quo for receipt of identical benefits and is in effect a free rider on the concessions that A and B have made to each other. This weakens the negotiating position of A or B in subsequent negotiations with C and may reduce incentives for A or B to make initial concessions to each other. Because the MFN Principle does not contemplate complete reciprocity, this is part of the motivation that explains the proliferation of preferential trade agreements between much smaller numbers of parties in recent years (discussed in the next chapter).

While theoretical rationales for the MFN Principle present something of a mixed balance sheet, nevertheless it needs to be acknowledged that tariff negotiations, at least with respect to industrial goods, under the GATT have been its most signal achievement.

3.4.2   Interpretive issues in the application of the MFN principle

3.4.2.1   *Scope of Article I*

Case law has made it clear that the MFN Principle applies not only to imports but exports, and applies not only to tariffs but to various rules and formalities applicable to imports and to internal taxes and regulatory measures that are covered by Article III(2) and (4) of the GATT (the National Treatment Principle).

3.4.2.2   *Unconditionality*

This has been a major matter of contention in a long line of trade disputes that have come before the Dispute Settlement Body of the GATT/WTO. Various interpretations have been adopted of the requirement that all advantages, favours, privileges, and immunities extended by one Contracting Party to another shall be immediately and unconditionally extended to all other members. One interpretation is that no conditions can be imposed that require other countries to provide quid pro quos. Another interpretation is that no conditions at all can be attached to the extension of MFN treatment. A yet further interpretation is that conditions are permitted but cannot discriminate by country of origin. A further possible interpretation is that conditions are permitted but that these must relate to the characteristics of the goods themselves (and not, for example, to differences in production and processing methods – PPMs).

In the *Belgium – Family Allowances* case (1952),[3] Belgian law imposed a charge on foreign goods purchased by public bodies when these goods originated in a country whose system of family allowances did not meet specific requirements that rendered their system comparable to that in place in Belgium. A number of countries had been granted an advantage – that is, an exemption – from the levy, but not others. A GATT panel held that conditioning the imposition of this internal tax on what kind of system of family allowances foreign countries had adopted violated Article I, in that this condition had nothing to do with the nature of the goods in question. In the

---

3 *Belgian Family Allowances (allocations familiales)*, adopted 7 November 1952, G/32 – BISD 1S/59 [*Belgium – Family Allowances 1952*].

Indonesia – Auto case (1998),[4] various exemptions from customs duties and internal taxes turned on various conditions and criteria not related to the nature of the imports themselves but rather, in effect, to the country of origin. The panel held that these conditions discriminated on the basis of country of origin and not product characteristics and hence violated Article I. In the *Canada – Auto* case (2000),[5] various duty remission rules on imported cars were conditioned on the manufacturers meeting various domestic content requirements in the production of other cars. Here the panel, after analyzing the *Indonesia – Auto* case, concluded that the fact that conditions are attached to a particular advantage and are not related to the imported product itself does not necessarily imply that such conditions are discriminatory with respect to the origin of imported products. This seems to imply that only conditions that discriminate on the basis of origin (and not, for example, differences in PPMs) violate Article I.

3.4.2.3   Like products

The MFN Principle only requires that any advantage, favour, privilege or immunity extended to one class of product from an exporting country be extended to exporters of like products from other foreign countries. The concept of "like products" has been enormously contentious both in the GATT/WTO case law and in scholarly commentary. Some cases, particularly in disputes over tariff classifications, have adopted quite narrow interpretations of like product, essentially requiring products to be (almost) identical in their physical characteristics. This view is reflected in the panel decisions in *Australia – Ammonium Sulphate* (1950),[6] *Germany – Sardines* (1952),[7] *EC – Animal Feed Protein* (1978),[8] and *Japan – SPF*

---

4 *Indonesia – Certain Measures Affecting the Automobile Industry*, WT/ DS54/R, WT/DS55/R, WT/DS59/R, WT/DS64/R and Corr. 1, 2, 3 and 4, adopted 23 July 1998, DSR 1998; VI, 2201. [*Indonesia – Autos* 1998].

5 *Canada – Certain Measures Affecting the Automotive Industry*, WT/ DS139/R, WT/DS142/R, adopted 19 June 2000, as modified by the Appellate Body Report, WT/DS139/AB/R, WT/DS142/AB/R [*Canada – Automobiles* 2000].

6 Working Party Report, *The Australian Subsidy on Ammonium Sulphate*, GATT/CP.4/39, adopted 3 April 1950, BISD II/188 [*Australia – Ammonium Sulphate* 1950].

7 *Treatment by Germany of Imports of Sardines*, adopted 31 October 1952, G/26 – BISD 1S/53 [*Germany – Sardines* 1952].

8 *EEC – Measures on Animal Feed Proteins*, adopted 14 March 1978, L/4599 – BISD 25S/49 [*EEC – Animal Feed Proteins* 1978].

Dimension Lumber (1989)[9] (which involved different species of soft-wood lumber used in home construction and which were held not to be "like" products). Other cases have taken a broader, more functional approach to the interpretation of like product, applying something closer to an antitrust law conception of whether given products fall into a relevant product market, which largely turns on their degree of functional substitutability from the perspective of consumers of those products despite significant physical differences (for example, butter and margarine). Cases that appear to favour this view include *Spain – Unroasted Coffee* (1981)[10] – different species of coffee were treated as like products – and *Indonesia – Autos* (1998).[11] An argument favouring narrow interpretations of the like product requirement in Article I is that tariff negotiations, which depend on reciprocity, put a high premium on issues of manageability and reciprocity in tariff administration. Products should not be defined so broadly that a variety of third countries who have offered no quid pro quos are able to benefit from tariff concessions (the free rider problem). An argument for a broader functional conception of like products is that it can be more coherently and consistently applied, as in antitrust law, than simply comparing the physical characteristics of products. An important and unresolved policy issue that flows from this difference in approaches to the interpretation of the like product requirement is whether countries are able to distinguish or discriminate between imported products on the basis of differences in production and processing methods (for example, with respect to differences in labour or environmental standards in the exporting country).

3.4.2.4   De facto discrimination

A number of cases have now recognized that Article I applies not only to de jure or explicit forms of discrimination between or amongst foreign imports but also to forms of de facto discrimination (*EC – Beef from Canada* (1981);[12] *Spain – Unroasted Coffee* (1981);[13]

---

9 *Canada/Japan – Tariff on Imports of Spruce, Pine, Fir (SPF) Dimension Lumber*, adopted 19 July 1989, L/6470 – BISD 36S/167 [*Japan – SPF Dimension Lumber* 1989].

10 *Spain – Tariff Treatment of Unroasted Coffee*, adopted 11 June 1981, L/5135 – BISD 28S/102 [*Spain – Unroasted Coffee* 1981].

11 *Indonesia – Autos* 1998, supra note 4.

12 *European Economic Community – Imports of Beef from Canada*, adopted 10 March 1981, L/5099 – BISD 28S/92 [*EC – Beef from Canada* 1981].

13 *Spain – Unroasted Coffee* 1981, supra note 10.

EC – Bananas (1999);[14] *Indonesia – Automobiles* (1998);[15] *Canada – Automobiles* (2000)[16]). Thus, a domestic measure that is facially neutral as amongst imports from different foreign countries may nevertheless have a disparate impact on imports of like products (however defined) from some foreign countries relative to others.

This interpretation seems obviously necessary to prevent formalistic circumventions of the MFN requirement.

3.4.2.5   MFN obligations under Article XIII of the GATT

Under Article XIII of the GATT, "no prohibition or restriction (such as quotas) shall be applied by any Contracting Party on the importation of any product of the territory of any other Contracting Party or on the exportation of any product destined for the territory of any other Contracting Party, unless the importation of the like product of all third parties or the exportation of the like product to all third countries is similarly prohibited or restricted".

In *EC – Bananas III* (1999),[17] among several other MFN complaints, the complainants (the USA and various Latin American countries) claimed that the EC regime for the allocation of tariff rate quotas (TRQs) with respect to bananas violated Article XIII. The *EC – Banana* import regime established three categories of banana imports: (1) traditional ACP bananas (from Lomé Convention ex-colonies in Africa, the Caribbean, and the Pacific); (2) third country bananas; and (3) non-traditional ACP bananas. Quotas were allocated to each of these categories, heavily favouring category (1). The EC had previously been granted a waiver from the MFN provisions of the GATT in Article I with respect to its Lomé Convention obligations to former colonies in Africa, the Caribbean and Latin America. However, the Appellate Body held that the exemption from Article I did not also imply an exemption from Article XIII and held that the allocation of tariff rate quotas violated Article XIII.

---

14 *European Communities – Regime for the Importation, Sale and Distribution of Bananas – Recourse to Article 21.5 by the European Communities*, 12 April 1999, WT/DS27/RW/EEC [*EC – Bananas* 1999].

15 *Indonesia – Autos* 1998, supra note 4.

16 *Canada – Automobiles*, 2000, supra note 5.

17 *European Communities – Bananas III*, 1999, supra note 14.

3.5   Conclusion

While the MFN principle has often been called the "corner-stone" of the multilateral trading system, two major exceptions to the principle increasingly challenge its pre-eminence: first, the proliferation of Preferential Trade Agreements (PTAs), negotiated on a bilateral, regional, or cross-regional basis amongst sub-sets of members of the WTO, that by their nature treat members more favourably than non-members; and second, special and differential treatment of developing countries, including the existence of unilateral, non-reciprocal preferences granted to many such countries by developed countries. Both of these phenomena are sufficiently important to warrant treatment in separate chapters of this book.

4   Preferential trade agreements

4.1   Introduction

Preferential trade agreements (PTAs) are treaties between two or more countries granting preferential market access to each other's markets. PTAs may be bilateral, regional, or cross-regional. PTAs have proliferated rapidly in recent years. Since 1948, 474 PTAs have been notified to the GATT/WTO, amongst which over 350 have been notified since 1990. In 1990, the WTO had an average of two PTA partners, but this has increased to twelve in the past two decades. Today, there are approximately 300 PTAs in force, of which most are bilateral, involving only two countries. Most of these are free trade agreements; few customs unions have formed. PTAs increasingly involve developing countries, whether in north-south or south-south agreements. In the late 1970s, the vast majority of PTAs involved developed countries – 60 per cent of PTAs were between developed and developing countries and 30 per cent between developed countries only. This has changed dramatically. Today, approximately two-thirds of PTAs in force are between developing countries, while only one quarter include both developed and developing countries, and only 10 per cent are between developed countries. In addition, cross-regional PTAs are increasingly common, comprising half of all PTAs in force. Finally, PTAs covering trade in goods are more common than those covering trade in services, but this tendency is becoming less pronounced. Less than 1 per cent of PTAs address only trade in services, but the proportion of PTAs addressing both trade in goods and services has more than doubled between 2000 and 2010, reaching 31 per cent.[1]

---

1 See Roberto V. Fiorentino, Jo-Ann Crawford and Christelle Toqueboeuf, "The Landscape of Regional Trade Agreements and WTO Surveillance", in Richard E. Baldwin and Patrick Low (eds), *Multilateralizing Regionalism* (New York: Cambridge University Press, 2009); Adrian Johnston and Michael Trebilcock, "The Proliferation of Preferential Trade Agreements: the Beginning of the End of the Multilateral Trading System?", in Rainer Hofmann, Stephan Schill and Christian Tams (eds), *Preferential Trade and Investment Agreements from Recalibration to Reintegration* (Baden-Baden: Nomos, 2013).

Preferential trade agreements have been provided for under Article XXIV of the GATT since its inception in 1947, raising a puzzle as to why the founders of the GATT would have wished to accommodate arrangements that are, on their face, discriminatory between members and non-members and hence in tension with the GATT's foundational non-discrimination principles, in particular the Most Favoured Nation Principle. In part, the explanation appears to be that customs unions (but not free trade areas) were viewed as analogous to a single country for trade purposes in their dealings with outside states by virtue of their common external tariff. In the immediate post-war years greater economic and political integration within Western Europe had emerged as a major policy objective not only within Europe but in the USA and other foreign policy circles and required special accommodation within the GATT system.[2]

However, developing countries viewed free trade areas as better suited to their interests and argued that any special dispensations for PTAs should embrace both customs unions and free trade areas. Moreover, the USA, which was the most vigorous proponent of multilateralism, had negotiated a secret free trade agreement with Canada and sought to have this accommodated within the GATT exception for PTAs (although it was never ratified).

4.2   The legal framework for preferential trade agreements under the GATT[3]

Article XXIV of the GATT sets out the key conditions that PTAs must satisfy in order to be GATT-compliant. These provisions are supplemented by the Understanding on the Interpretation of Article XXIV of the General Agreement on Tariffs and Trade 1994, which was adopted by the member countries as part of the Uruguay Round Final Act. Parties entering into PTAs must notify these agreements to the WTO under Article XXIV:7. Until 1996, GATT ad hoc working parties were

---

2 See David A. Gantz, *Regional Trade Agreements: Law, Policy, and Practice* (Durham, N.C.: Carolina Academic Press, 2009); Kerry A. Chase, "Multilateralism Compromise: The Mysterious Origins of GATT Article XXIV", (2006) 5 *World Trade Review* 1; Kyle Bagwell and Petros Mavroidis (eds), *Preferential Trade Agreements: Law, Policy and Economics* (New York: Cambridge University Press, 2011).

3 See generally, Joel P. Trachtman, "International Trade: Regionalism", in Andrew T. Guzman and Alan O. Sykes (eds), *Research Handbook in International Economic Law* (Cheltenham, UK: Edward Elgar, 2007).

convened to assess the compliance of PTAs with Article XXIV. In 1996, the Committee on Regional Trade Agreements (CRTA) was created by the WTO General Council, replacing the working parties in executing this function. The CRTA is empowered to conduct a full review and make recommendations to the General Council of the WTO on compliance of a notified PTA with the requirements of Article XXIV. However, despite this broad scope of PTA review, GATT contracting parties have never in the history of the GATT reached by consensus a decision that a notified scheme is inconsistent with the multilateral rules. The second avenue for review of PTAs is through a formal complaint to the Dispute Settlement Body of the WTO, followed by the convening of a panel and then a potential appeal to the Appellate Body. However, the only case directly addressing the issue of PTA consistency with the GATT is *Turkey – Textiles* (discussed below). Thus, despite the rapidly growing importance of the phenomenon of PTAs, and despite substantial ambiguities in a number of the key conditions for PTAs set out in Article XXIV, there has been remarkably little guidance on the interpretation and application of these requirements either by the CRTA or the GATT/WTO dispute-settlement system.

Article XXIV:4 addresses the purpose of PTAs and their place within the multilateral trading system and provides:

> The Contracting Parties recognize the desirability of increasing freedom of trade by the development, through voluntary agreements, of closer integration between the economies of the countries parties to such agreements. They also recognize that the purpose of a customs union or of a free trade area should be to facilitate trade between the constituent territories and not to raise barriers to the trade of other Contracting Parties with such territories.

The Appellate Body in *Turkey – Textiles* clarified that while Article XXIV:4 does not create an operative test for the purpose of a PTA, the entire text of Article XXIV must be interpreted in light of the purposive language in paragraph 4.

Article XXIV goes on to stipulate two key requirements for PTAs: an internal requirement and an external requirement.

With respect to the internal requirement, Article XXIV:8(a) (in the case of customs unions) and Article XXIV:8(b) (in the case of free trade areas) require that duties and other restrictive regulations of commerce be eliminated with respect to "substantially all the trade" between the constituent countries. The legal meaning of "substantially all the trade" and "other restrictive regulations of commerce" has never been fully articulated or resolved by either the CRTA or GATT/WTO panels or the Appellate Body.

With respect to the external requirement, Article XXIV:5 applies slightly different standards for customs unions and FTAs, but for both forms of PTAs it is generally required that duties and other regulations of commerce on third parties should not be "higher or more restrictive" after the creation of the PTA than before. For customs unions, which entail the creation of a common external tariff, duties or other regulations of commerce must not be higher or more restrictive "on the whole" after the creation of a PTA than before. This requirement was interpreted by the Appellate Body in *Turkey – Textiles* to provide for an "economic test" of the overall effect of the customs union on third parties; however, application of such an overall economic test poses major methodological problems which remain unresolved. In contrast, the external requirement for FTAs omits the words "on the whole", indicating a measure-by-measure approach rather than an overall economic test; each FTA member must ensure that no duties or other regulations of commerce faced by third parties are higher or more restrictive than the "corresponding duties and regulations of commerce" prior to the formation of the FTA. An additional external requirement for customs unions is contained in Article XXIV:8(a)(ii). This provision requires that "substantially the same duties and other regulations of commerce are applied by each of the members of the union to the trade of territories not included in the union". However, the meaning of this standard remains unclear in GATT/WTO jurisprudence.

The Article XXIV disciplines on PTAs have been the subject of one important Appellate Body decision (the *Turkey – Textiles* case 1999),[4] which involved a complaint by India against Turkey with respect to quantitative restrictions that Turkey had imposed on imports of textiles and clothing from India. Turkey, as part of its efforts to negotiate accession to the EU, had entered into an arrangement with the EU to adopt a customs union and pursuant to these arrangements had committed itself to adopt substantially the same commercial policy as the

---

4 *Turkey – Restrictions on Imports of Textile and Clothing Products*, 22 October 1999, WT/DS34/R and WT/DS34/AB/R [*Turkey – Textiles* 1999].

EU on textiles. India alleged breaches by Turkey of Article XI and XII of the GATT and Article 2.4 of the Agreement on Textiles and Clothing. Turkey pleaded by way of defence Article XXIV of the GATT, arguing that the impugned quantitative restrictions were necessary in order to form a customs union with the EU and that the chapeau to Article XXIV:5 asserts that the provisions of the GATT shall not prevent the formation of a customs union.

While the Appellate Body held that Article XXIV could justify certain GATT inconsistent measures, it interpreted the chapeau of Article XXIV:5 to mean that such a defence would only be available where adherence to the GATT provisions in question would "make impossible" formation of a customs union. On the facts of the case, the Appellate Body held that this test of necessity for an Article XXIV defence was not satisfied since Turkey could have adopted rules of origin that precluded trans-shipment of Indian textiles through Turkey into the EU, enabling formation of the customs union without imposing GATT-inconsistent quantitative restrictions on Indian textile and clothing imports into Turkey.

Turkey – Textiles was an important case in several respects. The Appellate Body made clear that it considers the overall compatibility of PTAs with Article XXIV to be justiciable, despite prior conventional wisdom that compliance with the requirements of Article XXIV primarily entailed political judgments by the WTO Committee on Regional Trade Agreements. Moreover, the Appellate Body made clear that Article XXIV offers a possible defence to measures inconsistent with GATT provisions beyond the MFN principle in Article I:1. However, an Article XXIV defence will only be available where formation of the customs union would be impossible in the absence of the GATT inconsistent measures – a stringent standard to satisfy.

4.3   The contested case for preferential trade agreements

The literature debating the merits and disadvantages of PTAs is well developed and wide-ranging, but contentious. Three central issues are essential to understanding the welfare effects of PTAs. The first two concern the static welfare effects of PTAs: 1) are PTAs trade-creating or trade-diverting? And 2) does the proliferation of PTA trade rules increase transaction costs and therefore inhibit trade? The third issue concerns the dynamic welfare effects of PTAs: 3) how does the formation of PTAs affect the future course of international trade liberalization? The World Trade Organization recently reviewed the evidence on trade creation and diversion in PTAs, finding that, although the literature is not conclusive, evidence suggests that PTAs are likely to create more trade among members and, while trade diversion may play a role in some agreements and in some sectors, it is not a key effect of most preferential agreements.[5]

4.3.1   Trade diversion or trade creation

The distinction between trade creation and trade diversion derives from the seminal work of Jacob Viner in his 1950 book, *The Customs Union Issue*. The distinction drawn by Viner between trade creation and trade diversion hinges on whether removal of a trade barrier through formation of a customs union shifts the source of production of a good to a lower cost producer (for trade creation) or higher cost producer (for trade diversion), based strictly on the costs of production and abstracting from costs associated with tariffs. For example, if removal of internal trade barriers shifts production in good X from domestic producers to more efficient producers in the partner countries, then this would be trade creating and beneficial for global welfare. However, if PTA creation shifts imports from more efficient producers in third countries to less efficient producers in the customs union partner, whose comparative advantage is a function of their preferential market access, then this is trade diverting and detrimental to global welfare. In the decades following Viner's classic contribution, economic models have become considerably more sophisticated, although despite these theoretical advances the net welfare impact of PTAs remains ambiguous.[6] Empirical studies have produced similarly conflicting results.[7]

---

5 WTO, *World Trade Report 2011: The WTO and Preferential Trade Agreements: From Co-existence to Coherence* (Geneva: World Trade Organization, 2011) 105–6.

6 See Arvind Panagariya, "Preferential Trade Liberalization: The Traditional Theory and New Developments", (2000) 38:2 *Journal of Economic Literature* 287.

7 See Viet D. Do and William Watson, "Economic Analysis of Regional Trade Agreements", in Lorand Bartels and Federico Ortino (eds), *Regional Trade Agreements in the WTO Legal System* (New York: Oxford University Press, 2006).

4.3.2   Transaction costs

Each PTA includes a unique set of trade rules with which importers and exporters must comply. Bhagwati likens the global web of PTAs as a "spaghetti bowl", with each additional PTA adding complexity to international trade rules and raising the transaction costs of international trade. As PTAs multiply, a single product will be subjected to different tariff rates under different PTAs; moreover, tariff treatment will hinge on compliance with each PTA's unique, and inherently arbitrary, rules of origin.[8] Other authors challenge the scale of these transaction costs as an impediment to trade, noting that producers always have the option of exporting under the MFN tariff rate, meaning that at worst the "spaghetti bowl" cannot diminish welfare beyond the original MFN starting point.[9]

4.3.3   Dynamic effects: building blocks or stumbling blocks?

The dynamic effects of PTAs concern the impact of each PTA on the subsequent path of international trade liberalization, either through the expansion of PTAs or through multilateral liberalization. Bhagwati argues that in modelling the dynamic effects of PTAs, the incentives faced by three key groups of agents must be considered. First, governments of member countries, once participating in a PTA, may avoid incurring the transaction costs of further PTA expansion due to a belief that the PTA market is already large enough. Second, interest groups in member countries, especially producer interest groups, may in some cases lobby for PTA expansion, but in others will seek protection from increased competition and oppose PTA expansion. Finally, interest groups and governments of outside countries may seek entry to, or emulation of, existing PTAs.[10] There are also reasons to suspect that PTAs could stall momentum for multilateral trade liberalization. Countries with existing or potential avenues for preferential market access are likely to have weaker incentives to pursue new markets through multilateral liberalization, a view for which there appears to be some empirical evidence.[11] It

---

8 Jagdish Bhagwati, *Termites in the Trading System* (New York: Oxford University Press, 2008).

9 See Do and Watson, supra note 7.

10 Jagdish Bhagwati, "Regionalism and Multilateralism: An Overview", in Jaime de Melo and Arvind Panagariya (eds), *New Dimensions in Regional Integration* (Cambridge: Cambridge University Press, 1993).

11 See Nuno Limão, "Preferential Trade Agreements as Stumbling Blocks for Multilateral Trade Liberalization: Evidence for the United States", (2006) 96:3 *The American Economic Review* 896.

is also often argued that negotiating and managing many PTAs is likely to strain the scarce economic, legal and diplomatic resources of countries, especially developing countries, and divert resources from advancing multilateral trade liberalization initiatives. Current gridlock in multilateral trade negotiations may be, in part, either a cause or an effect of the proliferation of PTAs.

4.3.4   Additional factors

Beyond these three key issues of trade diversion, transaction costs and dynamic effects of PTAs on global trade liberalization, a number of additional arguments are frequently advanced regarding the implications of PTAs. First, it has been claimed that PTAs offer the potential for deeper and broader liberalization, given that negotiations occur within or among smaller numbers of parties, often sharing common regional histories, backgrounds, and interests; however, deeper trade liberalization within PTAs may in some cases create more trade diversion than trade creation, which is not a desirable outcome from a global welfare perspective. Second, it is sometimes claimed that PTAs enable countries to advance the liberalization agenda into new issue areas, for many of the same reasons that may motivate deeper liberalization with respect to existing impediments to trade, and in this respect PTAs may function as laboratories of integration, serving as an example or a pathfinder for future multilateral disciplines.[12] Third, it may be argued that PTAs enable the advancement of important regional and domestic political objectives that are not directly trade related, such as greater political and economic integration in western Europe as a strategy for mitigating the risk of recurrence of the massive military conflicts that devastated Europe in the first half of the twentieth century. Fourth, on the negative side of the balance sheet, it is often pointed out that PTAs often group countries with significant disparities in wealth and political influence, and that these asymmetries between parties to a PTA can generate inequitable or inefficient outcomes, in contrast to the multilateral system where at least in principle decisions are made on a consensus basis, with one country-one vote, and the potential for coalition formation in negotiations within the multilateral system that may mitigate power asymmetries.

---

12 See Arie Reich, "Bilateralism versus Multilateralism in International Economic Law: Applying the Principle of Subsidiarity", (2010) 60:2 *University of Toronto Law Journal* 263.

4.4   Conclusion

The proliferation of PTAs in the global trading system is an empirical fact, but their economic impact, political implications, and legal status are contested. The legal disciplines on PTAs under Article XXIV are poorly defined, and the relative absence of GATT/WTO jurisprudence on PTAs is a symptom of the reluctance of WTO members to enforce the disciplines of Article XXIV, given that nearly all members are now party to a PTA and bear some risk if restrictive disciplines on PTAs are articulated by WTO panels or the Appellate Body. The consistency of PTAs with the multilateral trading system economically, politically, and legally is likely to constitute one of the most important and enduring challenges to the international trading system in the years ahead.

The proliferation of preferential trade agreements (PTAs) while in part, no doubt, reflecting paralysis within the multilateral system, also, in turn, undermines the centrality and vitality of the latter. One general line of response is to blur the boundaries between multilateralism and bilateralism, by providing much greater flexibility within the WTO for plurilateral agreements among sub-sets of members that are subject to a conditional MFN clause that permits subsequent accession by other members prepared to make similar commitments to those of existing members, along with an amendment to Article XXIV of the GATT that would permit signatories to preferential trade agreements to designate the WTO dispute settlement body as the dispute settlement body under a PTA, thus promoting coherence and integration of international trade law on similar issues.[13]

---

13 See Michael Trebilcock, "Between Theories of Trade and Development: The Future of the World Trading System", *Journal of World Investment and Trade Law* (*Journal of World Investment and Trade Law*, forthcoming); Bernard Hoekman and David Vines, "Multilateral Trade Cooperation: What Next?", (2007) 23:3 *Oxford Review of Economic Policy* 311–34.

5   The National Treatment Principle

5.1   Introduction

5.1.1   History

The National Treatment Principle has an ancient genesis in international trade law, arguably dating back to ancient Hebrew law and then appearing in agreements between Italian city-states in the eleventh century, in commercial treaties concluded during the twelfth century between England and continental powers and cities, and in agreements among German city-states constituting the Hanseatic League from the twelfth century onwards. The principle was also adopted in various shipping treaties entered into between European powers in the seventeenth and eighteenth centuries, and became commonplace in trade treaties drawn up in large numbers in the latter part of the nineteenth century.

5.1.2   The text of Article III of the GATT

(1) The Contracting Parties recognize that internal taxes and other internal charges, and laws, regulations and requirements affecting the internal sale, offering for sale, purchase, transportation, distribution or use of products in specified amounts or proportions, should not be applied to imported or domestic products so as to afford protection to domestic production.

(2) The products of the territory of any Contracting Party imported into the territory of any other Contracting Party shall not be subject, directly or indirectly, to internal taxes or other internal charges of any kind in excess of those applied, directly or indirectly, to like domestic products. Moreover, no Contracting Party shall otherwise apply internal taxes or other internal charges to imported or domestic products in a manner contrary to the principles set forth in paragraph 1.*

(. . .)

(4) The products of the territory of any Contracting Party imported into

the territory of any other contracting party shall be accorded treatment no less favourable than that accorded to like products of national origin in respect of all laws, regulations and requirements affecting their internal sale, offering for sale, purchase, transportation, distribution or use. The provisions of this paragraph shall not prevent the application of differential internal transportation charges which are based exclusively on the economic operation of the means of transport and not on the nationality of the product.

*A tax conforming to the requirements of the first sentence of paragraph 2 would be considered to be inconsistent with the provisions of the second sentence only in cases where competition was involved between, on the one hand, the taxed product and, on the other hand, a directly competitive or substitutable product which was not similarly taxed.

5.1.3 Interpretation of Article III

Over the history of the GATT/WTO, divergent approaches to the interpretation of Article III have been adopted, ranging from literalist or formalistic approaches; aims-and-effects approaches that focus on discerning protectionist intent; and economic or market-based approaches that focus on domestic fiscal or regulatory measures that upset competitive relationships between imports and domestic products.

5.2 The GATT (pre-WTO) case law

5.2.1 Internal taxes (Article III(2))

The first *Japanese-Alcohol Beverages* case (1987)[1] was the leading GATT case on internal taxes, and in interpreting the phrase "like products" in Article III(2) tended to focus on actual or potential substitutability between imported or domestic products on the part of consumers, as well as major differences in physical characteristics. This Panel adopted the criteria proposed by the GATT Working Party on Border Tax Adjustments in 1970, which emphasized: (i) product end-uses; (ii) consumers' tastes and habits; (iii) the products' properties, nature, and quality, to which later panels added a fourth criterion, that

---

1 *Japan – Customs Duties, Taxes and Labelling Practices on Imported Wines and Alcoholic Beverages*, adopted 10 November 1987, BISD 34S/83 [*Japan – Alcoholic Beverages* 1987].

is, common customs classifications. The other notable GATT Panel decision on internal taxes was *US – Taxes on Automobiles* in 1994[2] – an unadopted GATT Panel decision relating to gas guzzler and luxury excise taxes imposed by the US government on domestic and imported automobiles. Foreign exporters argued that this tax had a disparate impact on them, because of their different fleet composition. In this case the GATT Panel attached some weight to the "aims-and-effects" of the legislation in question and concluded that it was not motivated by protectionism and hence was not at variance with the objective of Article III, set out in Article III(1), which is to constrain the application of domestic measures "so as to afford protection to domestic production".

5.2.2   Regulatory measures (Article III(4))

The first major GATT Panel decision was the *US – Section 337 Tariff Act* case in 1989,[3] which related to special enforcement measures against allegedly patent-infringing imports. The Panel focused on the requirement in Article III(4) that, with respect to domestic legal and regulatory measures, imports of like products be treated "no less favourably" than domestic "like products". The Panel interpreted this requirement as prescribing "effective equality of competitive opportunities" for imports and domestic like products, which the measures in question were held to infringe. This decision has been followed in this respect by later GATT/WTO decisions.

The next important GATT Panel decision on Article III(4) was the *US – Tuna* case in 1991,[4] involving a US ban on imported tuna caught in ways that endangered dolphins. The GATT Panel in this case held that this ban violated Article XI and required justification under Article XX and also held that the measures in question could not be considered under Article III as they did not relate to tuna as a product, but rather the methods by which tuna was caught (implying that PPMs were not a legitimate basis for distinguishing between foreign and domestic products). This Panel decision was also not adopted by the GATT membership.

---

2 *United States – Taxes on Automobiles*, 29 September 1994, unadopted, DS31/R, 1–124 [*US – Taxes on Automobiles* 1994].

3 *United States – Section 337 of the Tariff Act of 1930*, adopted on 7 November 1989, L/6439 – 36S/345 [*US – Section 337 Tariff Act* 1989].

4 *United States – Restrictions on Imports of Tuna*, 3 September 1991, unadopted, DS21/R BISD 39S/155 [*US – Tuna* 1991].

Another important case was the *US – Malt Beverages* case in 1992[5] involving various US state fiscal and regulatory measures relating to wine and beer. With respect to various restrictions on the sale, distribution and marketing of high alcohol content beer, a Canadian complaint that these discriminated against Canadian imports was rejected on the grounds that the measures in question applied equally to domestic and foreign production and that the aims-and-effects of these measures were not protectionist but related to various health objectives.

5.3   WTO (post-1995) case law

5.3.1   Internal taxes

The first major case was the second *Japanese – Alcohol* case in 1996.[6] In this case both the Panel and the Appellate Body rejected the aims-and-effects test in the context of various fiscal measures that the European Union alleged discriminated against their alcohol exports to Japan. The Appellate Body held that the concept of "like product" meant different things in different GATT provisions, and invoked the analogy of an accordion that could be squeezed more widely or more narrowly depending on context. Both the Panel and the Appellate Body emphasized a market place test of "likeness" and the Appellate Body held that the second sentence of Article III(2), dealing with internal fiscal measures required an examination of the "design, architecture, and revealing structure" of the measures in question, in determining whether they had been adopted or applied so as to afford protection to domestic products (as required by Article III(1)) – a kind of objective test of legislative intention. The Appellate Body also emphasized that Article III is not limited in its purpose to preventing the undermining of prior bound tariff concessions by the adoption of subsequent protectionist domestic measures, but also applied where no tariff bindings existed.

In *Canada – Split Run Periodicals* (1997),[7] the Appellate Body overruled the Panel's finding on like products, deciding that in the context

---

5 *United States – Measures Affecting Alcoholic and Malt Beverages*, adopted 19 June 1992, DS23/R BISD 39S/206 [*US – Malt Beverages* 1992].

6 *Japan – Taxes on Alcoholic Beverages*, 11 July 1996, WT/DS8/R, WT/ DS10/R and WT/DS11/R; *Japan – Taxes on Alcoholic Beverages*, 4 October 1996, WT/DS8/AB/R, WT/DS10/AB/R, WT/ DS11/AB/R [*Japan – Alcohol* 1996].

7 *Canada – Certain Measures Concerning Periodicals*, 30 June 1997, WT/DS31/AB/R [*Canada – Split Run Periodicals* 1997].

of an 80 per cent excise tax on advertising content in foreign split-run periodicals, foreign split-run periodicals and domestic non-split run periodicals were not like products. However, the Appellate Body held that they fell within the ambit of the second sentence of Article III(2), and were competitive or directly substitutable products.

In *Korea – Taxes on Alcoholic Beverages* (1998),[8] the Panel and the Appellate Body largely followed the earlier decision in the second Japanese Alcohol case, and adopted a market-based test of likeness, and a *de minimus* test for "similarly taxed" under Article III(2) second sentence.

In *Chile – Taxes on Alcoholic Beverages* (1999),[9] the Panel adopted a consumer utility theory approach to deciding whether Pisco and various imported liquors were like products, using the analogy of butter and margarine to illustrate the point that differences in physical characteristics do not necessarily render products unlike if they serve similar functions in the utility function of consumers. A rather similar approach was taken by the Panel in *Indonesia – Autos* (1998),[10] where differences in treatment for internal tax purposes of certain domestically produced cars and various imported cars and car components were treated as violating Article III(2), again largely on grounds relating to the high degree of substitutability by consumers amongst these products.

5.3.2   Regulatory measures

In the first Appellate Body decision under the new dispute settlement regime: *US–Reformulated Gasoline* (1996),[11] different treatment of US and foreign refiners of gasoline in terms of base-line standards adopted for pollution abatement was held to violate Article III(4). There was no

---

8 *Korea – Taxes on Alcoholic Beverages*, 17 September 1998, WT/ DS75/R and WT/DS84/R; *Korea – Taxes on Alcoholic Beverages*, 18 January 1999, WT/DS75/AB/R and WT/DS84/AB/R [*Korea – Taxes on Alcoholic Beverages* 1998].

9 *Chile – Taxes on Alcoholic Beverages*, 15 June 1999, WT/DS87/R and WT/DS110/R [*Chile – Taxes on Alcoholic Beverages* 1999].

10 *Indonesia – Certain Measures Affecting the Automobile Industry*, WT/ DS54/R, WT/DS55/R, WT/DS59/R, WT/DS64/R and Corr. 1, 2, 3 and 4, adopted 23 July 1998, DSR 1998; VI, 2201. [*Indonesia – Autos* 1998].

11 *United States – Standards for Reformulated and Conventional Gasoline*, 29 January 1996, WT/ DS2/R [*US – Reformulated Gasoline* 1996], as modified by the Appellate Body Report, adopted 20 May 1996, WT/DS2/AB/R.

dispute that the products were like products. The Appellate Body held that the argument by the USA that it faced greater administrative difficulties applying the domestic measures in question to foreign refiners was not a sufficient justification for less favourable treatment under Article XX.

In *Korea – Beef* (2000),[12] where Korea had adopted a dual retailing system for domestic and imported beef, the Appellate Body held that formal differences in the way imports and domestic like products were treated were not in themselves sufficient to render the different treatment illegal under Article III(4), but some examination of disparate impacts was required, which the Appellate Body held that the Korean measures engendered.

In *EC – Asbestos* (2000),[13] probably the most important decision of the Appellate Body on Article III(4), the Appellate Body overruled findings by the Panel that asbestos fibres and asbestos-fibre products were "like products" relative to PCG Fibres, in the light of a French ban against the former but not the latter. While the Panel had upheld the measures under Article XX(b), the Appellate Body held that there was no violation in the first place of Article III(4). In the Appellate Body's view, all four criteria that had been adopted in prior Appellate Body and Panel decisions, largely based on the criteria proposed in the GATT Working Party Report on Border Tax Adjustments in 1970, had to be examined in order to reach an overall judgment on likeness. It held that the Panel had looked only at end-uses, and then only at a small number of overlapping end-uses without examining non-overlapping end-uses. The Appellate Body continued to emphasize, as it had in the second *Japanese – Alcohol*[14] case, the essentially economic test for likeness under Article III, with its focus on competitive relationships, but was of the view that there was a very heavy burden of proof on a complainant to demonstrate likeness in contexts where there were sharp differences in physical characteristics, particularly physical characteristics that related to health effects.

---

12 *Korea – Measures Affecting Imports of Fresh, Chilled and Frozen Beef*, 11 December 2000, WT/DS161/AB/R and WT/DS169/AB/R [*Korea – Beef* 2000].

13 *European Communities – Measures Affecting Asbestos and Asbestos-Containing Products*, adopted 5 April 2001, WT/DS135/R and Add. 1, as modified by the Appellate Body Report, *European Communities–Measures Affecting Asbestos and Asbestos-Containing Products*, adopted 5 April 2001, WT/DS135/AB/R.

14 *Japan – Alcohol* 1996, supra note 6.

In *Thailand – Cigarettes* (2011),[15] the Appellate Body held, with respect to assessing no less favourable treatment, that, with a condition that is formally more burdensome on imported products, one need not require empirical evidence on the actual effect on competitive conditions. Rather, assessment requires careful examination grounded in close scrutiny of the "fundamental thrust and effect of the measure", which might involve empirical evidence or might include those implications discernible from the design, structure, and expected operation of the measure.[16]

5.4   Critique of GATT/WTO case law

5.4.1   A literalist/formalistic approach

This approach seems to have very little to recommend it in that comparing and contrasting physical characteristics, without having some purpose or rationale in mind for the comparisons, is likely to be hopelessly indeterminate (in effect a "smell" test).

5.4.2   The aims-and-effects approach

Both the Panel and the Appellate Body in the second *Japanese – Alcohol* case emphasized the indeterminacy of an approach that focuses on the subjective intent of legislators and regulators, often operating with very mixed motives (for example, Baptist-bootlegger coalitions). However, the Appellate Body appears to have adopted something like an objective test of legislative intention in the second *Japanese – Alcohol*[17] case.

5.4.3   An economic approach

An economic approach would emphasize that whether the products are like or not is an empirical question involving an evaluation of the actual cross-elasticity of demand on the part of consumers vis-à-vis the products in question, as is conventionally undertaken in determining relevant product markets in antitrust law. As to whether imported

---

15 *Thailand – Customs and Fiscal Measures on Cigarettes from the Philippines*, 15 November 2010, WT/DS371/R [*Thailand – Cigarettes*], as modified by the Appellate Body Report, adopted 15 July 2011, WT/DS371/AB/R.

16 William Davey and Keith Maskus. "Thailand – Cigarettes (Philippines): A More Serious Role for the 'Less Favourable Treatment' Standard of Article III:4", 12(2) *World Trade Review*, 2013.

17 *Japan – Alcohol* 1996, supra note 6.

products have been treated less favourably than domestic products, one might also adopt from antitrust law a "raising rivals costs" approach in determining whether the measures in question have imposed greater costs on foreign producers relative to domestic producers. Under this approach differential treatment relating to health and environmental effects would require justification by the respondent under Article XX, on the theory that the respondent has better information than the complainant as to purported non-trade justifications for trade restrictive measures.[18]

5.4.4   Residual problems

A number of difficult residual problems remain unresolved in GATT/ WTO case-law interpreting and applying the National Treatment Principle.

How should one approach the question of domestic measures that distinguish between foreign and domestic products on the basis of differences in production and processing methods (PPMs)? What if these measures are imposed on both domestic and foreign products equally? What if these measures are imposed on domestic and foreign products sequentially? What if domestic measures do not relate either to product characteristics or to production and processing methods, but rather background differences in conditions in foreign and domestic countries, for example, human rights abuses? What scope is there for permitting incidental adverse impacts on imports from a non-protectionist domestic measure? Finally, how should one resolve the relationship between Article III and Article XX in terms of: a) the burden of proof; b) the scope of GATT exceptions?

---

18 See Michael J. Trebilcock and Shiva K. Giri, "The National Treatment Principle in International Trade Law", in E. Kwan Choi and James C. Hartigan (eds), *Handbook of International Trade*, Volume 2 (Blackwell Publishing, 2005).

6 Antidumping laws

6.1 Introduction

Antidumping laws are by far the most widely invoked of a trilogy of trade remedy or contingent protection regimes: antidumping laws; countervailing duties; and safeguards.[1] While Article VI of the GATT permitted member countries to impose antidumping laws from the outset of the GATT, up until the late 1970s antidumping laws were a relatively minor form of trade restriction, mostly because the bulk of protection was ensured by tariffs, quantitative restrictions (or voluntary export restraints), subsidies, or a mix of all these instruments. However, starting from the late 1970s both the total number of antidumping investigations and antidumping orders, as well as the number of countries that have introduced antidumping regimes have dramatically increased. As of December 2013, 2894 antidumping measures were in force around the world.[2] In many respects, it has become the protectionist remedy of choice.

India, followed by the USA, were the leading initiators of antidumping proceedings over the period of 1995 to 2013 (a total of 4358 initiations by all countries), in contrast to the period 1980 to 1988 when the actions of the USA, Australia, Canada, and the EU accounted for 97.5 per cent of all actions.[3]

---

1 See generally, Alan O. Sykes, "International Trade: Trade Remedies", in Andrew T. Guzman and Alan O. Sykes (eds), *Research Handbook in International Economic Law* (Cheltenham, UK: Edward Elgar, 2007); Petros C. Mavroidis, Patrick A. Messerlin and Jasper M. Wauters, *The Law and Economics of Contingent Protection in the WTO* (Cheltenham, UK: Edward Elgar, 2008).

2 World Trade Organization, "AD Measures: By Reporting Member 01/01/1995–31/12/2013", Online: http://www.wto.org/english/tratop_e/adp_e/AD_MeasuresByRepMem.pdf. Accessed 14 July 2014.

3 World Trade Organization, "AD Initiations: By Reporting Member 01/01/1995 – 30/06/2013", Online: http://www.wto.org/english/tratop_e/adp_e/AD_InitiationsByRepMem.pdf. Accessed 14 July 2014.

6.2   GATT/WTO provisions on antidumping

Article VI authorizes member countries to introduce antidumping regimes to address cases where the products of one country are introduced into the commerce of another country at less than the normal value of the products where this causes or threatens material injury to an established industry in the territory of a contracting party or materially retards the establishment of a domestic industry producing like products. A product is to be considered as being introduced into the commerce of an importing country at less than its normal value if the price at which the product is exported from one country to another is: a) less than the comparable price, in the ordinary course of trade, for the like product when destined for consumption in the exporting country, or b) in the absence of such domestic price, is less than either 1) the highest comparable price for the like product for export to any third country in the ordinary course of trade, or 2) the cost of production of the product in the country of origin plus a reasonable addition for selling costs and profit. Thus, under 1) export prices are compared with prices at the same level of trade in the country of origin, while under 2), the principal comparison is between the export prices and cost of production in the country of origin (often referred to as the "constructed cost" measure). Where these conditions are met, the importing country may levy on any dumped product an antidumping duty not greater in amount than the margin of dumping in respect of such products, where the margin of dumping is the price difference determined by comparisons between the export price and either of the two country-of-origin measures noted above.

These rather cursory provisions left open many ambiguities surrounding the determination of the relevant price comparators, the concept of injury, the concept of causation, the definition of like products, and the definition of a domestic industry. In the course of the Kennedy Round that closed in the late 1960s, the Tokyo Round that closed in the late 1970s, and the Uruguay Round that closed in 1993, a much more detailed antidumping agreement has been elaborated that attempts to provide more detailed specifications of all of these key concepts. Article 2.1 of the Uruguay Round Anti-Dumping Agreement defines products as being dumped – that is, introduced into the commerce of another country at less than their normal value – if the export price is less than the comparable price, in the ordinary course of trade, for the like product when destined for consumption in the exporting country. Where there are no sales of the like product in the ordinary course of trade in the domestic market of the exporting country, or when because of the particular market situation or the low volume of sales in the domestic market of the exporting country (a sufficient quantity must normally constitute 5 per cent or more of the sales of the product to the importing country) such sales do not permit a proper comparison, the margin of dumping shall be determined by comparison with a comparable price of the like product when exported to an appropriate third country, or with the cost or production in the country of origin plus a reasonable amount for administrative, selling and general costs, and for profits. Sales in the domestic market of the exporting country below per unit (fixed and variable) costs of production plus administrative, selling and general costs, may be disregarded in determining normal value if made for an extended period of time (normally one year) in substantial quantities (more than 20 per cent of transactions). Thus, all export sales, whether above or below total costs, will be averaged to obtain the export price, while generally only domestic sales above total costs will be averaged (increasing the likelihood of a finding of dumping). Where there are no home market or third country sales on which to base price comparisons, constructed value may be used, which includes materials and labour costs and an amount for selling, general and administrative expenses (SG and A) plus profit. These latter costs – SG and A plus profit – must now generally be based on actual data pertaining to production and sales in the ordinary course of business by the exporter (Article 2.2). In the case of designated non-market economies, importing countries may choose domestic prices in surrogate third countries as a foreign reference point (which may reflect quite arbitrary choices).

Comparison between the export price and the normal value should be "fair" as stipulated under Article 2.4, which provides that the existence of margins of dumping shall normally be established on the basis of a comparison of weighted average domestic sale prices and weighted average export market prices, or by a comparison of domestic prices and export prices on a transaction-to-transaction basis. This precludes comparing isolated low priced export transactions with weighted average domestic prices to establish dumping.

Under Article 3, determination of injury for purposes of Article VI of GATT 1994 shall be based on positive evidence and involve an objective examination of both a) the volume of the dumped imports and the effect of the dumped imports on prices in the domestic market for like products, and b) the consequent impact of these imports on domestic producers of such products. Where imports of a product from more than one country are simultaneously subject to antidumping investigations, the investigating authorities may cumulatively assess the effects of such imports if they exceed certain *de minimus* thresholds. The examination of the impact of the dumped imports on the domestic industry concerned shall include an evaluation of all relevant economic factors having a bearing on the state of the industry (which are enumerated in Article 3.4). The authorities shall also examine any known factors other than the dumped imports, which at the same time are injuring the domestic industry, and the injuries caused by these other factors must not be attributed to the dumped imports. A determination of the threat of material injury shall be based on facts and not merely on allegation, conjecture or remote possibility. The change in circumstances which would create a situation in which the dumping would cause injury must be clearly foreseen and imminent.

Under Article 5.8, investigations shall be terminated when a dumping margin is *de minimus* (less than 2 per cent of the normal value) or when the volume of dumped products is negligible (in other words, if the volume of dumped imports from a particular country accounts for less than 3 per cent of imports of the like product in the importing country, unless countries that individually account for less than 3 per cent of imports collectively account for more than 7 per cent of imports).

Under Article 7, provisional measures may be applied if an investigation has been initiated and a preliminary affirmative determination has been made of dumping and injury to a domestic industry. Provisional measures may take the form of a provisional duty or a security (a cash deposit or bond) equal to the amount of the antidumping duties provisionally estimated.

Under Article 8, proceedings may be suspended or terminated on receipt of the satisfactory voluntary undertaking from any exporter to revise its prices or to cease exports at dumped prices. Price undertakings may not be sought or accepted unless preliminary determinations of dumping and injury have been made and, even if then sought and accepted, the exporter may elect to have the investigation completed. In the event of a negative determination, undertakings lapse.

Under Article 17.6, in dispute settlement proceedings before the WTO under the Antidumping Agreement, a WTO Panel in its assessment of the facts of the matter shall determine whether the domestic authorities' establishment of the facts was proper and whether their evaluation of those facts was unbiased and objective. If the establishment of the facts was proper and the evaluation was unbiased and objective, even though the Panel might have reached a different conclusion, the evaluation shall not be overturned. WTO Panels shall interpret the relevant provisions of the Agreement in accordance with customary rules of interpretation of public international law. Where the Panel finds that a relevant provision of the Agreement admits of more than one permissible interpretation, the Panel shall find the domestic authorities' measures to be in conformity with the Agreement if it rests upon one of those permissible interpretations.

Despite these attempts at a greater specification of key requirements for the imposition of antidumping duties, in recent years formal trade disputes over the imposition of antidumping duties by member countries have accounted for a substantial part of the workload of WTO Panels and the Appellate Body. Between 1995 and the end of 2013, Leitner and Lester report 102 formal complaints relating to the application of antidumping measures, exceeded only by complaints relating to general GATT provisions.[4] Many of these disputes have related to the determinations of the two price or cost comparisons noted above. For example, the practice of the USA of attaching zero weight in determining country of origin prices to prices that entail negative dumping margins ("zeroing") – rendering home market prices lower than export market prices – have been repeatedly challenged before WTO Panels and the Appellate Body, and have been repeatedly found non-compliant. The USA recently signed agreements with the EU and Japan aimed at ending its practice of zeroing, in exchange for which the EU and Japan agreed to drop claims for trade retaliation.[5]

In addition, in two dispute-settlement proceedings, the remedies applied by the USA, once an affirmative determination of dumping, material injury, and causation has been made, have also been challenged in dispute-settlement proceedings. In the *US – Antidumping*

---

4 Kara Leitner and Simon Lester, "WTO Dispute Settlement 1995–2013 – A Statistical Analysis", (2014) 17:1 *Journal of International Economic Law* 196.

5 Office of the United States Trade Representative, "United States Trade Representative Ron Kirk Announces Solution to Years-Old Zeroing Dispute, Demonstrating Commitment to Export Growth and Job Creation", *Executive Office of the President*, February 2012.

Act 1916 in 2000,[6] the Appellate Body held that the treble damages complainants were authorized to recover under this Act for injury caused by dumping were not one of the three authorized remedies for dumping under the WTO Antidumping Agreement, that is, provisional duties, price undertakings, or definitive duties. Similarly, in the *US – Continued Dumping and Subsidy Offset Act* of 2000[7] (often referred to as the Byrd Amendment), the Appellate Body held that an amendment to USA antidumping legislation that required anti-dumping duties to be distributed to members of the injured domestic industry was non-compliant with the WTO Antidumping Agreement on similar grounds. Subsequent arbitration proceedings were brought under Article 22.6 of the Dispute Settlement Understanding as to the scale of the trade retaliation that many of the complainant countries in these proceedings were authorized to impose on the USA, given its continuing failure to bring its antidumping laws into compliance with the Appellate Body's decision. These revealed a new set of complexities in determining the equivalence of trade sanctions to the adverse trade effects caused to these complainants by the distribution of antidumping duties to members of the domestic US industries in question.

6.3   Domestic administration of antidumping duties

In Canada and the USA, a similar bifurcated determination process is employed. The determination of whether dumping is occurring and what the margin of dumping is are decided, in the case of Canada, by Revenue Canada, and in the case of the USA by the International Trade Administration of the Department of Commerce. Material injury determinations, in the case of Canada, are made by the Canadian International Trade Tribunal, and in the case of the USA, by the International Trade Commission, both specialized administrative agencies that typically hold elaborate hearings and review large bodies of documentary and oral evidence in the course of reaching their determinations. In the case of the European Union, the European Commission makes both of these sets of determinations in a much less public or transparent process than that which obtains in Canada and the USA, subject to appeals to the European General Court and

---

6   *United States – Anti-Dumping Act of 1916*, WT/DS136, D162/AB/R (00–3369), adopted by the Dispute Settlement Body, 26 September 2000 [*US 1916* 2000].

7   *US – Continued Dumping and Subsidy Offset Act 2000*, WT/DS217/AB/R and WT/DS234/AB/R [*US Byrd Amendment* 2000].

ultimately the European Court of Justice, which have been typically deferential to the European Commission.

In terms of the substantive issues to be resolved in domestic antidumping proceedings, the key issues are as follows.

6.3.1   The dumping determination

This entails estimating the normal value of the goods by reference to country-of-origin prices, constructed costs, or surrogate third country export prices in the case of transition economies and comparing this normal value with export prices in the country of importation. This comparison in turn yields the margin of dumping.

6.3.2   Injury determination

The injury determination requires an evaluation of the impact of dumping on the domestic producers of a majority of like products. Indicators of material injury, according to Article 3.4 of the Uruguay Round Antidumping Agreement, can include a variety of factors, such as actual and potential decline in sales, profits, output, market share, productivity, return on investments, or utilization of capacity; factors affecting domestic prices; the magnitude of the margin of dumping; actual and potential negative effects on cash flow, inventories, employment, wages, growth and ability to raise capital or investments.

6.3.3   Causation

Under Article 3.5 of the Antidumping Agreement it must be demonstrated that the dumped imports are, through the effects of dumping, causing injury within the meaning of this Agreement. The demonstration of a causal relationship between the dumped imports and the injury to the domestic industry must be based on an examination of all relevant evidence before the authorities. The authorities must also examine any known factors other than the dumped imports which at the same time are injuring the domestic industry, and the injuries caused by these other factors must not be attributed to the dumped imports (a non-attribution requirement).

Causation has been a source of persistent controversy in domestic antidumping proceedings, in WTO dispute-settlement proceedings, and in the scholarly literature. The generally prevailing approach in the USA and many other countries is to adopt a bifurcated approach to the determination of the causation issue by, on the one hand, determining the existence of dumping and the margin of dumping, while on the other hand looking at trends over some recent representative period, for example three years, relating to the condition of the domestic industry. If the volume of dumped imports or the margin of dumping has been increasing, while the financial condition of the domestic industry, in various dimensions, has been deteriorating, causation will typically simply be inferred. This technique essentially equates correlation with causation, and has been trenchantly criticized by law and economics scholars on that account.[8]

An alternative approach that is more economically defensible is the so-called unified or integrated approach where one asks what the condition of the domestic industry would be if dumping had not been occurring. This approach typically involves constructing a counterfactual where the price of imports is hypothetically raised so as to eliminate any margin of dumping, and then in the light of estimates of elasticities of domestic supply and demand and foreign supply, one reaches some judgment about the relative condition of the domestic industry with dumping and without dumping. This approach, for example, rules out attributing causation of material injury to dumped imports where the margin of dumping may be very small and where the domestic industry is really simply complaining about low-priced imports (whether dumped or not), and opportunistically seizes onto the fact that some small margin of dumping can be demonstrated.

Canadian antidumping law, contained in the *Special Import Measures Act*, includes an unusual provision authorizing the Canadian International Trade Tribunal (CITT), after making the foregoing determinations, to hold a public interest hearing to determine whether imposing antidumping duties would be contrary to the public interest, despite the fact that they meet all of the foregoing conditions. The Tribunal reports to the Minister of Finance who has discretion to lower or remove the duty. A prominent example of the exercise of this discretion is a 1998 case in which Revenue Canada found dumping of prepared baby food by Gerber US and

---

8   See Ronald Cass and Michael Kroll, "The Economics of 'Injury' in Antidumping and Countervailing Duty Cases: A Reply to Professor Sykes", in J.S. Bhandari and Alan O. Sykes (eds), *Economic Dimensions in International Law: Comparative and Empirical Perspectives* (Cambridge: Cambridge University Press, 1997).

the CITT found material injury to the only other supplier of baby food in Canada, Heinz Canada. The public controversy that resulted when Gerber left the Canadian market led the CITT to hold a public interest hearing and to recommend that 60 per cent antidumping duties be reduced by approximately two-thirds due to concerns about the impact of price increases on low income families, lack of consumer choice, security of supply, rates of innovation and quality of service with only one supplier to the Canadian market. Despite the implementation of this reduction, Gerber did not return to the market. Following the five-year expiry review mandated by the WTO Antidumping Agreement to determine whether material injury to the domestic industry was likely to result from an expiry, the CITT in 2003 refused to extend the duties, finding that any injury that Heinz might suffer from Gerber's re-entry into the Canadian market would be due, for the most part, to the effects of renewed competition into the market, not to dumping.[9]

6.3.4   Chapter 19 NAFTA binational panel reviews

One of Canada's principal negotiating objectives in entering into negotiations for a Canada–US Free Trade Agreement in the mid-1980s was to secure relief against harassment of Canadian exports under US trade remedy laws.

The result of these negotiations was that under Chapter 19 of the Canada–US Free Trade Agreement of 1988 and Chapter 19 of NAFTA, which largely superseded it in 1993, binational panel reviews of domestic antidumping and countervailing duty determinations have been instituted. Panels of five adjudicators drawn from the two countries involved in the antidumping proceedings are authorized to review determinations by domestic agencies on dumping issues, in accordance with the legal standard of review obtaining in the respondent country before domestic courts reviewing decisions of such agencies. Where the Panel finds deficiencies in these determinations, it remands the issues back to the domestic agency for redetermination. This process of binational panel review has been widely utilized since it was first introduced under the Canada–US Free Trade Agreement in 1988. Indeed, most Canada–US antidumping determinations have led to the

---

9 See Michael Trebilcock and Andrew Tepperman, "The CITT's Baby Foods Decision: Evaluating Dumping-Related Injury When the Domestic Producer is a Monopolist", (Fall 2004) *The Competition Policy Record* 38.

initiation of binational panel review proceedings, in turn resulting in a high remand rate.[10]

6.4 Normative rationales for antidumping duties

6.4.1 Economic rationales[11]

6.4.1.1 Price discrimination

In a typical dumping case, foreign exporters charge less for their goods in export markets than they charge in their country of origin, despite the fact that presumably selling in export markets involves some additional costs, such as transportation. These price discrepancies may be explained by a number of factors, including the fact that the foreign exporter may have a more firmly established reputation in its own domestic market and hence be able to sustain higher prices than when it is attempting to establish a presence in foreign markets for the first time; the foreign exporter's domestic market may be regulated in such a fashion or be subject to such weak or ineffective competition laws that the foreign exporter has some degree of market power in its own domestic market; or its own domestic market position may be protected by trade barriers of one kind or another. Hence, the foreign exporter may face more intense competition in export markets than in its home market. Domestic price discrimination is often prohibited under domestic competition or antitrust laws, in a limited range of circumstances, although the Canadian *Competition Act* has recently been amended to remove this prohibition from the Act. Domestic price discrimination is ubiquitous, for example, airlines, movie theatres, telephone calls, and so on. Most competition/antitrust law specialists generally regard the case for constraints on domestic price discrimination as dubious at best, as price discrimination tends to raise output toward competitive levels. However, whatever the merits of disciplining domestic price discrimination, the case for disciplining interna-

---

10 See John Mercury, "Chapter 19 of the United States – Canada Free Trade Agreement 1989–95: A Check on Administered Process?", (1995) 15 *Northwestern Journal of International Law and Business* 525; Juscelino F. Colares and John W. Bohn, "NAFTA's Double Standards of Review", (2007) 2 *Wake Forest Law Review* 199; William J. Davey, *Pine and Swine – Canada – US Trade Dispute Settlement: The FTA Experience and NAFTA Prospects* (Ottawa: Centre for Trade Policy and Law, 1996).

11 For an excellent treatment of these rationales, see Mavroidis, Messerlin and Wauters, supra note 1.

tional price discrimination (such as antidumping often entails) is even weaker, in that geographic price discrimination that yields both high-priced and low-priced markets (depending on differences in demand elasticities), in the case of international price discrimination yields a low-priced market in the importing country and a high-priced market in the exporting country, which would seem of little or no concern to importing countries that benefit from the lower-priced imports.

6.4.1.2   Predation

Under many countries' domestic competition or antitrust laws, preda-tory pricing is either prohibited on a stand-alone basis or is viewed as symptomatic of abuse of dominance. In most cases of predatory pricing, a dominant firm, in the face of price competition from rivals, may cut its prices below its costs, incurring a loss in the short-run, with a view to driving actual or potential rivals out of the market, and then raising prices subsequently to supra-competitive or monopolistic levels, enabling it to recoup any short-run losses and make mono-poly profits in the longer term. As with price discrimination, most competition/antitrust law specialists regard anti-competitive forms of domestic predation as a relatively rare occurrence, largely because it is likely to prove an unsuccessful or at least highly risky strategy, given the certainty of short-run losses and the uncertainty of future monopoly profits in the face of the prospect of future competitive entry. However, even amongst those commentators who believe that a domestic anti-predation law is warranted, it is widely accepted that it is generally symptomatic of abuse of a dominant position in the market. In the case of international dumping, where historically most antidumping actions have been brought by major importing countries, often against exporters in smaller countries, it seems totally implau-sible to assume that the foreign exporters could realistically aspire to monopolizing the importing country's market. One illustrative case is the antidumping complaint brought in Canada by General Motors and Ford against Hyundai for allegedly selling cars in Canada in the mid-1980s, at the time it was first entering the Canadian market, at 36 per cent less than it sold them for in South Korea. It is not seriously arguable that Hyundai was using supra-competitive profits garnered in its protected South Korean market to finance below-cost exports to the Canadian market, where it held a market share of 2 or 3 per cent, with a view to predating (monopolizing) the latter market.[12] Moreover,

---

12 Mathew Kronby, "Kicking the Tires", (1991) 18 *Canadian Business L.J.* 95.

a study by Hutton and Trebilcock of the 30 cases between 1984 and 1989 in which Canada imposed antidumping duties found that none could be supported on predatory pricing grounds.[13] An unpublished study for the OECD of a much larger sample of antidumping cases apparently reached similar conclusions.[14]

6.4.1.3   *Intermittent dumping*

Jacob Viner, in an early economic analysis of dumping, was concerned that some dumping could be characterized as intermittent, reflecting gluts or surpluses of, for example, perishable agricultural products in exporting countries, but as not reflecting a sustainable source of supply, while arguably disrupting more efficient domestic industries, and hence leading to higher costs for consumers in the long run.[15] While Viner may have been correct that intermittent dumping is inefficient in that it reduces total social welfare in the importing country, the concern seems applicable to a very narrow range of circumstances and moreover is not an explicit focus of domestic antidumping proceedings. Indeed, Hutton and Trebilcock find that the only Canadian antidumping cases, of the 30 that they analyzed in detail, that exhibited any indication of intermittent dumping were a handful of cases involving agricultural imports.

6.4.2   Non-economic rationales

6.4.2.1   *Distributive justice*

It might be argued that antidumping duties serve to advance distributive justice goals by protecting "least advantaged" groups in importing countries (in a Rawlesian sense). These groups might include low-skilled, low-paid, immobile workers. However, the problem with this argument is that such impacts, while a perfectly legitimate source of concern, are not limited to dumped imports but any low-priced imports, dumped or not, and would seem to call for quite different policy responses than antidumping laws, including safeguard laws and other forms of domestic adjustment assistance. Moreover, Hutton and Trebilcock find that only a very small number of the 30 cases they

---

13 Susan Hutton and Michael Trebilcock, "An Empirical Study of the Application of Canadian Antidumping Laws: A Search for Normative Rationales", (1990) 24 *Journal of World Trade* 123.

14 See "Attack on Antidumping Laws Sparks OECD Row", *Financial Times*, 21 September 1995.

15 See Jacob Viner, *Dumping: A Problem in International Trade* (University of Chicago Press, 1933).

examined seem to fit within this rationale – in many cases the workers involved in the domestic industry were better paid than average workers in Canada.

6.4.2.2   Communitarianism

A related concern is that the dumping laws may advance the objective of protecting long-standing communities that are dependent on particular industries and are threatened by import competition, along with the social ties and networks that are valuable to members of such communities. Again, as with distributive justice concerns, it is not obvious why this concern should be restricted to dumped imports, as opposed to low-priced imports generally (dumped or not), and again other policy responses are likely to be much more effective. Hutton and Trebilcock find very few cases in their sample of 30 cases where this concern seems legitimately engaged.

6.4.2.3   Political rationales

Alan Sykes argues that rather than attempting to ascribe an economic logic to antidumping laws, it is more persuasive to view them as part of a grand political compact among major trading nations where in order to facilitate major trade liberalization concessions with respect to border measures such as tariffs and quantitative restrictions, member countries by agreement reserved to themselves various unilateral "opt-out" regimes, including antidumping duties, against the contingency that the discrete impacts of import competition in particular sectors would prove politically unsustainable. He argues that in the absence of these opt-outs or safety valves, governments would have been more reluctant to assume the political risks of trade liberalization initiatives in the first place.[16] Sykes' argument is a subtle and disconcerting one, in that it is inherently non-refutable through any decisive *a priori* analysis. However, it seems to assume that there is some constant quotient of protectionism in the world which needs to be preserved, so that if tariffs or other border measures are reduced other outlets need to be found for this fixed quotient of protectionism. This seems empirically a highly suspect hypothesis, given the extensive forms and degrees of trade liberalization that have occurred in the post-war years. Moreover, even if the argument is correct in its own terms, it is not clear why this

---

16 See Alan O. Sykes, "The Economics of Injury in Antidumping and Countervailing Duty Cases", (1996) 16 *International Review of Law and Economics* 5.

justifies antidumping duties rather than a well-conceived safeguards regime.

6.5   Reforming antidumping duty regimes

Various reform options are open to consideration, ranging from the modest to the ambitious. At the modest end of the spectrum, one could tinker with the existing WTO rules in various ways; for example, prohibiting "zeroing"; introducing a public interest exception as in Canadian antidumping laws; or adopting a unified or integrated causation test. It is doubtful that any of these reforms would have a dramatic impact on the utilization of antidumping laws. One could also imagine strengthening the role of binational or multilateral review of the domestic application of antidumping laws, for example by giving binational panels under Chapter 19 of NAFTA dispositive power over antidumping determinations, rather than merely remand power, and perhaps creating some form of regional equivalent of the Appellate Body to replace the current Extraordinary Challenge Committees. One could also remove Article 17.6 from the Antidumping Agreement, which requires the Dispute Settlement Body to show deference to domestic agencies, both on factual determinations and in the interpretation of provisions of the Antidumping Agreement. However, again it is hard to imagine that such reforms are likely to have a dramatic impact on the utilization of antidumping laws.

A much more ambitious reform would be to contemplate the repeal of current antidumping laws and replacing them with a harmonized anti-predation law, whereby a country is authorized to enact domestic legislation (if such does not already exist) that penalizes or prohibits international forms of predatory pricing. This is likely to have a dramatic impact on the scope of antidumping laws, given the rarity of successful predation prosecutions or civil suits under domestic competition or antitrust law and would probably reduce positive antidumping determinations by upwards of 90 per cent. This is the course that has been taken by Australia and New Zealand under their regional free trade treaty, and predictably has led to the end of antidumping actions between the two countries. In this way, the National Treatment Principle would be fully respected, in that domestic and foreign producers of competitive products would be put on exactly the same footing in terms of the pricing practices in which they are permitted to engage. Current antidumping laws are flagrantly discriminatory by imposing much more stringent disciplines on the pricing behaviour of foreign producers than the pricing constraints imposed under domestic competition/antitrust laws on domestic producers. One might end with a final question: is reform along these lines remotely feasible in the future, and if not why not?

7 Subsidies, countervailing duties and government procurement

7.1 Introduction

Allegedly trade-distorting subsidies conferred on domestic industries by member countries have been a longstanding issue of contention in trade policy circles, and according to Leitner and Lester[1] accounted for 99 issues in dispute in formal trade dispute proceedings between 1995 and 2013 – more than any other GATT/WTO agreement, aside from the basic GATT itself. A number of these disputes have been high profile, including the long-running softwood lumber dispute between Canada and the USA; the dispute between Brazil and Canada over aircraft subsidies by both countries; the dispute between the EU and the USA over US taxation of Foreign Sales Corporations; the dispute between Brazil and the USA over US subsidies to domestic cotton production; the dispute over EU subsidies to sugar production; and the dispute between the USA and the EU over subsidies to Boeing and Airbus.

It is useful to keep in mind three basic subsidy scenarios:

a. Country A subsidizes exports of products to Country B, allegedly causing material injury to domestic producers of like products in Country B. This is the classic countervailing duty scenario.
b. Country A subsidizes exports to Country C and as a result squeezes out exports from Country B to Country C's market.
c. Country A subsidizes domestic production of products for its own market, having the effect of squeezing out imports from Country B into Country A's market.

The latter two scenarios do not implicate the potential imposition of unilateral countervailing duties given that the subsidized products are

---

1 Kara Leitner and Simon Lester, "WTO Dispute Settlement 1995–2013 – A Statistical Analysis", (2014) 17:1 *Journal of International Economic Law* 196.

not moving from Country A to Country B's market, but instead raise the potential for a formal complaint under the Dispute Settlement Provisions of the WTO.

7.2   The GATT subsidies regime

Under Article VI of the GATT, member countries may impose countervailing duties on imports into their domestic markets in an amount not in excess of the estimated bounty or subsidy determined to have been granted, directly or indirectly, on the manufacture, production, or export of such product in the country of origin or exportation. Under Article VI, as with dumping, no countervailing duties may be imposed unless there has been a determination that the effect of subsidization is such as to cause or threaten material injury to an established domestic industry, or is such as to retard materially the establishment of a domestic industry producing like products. No product should be subject to countervailing duties by reason of the exemption of such product from duties or taxes borne by the like product when destined for consumption in the country of origin, or by reason of the refund of such duties or taxes, reflecting the theory that countries of importation may well wish to impose consumption taxes on such imports and that exemption from payment of such taxes in countries of origin simply avoids double taxation. After antidumping actions, countervailing duty actions are generally the most frequently initiated type of trade remedy. Between 1995 and 2011, the USA reported the most initiations, with 109 of 262, followed by the EU with 60. Developed countries were responsible for 215, or 82 per cent of countervailing duty initiations. Between 1995 and 2008, developing countries were the object of the majority of initiations.[2]

Under Article XVI of the GATT, if any contracting party grants or maintains any subsidy which operates directly or indirectly to increase exports of any product from, or to reduce imports of any product into, its territory, it must notify the contracting parties of the nature and extent of the subsidization and of its likely effects on imports and exports and upon request discuss with other contracting

---

2 WTO. "CV Initiations by Reporting Member 01/01/1995 – 30/06/2011", World Trade Organization. Online: http://www.wto.org/english/tratop_e/scm_e/cvd_init_rep_member_e.pdf. Accessed 12 July 2014.

parties concerned the possibility of limiting subsidization. Additional provisions were added to Article XVI in 1955 dealing with export subsidies, whereby contracting parties agreed not to grant either directly or indirectly any form of subsidy on the export of any product other than a primary product, where such a subsidy results in the sale of such a product at a price lower than the comparable price charged for the like product to buyers in the domestic market. In the case of subsidies on the export of primary products, contracting parties agreed that such subsidies should not be applied in a manner which results in the subsidizing party having more than an equitable share of world export trade in that product, taking account of the shares of the contracting parties in such trade in the product during a previous representative period. However, the consultation provisions of Article XVI have proved largely ineffectual, and the additional provisions on export subsidies were not adopted by many members of the GATT, in particular most developing country members.

During the Tokyo Round of multilateral negotiations that ended in the late 1970s a more detailed subsidies code was negotiated that attempted to set out some basic disciplines for two tracks or avenues of complaints – first, unilateral imposition of countervailing duties by member countries pursuant to domestic countervailing duty laws; and second, subsidies falling into all three of the scenarios described above could constitute the subject of a formal complaint under the Dispute Settlement provisions of the GATT which, if upheld, could eventually lead to the authorization of retaliatory trade sanctions against the country whose subsidies were held in violation of the disciplines set out in this code. However, many of the rules contained in this agreement remained vague. For example, export subsidies on primary products were subject to a rule that was not much more specific than the rule contained in Article XVI of the GATT, and disciplines on domestic subsidies were subject to a wide range of exceptions or qualifications which permitted member countries to provide such subsidies, subject only to the vague requirement that they take into account possible adverse effects on trade. Moreover, the Tokyo Round Subsidies Code was a plurilateral, not a multilateral, agreement and was adopted mostly by OECD countries and not by most developing countries.

7.3   The Uruguay Round Subsidies and Countervailing Measures (SCM) Agreement

In the course of the Uruguay Round of multilateral trade negotiations that ended in December 1993, a much more detailed subsidies agreement was negotiated (henceforth the SCM Agreement). This agreement is part of the single undertaking that all members of the WTO were required to commit themselves to, and hence is a multilateral and not plurilateral agreement (in contrast to the Tokyo Round Subsidies Code). Like the Tokyo Round Code, the SCM Agreement preserves two tracks or avenues for objection to other countries' subsidies policies: the unilateral imposition of countervailing duties on subsidized imports, and the filing of a formal complaint with the WTO Dispute Settlement Body, with the possibility for the imposition of retaliatory sanctions in the event that the complaint is upheld.

The SCM Agreement essentially adopts what has been described as a red light, yellow light, and green light approach to subsidies. Under Article 3 of the SCM Agreement, two classes of subsidies are prohibited outright: a) subsidies contingent, in law or in fact, upon export performance; and b) subsidies contingent upon the use of domestic over imported goods (the red light category of subsidies). Under Article 8 of the SCM Agreement, certain subsidies are declared to be non-actionable, including certain subsidies for research and development, certain types of assistance to disadvantaged regions, and certain subsidies for compliance with environmental regulations. These green light provisions were scheduled to expire in 2000 unless renewed (Article 31), which the members have not chosen to do. This, then, focuses our attention on the intermediate or yellow light class of subsidies, deemed to be actionable subsidies under Part III of the SCM Agreement.

Article 1 of the SCM Agreement contains a fairly detailed definition of a subsidy which must entail a financial contribution by government, including direct transfers of funds (for example, grants, loans and equity infusions), potential direct transfers of funds or liabilities (for example, loan guarantees); government revenue otherwise due that is foregone or not collected; government provision of goods or services other than general infrastructure; government purchases of goods. In addition, a benefit must thereby be conferred by the subsidy in question.

With respect to actionable subsidies, a subsidy must also be "specific" as defined in Article 2, whereby the granting authority either explicitly or implicitly limits access to a subsidy to certain enterprises (prohibited subsidies are deemed to be specific). In the case of actionable subsidies, Article 5 provides that no member shall cause, through the use of any subsidy, the following adverse effects to the interests of any other member: that is: a) injury to the domestic industry of another member; b) nullification or impairment of benefits accruing directly or indirectly to other members, in particular the benefits of tariff concessions bound under Article II of the GATT; and c) serious prejudice to the interests of another member. Serious prejudice is defined, in turn, in Article 6 as arising in any case where one or several of the following apply:

a) the effect of the subsidy is to displace or impede the imports of a like product of another member into the market of the subsidizing member;
b) the effect of the subsidy is to displace or impede the exports of a like product of another member from a third country market;
c) the effect of the subsidy is a significant price undercutting by the subsidized product as compared with the price of a like product of another member in the same market or significant price suppression, price depression, or lost sales in the same market; or
d) the effect of the subsidy is an increase in the world market share of the subsidizing member in a particular subsidized primary product or commodity as compared to the average share it had during the previous period of three years and this increase follows a consistent trend over a period when subsidies have been granted.

The SCM Agreement contains various transitional provisions that provide various dispensations to developing countries or countries in transition from command to market economies, particularly with respect to the time within which they are required to bring their subsidy practices into compliance with the provisions of the SCM Agreement. In the case of actionable subsidies, the relevant provisions in the SCM Agreement do not apply to subsidies maintained on agricultural products as provided in Article 13 of the Agreement on Agriculture (the so-called "Peace Clause", which expired at the beginning of 2004). Part 7 of the SCM Agreement sets out detailed annual reporting requirements for members with respect to actionable subsidies granted or maintained within their territories to the Committee on Subsidies and

Countervailing Measures. Finally, Part V of the SCM Agreement sets out a number of detailed procedural provisions governing the unilateral imposition of countervailing measures, which broadly parallel the procedures applicable to antidumping actions.

7.4   WTO case law on the interpretation and application of subsidy rules

A substantial body of complex WTO case law (both Panel and Appellate Body decisions) has developed since 1995 on some of the key provisions in the SCM Agreement. A number of the key interpretive issues that have required resolution are briefly summarized below.

7.4.1   Subsidy

First, as to the definition of a subsidy, Article 1.1 of the SCM Agreement defines a subsidy as a financial contribution by a government or any public body within the territory of a member whereby a benefit is thereby conferred. In *EC– Large Civil Aircraft*,[3] the Panel discussed potential direct transfers of funds under particular loan guarantees. The Panel noted that loan guarantees benefit their recipients because they enable them to obtain lower prices for the loans guaranteed. Thus, according to the Panel, an assessment regarding potential direct transfers of funds should focus on the existence of a government practice that involves an obligation to make a direct transfer of funds which, in and of itself, is claimed to be capable of conferring a benefit on the recipient that is separate and independent from the benefit that might be conferred from any future transfer of funds. The *US – FSC*[4] dispute involved a challenge by a number of countries of billions of dollars of tax exemptions given to offshore "foreign sales corporations" by the United States. These corporations were typically subsidiaries of US-based corporations selling goods into foreign markets. The Appellate Body was required to address the meaning of "otherwise due" in the phrase "government revenue that is otherwise due, is foregone, or not collected" in Article 1.1 of the SCM Agreement. The principal issue was whether a comparator may be found in the actions of other members or solely the member whose actions are being challenged. The

---

3 *European Communities–Measures Affecting Trade in Large Civil Aircraft*, (2010) WT/DS 316/R.

4 *United States – Fair Treatment of Foreign Sales Corporations* (2000) WT/DS108/AB/R.

Appellate Body found that "otherwise due" requires, on the basis of a normative benchmark, a comparison between revenues raised and those which would otherwise have been raised and that this benchmark varies between members according to their own tax scheme. The US tax exemptions were held to diverge from revenue otherwise due under US law. In *US – Softwood Lumber IV*,[5] the Appellate Body upheld the Panel's determination that Canadian provincial governments made "financial contributions" to timber producers by providing them with rights to harvest standing timber through government stumpage programmes in return for royalties. As to the meaning of "general infrastructure" in Article 1.1, the Panel in *EC – Large Civil Aircraft* held that the determination of whether or not a measure involves general infrastructure must be made on a case-by-case basis, taking into account the existence of de jure or de facto limitations on access or use, and any other factors that tend to demonstrate that the infrastructure was or was not provided to or for the use of only a single entity or a limited group of entities. On the facts of this case, the Panel found that the EC had provided specific forms of infrastructure assistance to Airbus.

7.4.2   Benefit

With respect to the interpretation of the phrase "benefit thereby conferred" in Article 1.1, the Appellate Body in *Canada – Aircraft*[6] affirmed the Panel's interpretation of this term that in order to confer a "benefit", a financial contribution must be provided on terms that are more advantageous than those that would have been available to the recipient on the market. This in turn raises questions of what is the relevant market comparison. In the softwood lumber dispute between Canada and the USA, the USA argued that the prevailing market conditions in Canada did not reflect the fair market value of timber in Canada because of the large involvement of Canadian governments in that market. Reversing the decision of the Panel that prevailing market prices may not be disregarded simply because they are distorted, the Appellate Body held that an investigating authority may use a benchmark other than private prices in the country of provision where it has been established that private prices in that country are distorted. This decision was recently relied on in *United States – Definitive*

---

5 *United States – Final Countervailing Duty Determination with Respect to Certain Softwood Lumber from Canada* (2004) WT/DS257/AB/R.

6 *Canada – Measures Affecting the Export of Civil Aircraft* (1999) WT/ DS70/AB/R.

Anti-Dumping and Countervailing Duties on Certain Products from China,[7] where the Appellate Body upheld the Panel's finding that the USA was able to reject in-country prices as a benchmark in analyzing the conferral of a benefit, given that the Chinese government was the predominant supplier of the relevant goods and as such prices were likely to be distorted.[8] Other WTO cases have wrestled with the question of the effect of subsidies on state-owned enterprises once they are privatized in an arm's length transaction. In *US – Countervailing Measures on Certain EC Products,*[9] the Appellate Body held that although there should be a presumption that a benefit no longer exists after a firm is privatized at market value in an arm's length transaction, there may be market conditions where the value of a continuing benefit from a past financial contribution to the pre-privatized firm is not fairly reflected in the market price at which a new owner purchases an entity from the government.

A recent dispute, *Canada – Feed-in Tariff Program,*[10] addressed the question of how to apply a benchmark in order to determine whether a benefit has been conferred, in the situation of a market (in this case, renewable energy) that would not exist but for government intervention designed to create such markets. In this dispute, Japan and the EU argued that minimum domestic content requirements in Ontario's feed-in tariff programme constituted a subsidy inconsistent with Article 3 of the SCM Agreement. Neither the Panel nor the Appellate Body were able to find that wind power and solar generators received benefits in excess of those available to other electricity producers, given the heavy extent of government intervention in most electricity markets and hence the lack of an undistorted market benchmark. Given that renewable energy markets would not exist in many cases absent government intervention, because cost structures are such that renewables often cannot compete with conventional sources of electricity, the Appellate Body took the view that government intervention to create a market that would otherwise not exist should be distinguished from other types of government interventions in support of

---

7 *United States – Definitive Anti-Dumping and Countervailing Duties on Certain Products from China* (2011) WT/DS379/AB/R.

8 Thomas Prusa and Edwin Vermulst. "United States – Definitive Anti-Dumping and Countervailing Duties on Certain Products from China: Passing the Buck on Pass-Through", 12(2) *World Trade Review,* 2013, 199.

9 *United States – Countervailing Measures Concerning Certain Products from the European Communities* (2002) WT/DS212/AB/R.

10 *Canada – Measures Relating to the Feed-in Tariff Program* (2013) WT/DS426/AB/R.

certain firms within markets that already exist. It therefore concluded that the benefit benchmarks for wind and solar generated electricity should be found within the market for wind and solar electricity that results from the supply mix definition.

7.4.3   Specificity

With respect to the requirement of specificity that must be satisfied in order for a subsidy to be actionable (prohibited subsidies are deemed to be specific), Article 2 of the SCM Agreement indicates that subsidies may be de jure or de facto specific, but as demonstrated in the long-running *Canada – US Softwood Lumber* dispute, where US authorities reached divergent findings on this issue in successive countervailing duty proceedings, how small a number of firms or industries must benefit from a subsidy in order for it to be specific has an element of arbitrariness to it, with a focus on upstream input markets yielding a smaller number of recipients on the facts of this case than a focus on the number of firms or industries involved in using softwood lumber as inputs into the production of downstream products. The decisions by the Panel and Appellate Body in *US – Upland Cotton*[11] generally suggest that the appropriate focus is on subsidies conferred on upstream input producers.

7.4.4   Export contingency[12]

With respect to prohibited subsidies that under Article 3 of the SCM Agreement encompass subsidies contingent upon export performance or the use of domestic over imported goods, both types of subsidies have been held to embrace both de jure and de facto contingency. In the case of export subsidies, according to the Appellate Body in *Canada – Aircraft*, facts that demonstrate a grant of a subsidy, a "tie to" exports, and actual or anticipated exportation or export earnings are necessary to demonstrate de facto contingency; it is not sufficient to demonstrate solely that a government granting a subsidy anticipated that exports would result. Annex 1 of the SCM Agreement lists 12 illustrative export subsidies. Export guarantee or insurance pro-

---

11 *United States – Subsidies on Upland Cotton* (AB-2004–5).

12 For an extensive review of the rules and case law of export subsidies, see Andrew J. Green and Michael J. Trebilcock, "The Enduring Problem of World Trade Organization Export Subsidy Rules", in Kyle W. Bagwell, George A. Berman and Petros C. Mavroidis (eds), *Law and Economics of Contingent Protection in International Trade* (Cambridge: Cambridge University Press, 2010).

grammes may constitute a prohibited subsidy under Item J of the Appendix if offered at rates that do not cover the long-term operating costs and losses of the programme. The Appellate Body in *US – Cotton 21.5*[13] held that to the extent relevant data are available, an analysis under Item J should involve a quantitative evaluation of the financial performance of a programme, taking into account historical data as well as projections regarding the future performance of a programme. In *Brazil – Aircraft*,[14] the Appellate Body made it clear that where export credit, insurance, or guarantee programmes did not meet these requirements, a country conferring such subsidies would not be excused simply because the withdrawal of such subsidies may entail breaches of contracts with foreign buyers.

An important issue that has emerged in the wake of the recent global financial crisis is the potential for currency wars over allegedly undervalued currencies (such as the Chinese yuan), which make exports relatively cheap and imports relatively expensive, leading to massive trade surpluses in the case of China and threatened invocation of countervailing duties by importing countries, especially the USA, on the grounds that undervalued currencies are an illegal export subsidy. However, it may be difficult to demonstrate that such "subsidies" are contingent on exports but affect all trade – both exports and imports.

7.4.5   Adverse effects

In the case of actionable subsidies, the complaining member must demonstrate adverse effects from such subsidies. In *US – Cotton*, these adverse effects were found to entail price suppression in the world market for upland cotton as a result of various US domestic subsidies to cotton producers. In the case of *EC – Large Civil Aircraft*, EC subsidies to Airbus were found to have adverse effects on Boeing in terms of displacement of imports into the EC market, displacement of exports from third country markets, and lost sales more generally.

7.4.6   Remedies

With respect to multilateral remedies, Article 4.7 of the SCM Agreement indicates that if a measure is found to be a prohibited

---

13 *United States – Subsidies on Upland Cotton – Recourse to Article 21.5 of the DSU by Brazil* (2008) WT/DS267/AB/RW.

14 *Brazil – Export Financing Programme for Aircraft 21.5* (1990) WT/ DS46/AB/R.

subsidy, the Panel is to recommend that the subsidy be withdrawn without delay. Where a member fails to withdraw a prohibited subsidy following the Panel's recommendation to this effect, a complaining party may take appropriate countermeasures. In *Brazil – Aircraft*,[15] the arbitrators determined that the scale of the countermeasures may equal the total amount of the subsidies, and in *Canada – Aircraft*[16] indicated that the penalties must be sufficiently large to bring about compliance and to this end added a 20 per cent penalty on top of the value of the subsidies when Canada indicated that it did not propose to withdraw the offending subsidies. In *US – FSC*, the complaining party (the EU) was permitted to take countermeasures equal to the full subsidy even though it was not the only party harmed. In the case of actionable subsidies, Article 7.9 of the SCM Agreement permits complaining parties only to take countermeasures commensurate with the degree and nature of the adverse effects determined to be caused by actionable subsidies.

7.5 Normative rationales for disciplines on subsidies

The scholarly literature on normative rationales for disciplines on subsidies does not yield a strong consensus.[17] The most straight-forward justification prohibiting some subsidies relates to their potential to nullify or impair prior tariff concessions. For example, if country A reduces its tariffs on a particular class of imports from 10 per cent to zero in return for reciprocal commitments by country B, country A could negate the benefit of these concessions by providing subsidies to domestic producers in the amount of 10 per cent of their production costs. This might well yield a claim for nullification and impairment of reasonably expected benefits to country B under Article XXIII of the GATT. In similar vein, it might be argued that if country A has bound its tariff on a particular class of imports to 10 per cent in prior tariff negotiations, then if country B subsidizes exports to country A in an amount equivalent to this tariff, this may undermine the ability of country A to set its tariffs in reciprocal negotiations, thus nullifying

---

15 *Brazil – Export Financing Programme for Aircraft Recourse to Arbitration by Brazil under Article 22.6 of the DSU* (2000) WT/DS46/AB R.

16 *Canada – Export Credits and Loan Guarantees for Regional Aircraft–Recourse to Arbitration under Article 22.6 of the DSU* (2003) WT/DS222/ AB R.

17 For a provocative recent review of this literature, see Alan O. Sykes, "The Questionable Case for Subsidies Regulation: A Comparative Perspective", Stanford Law and Economics Olin Working Paper Series No. 380 (2009).

or impairing this prerogative under the GATT. However, it will be obvious from the foregoing discussion that the disciplines on subsidies contained in the SCM Agreement range well beyond protecting benefits from prior tariff negotiations.

With respect to the *per se* prohibition on export subsidies, some commentators argue that these subsidies benefit consumers in importing countries more than any losses suffered by producers in these countries, and should be welcomed by importing countries rather than condemned through either countervailing duty actions or multilateral complaints, while recognizing that third country exporters may have a legitimate complaint that their exports are being squeezed out of the importing country's markets by subsidies originating in the first country. Along the same lines, it is argued that export subsidies increase trade, rather than reduce it (as in the case of tariffs) and may assist in mitigating sources of imperfect competition in importing countries. Other commentators argue to the contrary that pure export subsidies have no rationale other than distorting trade and cannot generally be justified on various non-trade related public policy grounds which might justify various forms of domestic subsidies. Moreover, it is argued that export subsidies may lead to subsidy wars (as with agricultural subsidies in various export markets in the 1980s and 1990s), reflecting a Prisoner's Dilemma or race-to-the-bottom, which a highly categoric prohibition agreed to by all member states can preempt.

With respect to actionable subsidies, it is argued that the distinction between specific and general subsidies is arbitrary and often unprincipled and does not recognize legitimate non-trade-related public policy rationales for many specific subsidies; that no effort is made to distinguish between competitively salient subsidies that affect a recipient firm's marginal cost function and hence output from subsidies that benefit it in other ways, for example off-setting the costs of decommissioning plants for environmental reasons, for underwriting severance payments, or retraining costs for redundant workers; that no attempt is made to net out the effect of subsidies against other special tax or regulatory burdens that recipient firms may be required to bear; and that in evaluating adverse effects from subsidies, no attempt is made to net out these effects from subsidies or other kinds of benefits to firms from governments in complainant countries.

One approach that has some appeal would be: 1) to facilitate sector-specific negotiations among members on subsidy constraints (for example, agriculture, civil aircraft) to minimize the risk of mutually destructive subsidy wars; 2) to continue the prohibition on export subsidies and import substitution subsidies, defining export subsidies (somewhat arbitrarily) as subsidies applied to the output of firms or an industry where, for example, 80 per cent of output is exported and confine the scope of unilateral countervailing duty remedies to such subsidies; 3) to retain the option of bringing a complaint for nullification and impairment where prior tariff commitments are allegedly being negated by subsidies; and 4) with respect to all other subsidies (specific or otherwise) that can be demonstrated to have adverse effects on other member countries to permit a range of non-trade-related justifications for such subsidies (analogous to those set out in Article 31 of the Tokyo Round Subsidies Code, Article 8 of the SCM Agreement on non-actionable subsidies, and Article XX of the GATT), provided that these are the least trade-restrictive means available for achieving such non-trade-related policy goals (analogous to the necessity test under Article XX), and provided that they meet conditions like those in the chapeau to Article XX, in particular that they are not a disguised restriction on or distortion of trade. The distinction between specific and non-specific subsidies drawn in the SCM Agreement purports to be a descriptive distinction but cannot be reasonably treated as a normative proxy for potential non-trade-related rationales for subsidies that have unavoidable trade spill-overs. Only in the event of adverse determinations on these issues would retaliatory sanctions be available. Such a regime would put subsidies and tariff and quota constraints on a similar legal footing.

7.6 Protectionism in government procurement[18]

Governments, in most countries, constitute the largest single purchaser in the economy.[19] Although government procurement is, on its face, similar to private contracting, it can be seen as akin to subsidies because

---

18 For a review of international trade and public procurement, see Arie Reich, *International Public Procurement Law: the Evolution of International Regimes on Public Purchasing* (The Hague, the Netherlands: Kluwer Law International, 1999); Sue Arrowsmith, *Government Procurement in the WTO* (The Hague, the Netherlands: Kluwer Law International, 2003); Simon J. Evenett and Bernard Hoekman (eds), *The WTO and Government Procurement* (Northampton: Edward Elgar, 2006).

19 Government procurement has been estimated to account for, on average, 15–20 per cent of gross domestic product in developed countries. See OECD, *The Size of Government Procurement Markets* (Paris: OECD, 2001), accessed at <www.oecd.org/dataoecd/34/14/1845927.pdf>. Accessed 12 September 2014.

governments often adopt a wide range of measures that qualify the objective of obtaining the best product or service for the lowest price in service of other policy goals such as: protecting employment in declining industries; protecting the supply of strategic defence goods; supporting emerging domestic industries; or advancing environmental standards.

A domestic preference in public procurement can be overt or hidden. Overtly discriminatory practices might include the application of a rule that a foreign bid may be accepted only if it is a certain amount lower than the lowest domestic bid; the use of selective sourcing policies in which only domestic firms are invited to bid; the provision of "set-aside" contracts wherein only certain businesses may compete; or the imposition of a policy requiring foreign suppliers to purchase goods or services in the domestic market as a condition of the contract, amongst others. Discrimination can also be more subtle, for example through the use of selective tendering processes, the manipulation of timing and method in a bidding process, the application of bid submission deadlines, or the imposition of product or service standard requirements in such a way that prevents foreign firms from competing.

7.6.1   Procurement under the GATT

Initially, the GATT refrained from regulating government procurement policies, by way of an exception to the National Treatment Principle under Article III(8). However, during the Tokyo Round this policy was revisited, resulting in a plurilateral agreement with 20 signatories – the Tokyo Round Government Procurement Code ("the Code") – that extended the obligation of nondiscrimination to procurement of goods by the central government entities of its signatories, and laid out transparency requirements as well as procedures for multilateral dispute settlement. The Code was limited in scope, as it excluded contracts below a certain, relatively high, value; service contracts; and procurements of sub-national governments.

7.6.2   Procurement under the WTO

The WTO Uruguay Round Government Procurement Agreement ("GPA"),[20] agreed to in 1994, maintained important aspects of the

---

20 For a review of the Uruguay Round Government Procurement Agreement, see Arie Reich, "The New GATT Agreement on Government Procurement: the Pitfalls of Plurilateralism and Strict Reciprocity", 31 *Journal of World Trade*, 125.

Code, but with an expanded scope that included service and construction contracts, as well as more entities, including sub-national government entities and government enterprises. Three types of procedures are contemplated in the Agreement: open, selective, and limited (the latter two are only allowed under certain conditions). Next, and arguably the most important improvement upon the Code, the GPA established mandatory bid challenge procedures enabling aggrieved foreign suppliers to challenge alleged breaches of the Agreement. Each Party must establish an impartial review body to adjudicate procurement disputes in a timely and effective fashion. Thus far, there have been only three WTO disputes under the GPA, the most recent of which, *Korea – Procurement*,[21] was concluded in 2000.

The GPA has been criticized for a number of deficiencies. First, like its predecessor, the GPA is only a plurilateral agreement, and includes few developing countries. Next, the compensation provided to an aggrieved supplier may be limited to the costs of tender or protest, an insufficient amount to deter a government from breaching its obligations. Third, because the scope and coverage of the GPA is complex (as each Party has its own Appendix I where entities, goods, services, and contract values that are included or excluded are identified) and different Parties have made different commitments (for example, some parties made access to procurement by sub-national governments and utilities dependent on reciprocity), GPA commitments can vary between different pairs of signatories, a structure which poses problems for the accession of countries with large state sectors.[22] Each Party can withdraw one of its listed entities at will (subject to objections from other Parties).

Although government procurement is not formally on the multilateral agenda of the Doha Development Round, a revised text of the GPA 1994 ("GPA 2014") entered into force on 6 April 2014.[23] The

---

21 WTO, "Government Procurement: the Plurilateral Agreement on Government Procurement (GPA) – Dispute Settlement under the Government Procurement Agreement", World Trade Organization. Online: http://www.wto.org/english/tratop_e/gproc_e/disput_e.htm. Accessed 12 July 2014.

22 See Wang Ping, "Coverage of the WTO's Agreement on Government Procurement: Challenges of Integrating China and Other Countries with a Large State Sector into the Global Trading System", 10 *Journal of International Economic Law* 887.

23 WTO. "Revised WTO Agreement on Government Procurement Enters into Force", World Trade Organization. Online: http://www.wto.org/english/news_e/news14_e/gpro_07apr14_e.htm. Accessed 12 July 2014.

revised Agreement expands the scope of coverage to more entities, services, and other procurement activities, including local governments and sub-central entities. GPA 2014 also includes standards pertaining to the use of electronic procurement tools, improved transitional measures to facilitate accession by developing countries,[24] language recognizing the aim of reducing corruption in procurement,[25] and provisions related to the promotion of environmental protection.[26]

7.6.3   Procurement outside of the WTO

Government procurement agreements also exist outside of the WTO. For example, Chapter 10 of the North American Free Trade Agreement (NAFTA) concerns government procurement. It built upon commitments made in the Tokyo Round Code and the Canada-US Free Trade Agreement. In 2010, Canada and the USA became Parties to a new procurement agreement, the Canada-US Agreement on Government Procurement, which exempts Canada from the Buy American provisions of the *American Recovery and Reinvestment Act* of 2009. In exchange, the USA gains temporary access to Canadian procurement commitments for construction projects for agencies not included in the WTO GPA, as well as some municipalities. Public procurement under the European Communities is governed by the EC Treaty, the WTO GPA, and directives (of which the two main directives are the Public Sector Directive and the Utilities Directive, which are designed to liberalize government procurement markets within the EU).

---

24 Timothy Keeler. "Revisions to WTO Agreement on Government Procurement Enter into Force", *Mondaq Business Briefing* 10 April 2013.

25 Krista Nadakavukaren Schefer and Mintewab Gebre Woldesenbet. "The Revised Agreement on Government Procurement and Corruption", 47(5) *Journal of World Trade*, 2013, 1129–61.

26 Luca Tosoni, "The Impact of the Revised WTO Government Procurement Agreement on the EU Procurement Rules from a Sustainability Perspective", 8(1) *European Public Private Partnership Law Review*, 2013, 41.

8 Safeguards and adjustment assistance policies

8.1 Introduction

Since the genesis of the GATT in 1947, the multilateral trade regime has provided for unilateral opt-outs from trade liberalization commitments in circumstances involving unforeseen developments causing serious injury to domestic producers in the importing country. Between January 1995 and March 2013, 255 safeguard initiations and 335 countervailing duty initiations were reported to the WTO compared to 4358 dumping actions reported to the WTO between 1995 and 2013.[1] While the "safeguards" regime has been much less frequently invoked than the other two major trade remedy regimes (especially antidumping), it has given rise to a number of high profile recent disputes.

Article XIX of the GATT sets out the basic safeguard regime:

> If, as a result of unforeseen developments and of the effect of the obligations incurred by a contracting party under this Agreement, including tariff concessions, any product is being imported into the territory of that contracting party in such increased quantities and under such conditions as to cause or threaten serious injury to domestic producers in that territory of like or directly competitive products, the contracting party shall be free, in respect of such product, and to the extent and for such time as may be necessary to prevent or remedy such injury, to suspend the obligation in whole or in part or to withdraw or modify the concession.

Article XIX goes on to provide that before any contracting party shall take action pursuant to this provision, it shall give notice to the

---

1 Chad Bown, *Self-enforcing Trade: Developing Countries and WTO Dispute Settlement* (Washington, D.C.: Brookings Institution, 2009), Table 4.3; WTO, "Safeguard Initiations by Reporting Member", World Trade Organization. Online: http://www.wto.org/english/tratop_e/safeg_e/SG-Initiations_By_Reporting_Member.pdf. Accessed 12 July 2014; WTO, "Countervailing Initiations by Reporting Member", World Trade Organization. Online: http://www.wto.org/english/tratop_e/scm_e/CV_InitiationsByRepMem.pdf. Accessed 12 July 2014.

contracting parties at large and afford those contracting parties having a substantial interest as exporters of the product concerned an opportunity to consult with it in respect of the proposed action. Such consultations may lead to the negotiation of compensatory trade concessions. If compensation cannot be agreed on, affected contracting parties may suspend substantially equivalent concessions or other obligations under the GATT.

Many of the terms and concepts employed in Article XIX are extraordinarily vague, and efforts were made during the Tokyo Round, culminating in the late 1970s, to negotiate a more detailed safeguards code. However, these negotiations foundered over disagreements as to whether safeguards should be permitted on a selective, as opposed to a non-discriminatory basis; whether compensation, in the form of offsetting trade concessions, or in the absence of agreement on compensation, retaliation should be permitted where legitimate safeguard action has been taken; how "serious injury" should be defined; whether there should be political discretion in the imposition of safeguard measures (as opposed to administrative determinations as under antidumping and countervailing duty laws); and the role for multilateral oversight of the invocation of safeguard measures.

At the time of these abortive negotiations and thereafter, circumventions of the requirements of the GATT safeguard regime began to proliferate through the negotiation of bilateral Voluntary Export Restraint agreements or Orderly Marketing Agreements between importing and exporting countries, typically initiated by importing countries with industries experiencing economic distress in the face of intensifying import competition.

During the Uruguay Round, a new multilateral Agreement on Safeguards was finally negotiated. Under Article 4, "serious injury" is defined to mean "a significant overall impairment in the position of a domestic industry". "Threat of serious injury" shall be understood to mean serious injury that is clearly imminent and shall be based on facts and not merely on allegation, conjecture or remote possibility.

Under Article 4(2)(a), in an investigation to determine whether increased imports have caused or are threatening to cause serious injury to a domestic industry, the competent domestic authorities must evaluate all relevant factors of an objective and quantifiable nature having a bearing on the situation of that industry, in particular the rate and amount of the increase in imports of the product concerned in absolute and relative terms, the share of the domestic market taken by increased imports, changes in the levels of sales, production, productivity, capacity utilization, profits and losses, and employment.

Under Article 4(2)(b), an affirmative determination must not be made under Article 4(2)(a) unless an investigation demonstrates, on the basis of objective evidence, the existence of a causal link between increased imports of the product concerned and serious injury or threat thereof. When factors other than increased imports are causing injury to the domestic industry at the same time, such injury shall not be attributed to increased imports.

Under Article 2.2, safeguard measures shall be applied to a product being imported irrespective of its source. Under Article 5.2, where a safeguard measure takes the form of a quota, the country adopting the safeguard measure shall allocate the quota to members having a substantial interest in supplying the product shares based upon the proportions of imports supplied by such members during a previous representative period. A country may depart from this requirement of non-discrimination if it can demonstrate to the WTO Committee on Safeguards that: 1) imports from certain members have increased disproportionately in relation to the total increase of imports of the product concerned in the representative period; 2) the reasons for the departure from a non-discriminatory allocation of quotas are justified; and 3) the conditions of such departure are equitable to all suppliers of the product concerned. The duration of any such exceptional measures shall not extend beyond four years.

Under Article 7, safeguard measures may not exceed four years in duration, unless the competent authorities of the importing country have determined that the safeguard measure continues to be necessary to prevent or remedy serious injury and that there is evidence that the industry is adjusting, in which case the measure may be renewed provided that it does not exceed eight years duration in total. Under Article 7, safeguard measures shall be progressively liberalized at regular intervals during the period of application. No safeguard measure shall be applied again to the products which have been subject of such measure for a period of time equal to that during which such measure had been previously applied.

Under Article 8, the right of exporting countries to suspend equivalent trade concessions shall not be exercised for the first three years that a safeguard measure is in effect (substantially reducing their ability to insist on compensatory offsetting trade concessions for this period).

Under Article 11, member countries shall not seek, take, or maintain any Voluntary Export Restraints, Orderly Marketing Agreements, or any other similar measures on the export or import side. Such measures must be phased out or brought into conformity with this Agreement within four years after the entry into force of the Agreement.

While this chapter focuses on the GATT safeguard regime under Article XIX of the GATT and the Uruguay Agreement on Safeguards, it is important to note specific safeguard regimes contained in the Uruguay Agreement on Agriculture (Article 5), in the General Agreement on Trade in Services (GATS) (Article X), in the Agreement on Apparel, Textiles, and Clothing (Article 6), and in a specific safeguard regime associated with acceding countries (particularly targeted at China).[2]

Despite these reforms, safeguard actions have led to a significant number of formal trade disputes.[3] A number of these cases have resulted in Panel or Appellate Body decisions.[4] In each of these cases

---

2   See Petros C. Mavroidis, Patrick A. Messerlin and Jasper M. Wauters, *The Law and Economics of Contingent Protection in the WTO* (Cheltenham, UK: Edward Elgar, 2008).

3   Kara Leitner and Simon Lester, "WTO Dispute Settlement 1995–2013 – A Statistical Analysis", (2014) 17:1 *Journal of International Economic Law* 196.

4   *Korea – Definitive Safeguard Measure on Imports of Certain Dairy Products* (1999) WTO Docs WT/DS98/R and WT/DS98/AB/R [*Korea – Dairy* 1999]; *Argentina – Safeguard Measures on Imports on Footwear* (1999) WTO Docs WT/DS121/R and WT/DS121/AB/R [*Argentina – Footwear*, 1999]; *United States – Safeguard Measures on Imports of Fresh, Chilled or Frozen Lamb Meat from New Zealand and Australia* (2000) WTO Docs WT/ DS/177/R and WT/DS178/R and (2001) WTO Docs WT/DS/177/AB/R and WT/DS178/AB/R [*US – Lamb*, 2001]; *United States – Definitive Safeguard Measures on Imports of Wheat Gluten from the European Communities* (2000) WTO Docs WT/DS166/R and WT/DS166/AB/R [*US – Wheat Gluten*, 2000]; *United States – Definitive Safeguard Measures on Imports of Circular Welded Carbon Quality Line Pipe from Korea* (2001) WTO Docs WT/DS202/R and (2002) WTO Docs WT/DS202/AB/R [*US – Line Pipe*, 2001]; *Argentina – Definitive Safeguard Measure on Imports of Preserved Peaches* (2003) WTO doc. WT/DS238/R [*Argentina – Peaches*, 2003]; *United States – Definitive Safeguard Measures on Imports of Certain Steel Products* (2003) WTO Docs WT/DS248/R, WT/DS249/R, WT/DS251/R, WT/DS252/R, WT/DS253/R, WT/DS254/R, WT/DS258/R, WT/DS25/R and WT/DS248–259/AB [*US – Steel*, 2003]; *Dominican Republic – Safeguard Measures on Imports of Polypropylene Bags and Tubular Fabric* (2012) WTO Docs WT/DS415/R, WT/DS416/R, WT/ DS417/R and WT/DS418/R [*Dominican Republic – Safeguard Measures*].

(except *Argentina – Peaches* and *Dominican Republic – Safeguard Measures*), WTO Panel decisions have been appealed to the Appellate Body. In not one of the cases did the safeguard measure in question survive challenge. In a withering critique of these decisions, Professor Alan Sykes argues that the current safeguard regime, as interpreted by the Appellate Body, has become essentially impossible to comply with, creating strong incentives for member countries to resort again to extra-legal arrangements, such as Voluntary Export Restraint Agreements or Orderly Marketing Agreements, which the Agreement on Safeguards sought to outlaw, or antidumping measures, which are in many cases more distorting of trade than formal safeguard measures.[5]

8.2   Substantive requirements of the GATT/WTO safeguards regime

In Canada, domestic producers petition the Canadian International Trade Tribunal and in the USA, the International Trade Commission, for determinations that safeguard measures are justified and consequential recommendations to the executive arm of government – in Canada, the Minister of Finance, in the USA, the President of the USA – for the negotiation of safeguard measures with affected exporting countries, and in the absence of negotiated agreements, the unilateral imposition of safeguard measures, with the possibility thereafter of affected exporting countries suspending trade concessions of equivalent value.

In order for a country validly to invoke the GATT/WTO Safeguard Regime, as set out in Article XIX of the GATT and the Uruguay Round Agreement on Safeguards, certain basic conditions must be met:

8.2.1   Unforeseen developments

Under Article XIX of the GATT, the increase in imports must be a result of "unforeseen developments". This raises the questions of at what point of time must developments have not been foreseen and by whom? As Sykes points out,[6] under US trade law and that of many other countries, this requirement had been progressively ignored, and

---

5   See Alan O. Sykes, "The Persistent Puzzles of Safeguards: Lessons from the Steel Dispute", (2004) 7:3 *Journal of International Economic Law* 523; Sykes, "The Safeguards Mess: A Critique of Appellate Body Jurisprudence", (2003) 2 *World Trade Review* 261.

6   Sykes, "The Persistent Puzzles of Safeguards", *ibid.*

the Uruguay Round Agreement on Safeguards notably fails to mention any such requirement. However, the Appellate Body in *Argentina – Footwear*[7] and *Korea – Dairy*[8] held that Article XIX of the GATT and the Agreement on Safeguards must be read cumulatively, and the Agreement on Safeguards should not be interpreted as abrogating this requirement in Article XIX. It now seems clear from the Appellate Body case law that the relevant point of time for determining whether developments have been unforeseen is when the last tariff concession was made with respect to the class of product in question. An unforeseen development is one that was "unexpected" by trade negotiators at the time when such concessions were negotiated.[9] In a series of cases, both WTO Panels and the Appellate Body have interpreted this requirement relatively strictly and have insisted that only increases in imports attributable to unforeseen developments can be considered in determining whether increasing imports are causing serious injury.

8.2.2   Prior obligations

As noted above, prior obligations have been interpreted to refer to the last point in time at which the importing country seeking to impose a safeguard measure made binding tariff or other commitments related to the product in question.

8.2.3   Increased imports

In *Argentina – Footwear*[10] the Appellate Body held that whether imports are increasing requires consideration of trends over a representative period (often five years), not simply the end points of this period and emphasized that not any increase is sufficient but must have been "recent enough, sudden enough, sharp enough, and significant enough, both quantitatively and qualitatively, to cause or threaten to cause serious injury".

8.2.4   Serious injury

The Appellate Body has held that "serious injury" connotes a significantly higher or more serious level of injury than "material injury"

---

7 *Argentina – Footwear* 1999, supra note 4.

8 *Korea – Dairy* 1999, supra note 4.

9 *Argentina – Footwear* 1999, supra note 4.

10 *Ibid.*

that is the counterpart requirement in antidumping and countervailing duty determinations.[11] Moreover, both WTO Panels and the Appellate Body have insisted that domestic authorities, pursuant to Article 4(2)(a) must, in their determinations, evaluate all relevant factors of an objective and quantifiable nature listed in this provision bearing on the condition of the domestic industry.

8.2.5 Causation

While the Appellate Body has held, somewhat confusingly, that increased imports need not be the only cause of serious injury, and other contributing factors may not necessarily preclude such a determination,[12] it has also insisted on a rigorous application of the non-attribution requirement in Article 4(2)(b), pursuant to which when factors other than increased imports are causing injury to the domestic industry at the same time, such injury shall not be attributed to increased imports, and has required domestic authorities to demonstrate that they have rigorously identified all causal factors bearing on a domestic industry's financial distress and carefully assigned relative weights to factors relating to serious injury that are properly attributable to imports and those that are not.

In addition, WTO Panels and the Appellate Body have insisted that where all exports are included in the serious injury determination, but that the safeguard measure itself excludes imports from certain countries (for example, pursuant to Free Trade Agreements with these countries), the injury determination will be viewed as flawed, in that there must be "parallelism" between the exports included in the injury determination and the exports included in the safeguard measure.

Finally, and more generally, Sykes is highly critical of what he regards as an economically incoherent conception of causation adopted by WTO Panels and the Appellate Body in many of their safeguard decisions by essentially equating correlation with causation. As Sykes points out, increasing imports are often the result of various factors that have caused a shift in either the domestic demand curve or the domestic supply curve (for example, an unexpected increase in the costs of domestic suppliers) and are not the cause of loss of domestic market share or other measures of the financial health of the domestic

---

11 *US – Lamb* 2000, supra note 4.

12 *US – Wheat Gluten* 2000, supra note 4.

industry. This critique parallels similar critiques of causation determinations in antidumping and countervailing duty determinations. Even with respect to correlation analysis, Sykes is critical of several WTO Panel and Appellate Body decisions for accepting, on the one hand, an arbitrary period of trend analysis by domestic authorities (for example, five years prior to the safeguard determination), while at the same time insisting that trends in the most recent months or year or so of this trend analysis be assigned much more weight than longer-term trends which may be a much more reliable indication of the need for the domestic industry to undergo long-term structural adjustment.

Alternatives to correlation analysis reviewed by Sykes include the hypothetical quota approach, where at the beginning of some representative time period (for example, the previous five years before the safeguard determination), a hypothetical quota is imposed on imports and then a determination is made as to whether the domestic industry would have suffered substantially less serious injury than the injury that it is in fact incurring with prevailing levels of imports (although this approach would, in some cases, provide relief to domestic industries that are suffering from some domestically originating factor). A yet further approach would be to examine over some representative time period shifts in domestic demand curves, domestic supply curves, and import supply curves, with a view to determining which of these three potential shifts has in fact been most responsible for the decline in the financial health of the domestic industry (although this implies data-intensive and potentially error-prone general equilibrium econometric analysis).

8.2.6   Standard of review

An overarching question confronting WTO Panels and the Appellate Body in reviewing determinations by domestic authorities in safeguard actions, as in antidumping and countervailing duty actions, as well as in many domestic regulatory contexts such as health, safety, and environmental regulation, is the standard of review that should be applied to these determinations by WTO Panels and the Appellate Body. While Article 11 of the Dispute Settlement Understanding requires Panels to make "an objective assessment of the facts", the Appellate Body seems to have accepted that this does not require Panels to make a *de novo* determination of the facts but rather the review is both a procedural review of the domestic authority's decision-making processes, and that the domestic authority's determinations must meet some minimum standard of substantive rationality ("a reasoned and adequate explanation of how the facts support their determination").[13]

8.3   Rationales for safeguard regimes

8.3.1   Economic rationales

Some authors argue that safeguard regimes permit domestic industries that have lost their competitiveness vis-à-vis imports a "breathing space" to restructure themselves and become competitive again, or at least contract in an orderly temporal fashion to a competitive core, hence moderating the adjustment costs faced by investors, workers, and dependent communities.

8.3.2   Political rationales

Authors such as Kenneth Dam and Alan Sykes argue that opt-out regimes, such as the safeguard regime, reduce the political risks associated with *ex ante* trade liberalization commitments and hence induce political negotiators to undertake such commitments more willingly, although then the question arises whether the same rationale can also justify antidumping and countervailing duty regimes.

8.3.3   Fairness rationales

One might argue that the adverse impacts of increasing imports of low-priced products may have distributionally and socially unfair consequences for low-paid, low-skilled, immobile workers, and dependent communities. Again, safeguard regimes may have the potential to mitigate these impacts. However, in this respect, it needs to be noted that many empirical studies have shown that safeguard and related forms of protectionist relief often entail costs for domestic consumers that are several orders of magnitude greater than the value of jobs preserved, at least as measured by wage levels in the industry in question. Moreover, it is not clear why the normative case for intervention to mitigate the impact of shocks from low-priced imports is stronger than domestically originating shocks, such as changes in consumer

---

13 *US – Lamb* 2000, supra note 4 at 18; see more generally, Andrew T. Guzman, "Determining the Appropriate Standard of Review in WTO Disputes", (2009) 42:1 *Cornell International Law Journal* 45.

preferences, technological innovation, exhaustion of natural resources, or various cost shocks. In any event, if this rationale is to be relied on as a justification for safeguard measures, the conception of serious injury embodied in the WTO Agreement on Safeguards would require radical revision to focus not primarily on injury to domestic industries, but injury to domestic workers and dependent communities.

8.4   Alternatives to safeguards

8.4.1   Industrial subsidies

In general, industrial subsidies have not been effective in avoiding the ultimate need for adjustment by uncompetitive domestic industries or moderating its severity. Pure output-sustaining subsidies have been the least effective in this respect. Other forms of industrial subsidies have been designed to facilitate the modernization of obsolete capital, but obsolete plants are often the result and not the cause of loss of international competitiveness and if an adequate return could be made on new fixed assets, presumably private capital markets would provide the funds required to make this investment. Less frequently, industrial subsidies have been provided to ease exit costs, where, as in the case of Japan, government plays an active role in managing contraction in demand for domestic industry's output, perhaps through recession cartels, active promotion of mergers or specialization agreements, or compensation for scrapping physical capacity, although such active involvement by government in orchestrating an industry's future shape and size raises questions about both institutional competence and the potential risks for facilitating anti-competitive forms of industry collusion under the guise of industry-wide coordination of efforts at restructuring.

8.4.2   Labour market adjustment policies

The normative case for such policies seems much stronger than for industrial subsidies, where workers are often less able to diversify the risks of future shifts in comparative advantage than investors in domestic firms. Most developed countries have introduced some form of unemployment insurance, while a smaller sub-set of such countries have tended to place much more weight on active labour market policies (ALMPs) focused on assistance with job search, relocation, and retraining (safety nets versus trampolines). In general, the latter class of policy seems to have been more effective in mitigating adjustment costs than purely passive forms of unemployment insurance, although the empirical evidence is mixed and in the case of unemployed youths, especially high school dropouts, and older workers, ALMPs seem to have been much less effective than in the case of other classes of workers.[14]

8.5   Reforming the safeguards regime

Various reforms could be contemplated, from the modest to the ambitious. At the modest end of the scale, there may be much to be said for Sykes' view that the unforeseen development requirement in Article XIX should be removed, and that the causation requirement, at least as interpreted by the Appellate Body, should be substantially relaxed or at least simplified, perhaps through the adoption of something as simple, albeit crude, as the hypothetical quota approach. At the more ambitious end of the reform spectrum, radical reconceptualization of the injury test might be justified, so as to focus on adverse impacts of imports on disadvantaged workers and dependent communities (taking into account other labour market adjustment policies in place).

---

14 See Michael Trebilcock, *Dealing with Losers: The Political Economy of Policy Transitions* (New York: Oxford University Press, 2014), chapter 5.

9   Trade and agriculture

9.1   Introduction

Trade in agricultural products has long been one of the most prominent and acrimonious issues on the global trade agenda. Prior to the
Uruguay Round, the GATT placed many fewer disciplines on agricultural trade than on any other product sector. Although Article XI of
the GATT prohibits quantitative restrictions, it contains a number of
exceptions which relate specifically to agricultural trade. In particular,
Article XI.2(a) permits export prohibitions or restrictions temporarily
applied to prevent or relieve critical shortages of foodstuffs or other
products essential to the exporting contracting party. Article XI.2(c)
permits import restrictions on any agricultural or fisheries product
necessary to the enforcement of government measures which operate:
i) to restrict the quantities of the like domestic product permitted to be
marketed or produced, or ii) to remove a temporary surplus of the like
domestic product. In principle, any restrictions applied under Article
XI.2(c)(i) shall not be such as will reduce the total of imports relative
to the total of domestic production, as compared with the proportion
that might reasonably be expected to prevail between the two in the
absence of restrictions, although this provision has not been rigorously
enforced. Article XI.2(c)(i) is particularly important, because it permits countries to restrict imports in order to sustain domestic supply
management schemes designed to increase the price of domestic
agricultural products.

Apart from Article XI, Article XVI of the GATT provides that contracting parties should seek to avoid the use of subsidies on the export
of primary products. Where such subsidies are used, they shall not
be applied in a manner which results in that contracting party having
more than an equitable share of world export trade in that product,
account being taken of the shares of the contracting parties in such
trade in the product during a previous representative period. This provision was largely carried over into the Tokyo Round Subsidies Code

negotiated at the end of the 1970s. Despite the relative laxity of these provisions, the US government sought and obtained a waiver of Article XI GATT obligations in 1955 with respect to a variety of agricultural products, including sugar, peanuts, and dairy products. In a series of cases in the 1980s, the USA challenged before GATT panels various EU export subsidies on wheat flour and pasta, and domestic subsidies for EU users of oil seeds, but adoption of panel decisions in these cases were vetoed by the losing party.

The instruments of agricultural protection are varied. The European Union's Common Agricultural Policy has traditionally employed a combination of minimum prices for sales within the EU protected through variable import levies, guaranteed sales (in other words, government purchase of oversupply), and rebates on export sales below EU prices. These policies tend to result in overproduction and displacement of foreign producers in third country markets. US agricultural protection has focused on price support measures coupled with production restrictions, and in recent years certain forms of export subsidies. Canada maintains marketing and production restrictions on poultry, eggs, and dairy products through the use of domestic quotas and high tariffs. As well, Japan employs a wide range of instruments including price stabilization, supply management, import quotas, and extremely high tariffs. Agricultural protection imposes substantial costs on consumers through higher food prices, on taxpayers who fund government subsidization programmes, and on society through allocative efficiency losses as resources are misdirected toward agricultural production when no comparative advantage exists in this sector. It has been estimated that the average cost of agricultural protection to non-farm households in Europe, the United States, and Japan is over $1000 per year. Moreover, agricultural protectionism stifles trade: a 2001 study estimated that removing all agricultural support and protection globally would result in an increase in the value of world agricultural trade of about 30 per cent.[1]

---

1   See Arvind Panagariya, "Agricultural Liberalisation and the Least Developed Countries: Six Fallacies", (2005) 28:9 *World Economy* 1277–99; Xinshen Diao, Agapi Somwaru and Terry Roe, "A Global Analysis of Agricultural Reform in WTO Member Countries", (2001) *Economic Research Service/USDA*. Online: file:///Users/Kristen/Downloads/aer802c.pdf. Accessed 13 July 2014.

9.2   The Uruguay Round Agreement on Agriculture

During the Uruguay Round, member countries of the GATT committed themselves to beginning an attempt at liberalization of trade in agricultural products. The negotiations were protracted and contentious, and raised major divisions between the USA and the EU and at various junctures threatened the collapse of the Round. The opening negotiating position of the USA was that all forms of agricultural support should be eliminated within 10 years, while the EU sought to defend major features of its Common Agricultural Policy (CAP). Ultimately, a compromise was cobbled together in the closing months of the Round in 1993. The Agreement addresses three key sources of distortion in agricultural trade: domestic support measures (price supports, payments to farmers, supply management), export subsidies, and tariffs and non-tariff border measures. Articles 1(a), 6, and Annex 3 to the Agreement attempt to quantify domestic support measures in terms of a common metric, the Aggregate Measure of Support (AMS), and commit members to 20 per cent reductions in their level of domestic support from a 1986–88 baseline. Articles 8–10 commit members to the reduction of export subsidies over a six-year period by 21 per cent in terms of the volume of products that receive subsidies and 36 per cent in terms of the cash value of such subsidies. Members also commit not to expand export subsidies beyond the levels reached after achievement of the six-year goal. It should be noted that this essentially overrides Article XVI of the GATT, which had theretofore largely permitted export subsidies on primary products. Article 4 requires members to convert non-tariff border measures (such as import quotas) into tariffs, and to reduce overall agricultural tariffs (including non-tariff measures which have been converted) by at least 36 per cent over a six-year period, with a minimum 15 per cent reduction in each product category. Furthermore, new non-tariff measures of any kind are prohibited. Members also commit to reduce border measures to an extent that allows foreign producers market access equivalent to 3 per cent of total domestic production, rising to 5 per cent by the end of the six-year phase-in period.

The Agreement also includes a system under which certain forms of subsidies are exempted from the reduction commitments. All forms of domestic support measures are classified into three categories: "Yellow Box", "Green Box", and "Blue Box". "Yellow Box" support measures are those which have clear market-distorting effects, such as price supports and other subsidies which encourage overproduction.

These measures are subject to reduction commitments. "Green Box" subsidies are defined in Annex 2 to the Agreement, and include measures directed at research, infrastructure, domestic food aid, disaster assistance, training and advisory services. "Green Box" subsidies are deemed to have no effect on trade or production and are exempt from the reduction commitments. "Blue Box" subsidies are listed in Article 6, and involve direct payments to farmers made under "production-limiting programs" and certain developing country subsidies designed to encourage agricultural production. "Blue Box" subsidies are not subject to reduction commitments, provided they adhere to certain requirements set out in Article 6.5(a). Article 13 of the Agreement, known as the "Peace Clause", states that domestic support measures which are exempt from reduction commitments (in other words, "Green Box" measures) are non-actionable for the duration of the peace clause. Furthermore, "due restraint" is to be exercised in initiating countervailing duty investigations into "Blue Box" subsidies. The Peace Clause expired in January 2004. In *United States – Subsidies on Upland Cotton*,[2] a complaint initiated by Brazil before this expiration date against the USA with respect to various US domestic and export subsidies to its cotton producers, users, and exporters, a WTO panel, largely affirmed by the Appellate Body, held that most of these subsidies failed to meet the conditions for immunity stipulated in Article 13 and violated various provisions of the Subsidies and Countervailing Measures (SCM) Agreement. Brazil had also earlier prevailed in a complaint against the EU with respect to export subsidies on sugar.[3]

Other important provisions in the Agreement include a safeguard clause (Article 5), which permits the imposition of additional duties where the volume of imports exceed a given trigger level or where import prices fall below a trigger price, and Article 15 which provides for special and differential treatment for developing countries. Generally, this treatment entails longer phase-in periods as well as exceptions from the Agreement's disciplines for certain forms of subsidies.

---

2 *United States – Subsidies on Upland Cotton* (2005) WT/DS267/AB/R, discussed in detail by Karen Halverson Cross, "King Cotton, Developing Countries and the Peace Clause", (2006) 9:1 *Journal of International Economic Law* 149.

3 *European Community – Export Subsidies on Sugar* (2005) WT/DS265/ AB/R, WT/DS266/AB/R, WT/DS283/AB/R [*EC – Export Subsidies on Sugar* 2005].

9.3 The Doha Round negotiations on agriculture

The OECD has estimated that its members' support for agriculture was about US $311 billion in 2000,[4] signifying the modesty of the liberalization efforts reflected in the Uruguay Round Agreement on Agriculture. With a view to launching further liberalization negotiations, Paragraph 13 of the Doha Declaration in 2001 commits member countries to build on the Uruguay Agreement on Agriculture and to negotiate "substantial improvements in market access; reductions of, with a view to phasing out, all forms of export subsidies; and substantial reductions in trade-distorting domestic support". It also agrees to special and differential treatment for developing countries, considering their food security and rural development needs, and to consider the non-trade concerns of member countries. However, these negotiations seem to have reached an impasse. While there appears to be some agreement on phasing out export subsidies (in 1995, the EU accounted for 89 per cent of export subsidies),[5] there is much less agreement on reducing domestic forms of support, and severe disagreement over the extremely high tariffs, tariff peaks and tariff escalation which still prevail in this sector and which constitute major barriers to market access. World Bank estimates in 2005 indicated that 90 per cent of the potential gains from further liberalization of agriculture would come from reducing import barriers and 10 per cent from reducing subsidies.[6] The conversion of quantitative restrictions into tariffs mandated by the Uruguay Round Agreement on Agriculture led many countries to substitute tariff rate quotas (TRQs) for former quantitative restrictions and out of quota tariffs sometimes run to several hundred per cent, largely preserving the previous quota system.

Attempts to agree on tariff cutting formulae that would require larger reductions in high tariffs or tariff peaks as well as escalating tariffs on processed agricultural products have foundered. As well, there are sharp disagreements as to the ability of both developed and developing countries to designate some number of agricultural products as "sensitive products" or "special products" respectively, to which tariff reduction commitments would not apply in full or at all and over

---

4 OECD, *Agricultural Policies in OECD Countries: Monitoring and Evaluation 2000* (Paris: OECD, 2000).

5 See Brett G. Williams, "The WTO Doha Round Draft Text on Agricultural Trade Liberalization: How did We Get into Such a Mess? Should We Walk Away?", (2009) 6:3 *Farm Policy Journal* at 6.

6 *Ibid.*

special safeguard regimes in the agricultural sector. There is also severe disagreement amongst members as to what special and differential treatment for developing countries should entail. Negotiations have been further compounded by large spikes in food prices in recent years that have led some countries to impose taxes or restrictions on some exports to stabilize domestic prices, although exacerbating global price fluctuations. As with the Uruguay Round of Multilateral Negotiations, these issues pertaining to agricultural trade liberalization have proven to be make-or-break issues in the Round.[7]

Nonetheless, Doha has regained some momentum. The Bali Package, agreed to in December 2013 at the most recent phase of the Doha trade talks (the WTO's ninth Ministerial Conference in Bali), includes agriculture – though there were no legally binding outcomes agreed to in the agriculture pillar of the package, reflecting the contentious nature of the topic. The Bali Package as it pertains to agriculture includes outcomes on two topics: tariff quota administration and food stockpiles (specifically, discussion on shielding public stockholding programmes for food security in developing countries such that they would not be challenged legally even if a country's agreed limits for trade-distorting domestic support were breached). On tariff quota administration, member states committed themselves to addressing issues of quota under-filling through simplifying procedures. On food stockpiles, members agreed to a "peace clause" in which countries will temporarily refrain from lodging a legal complaint if a developing country exceeds its Amber Box limits (the 10 per cent of production at which trade-distorting domestic supports are capped) as a result of stockholding for food security, until a permanent solution has been agreed.[8]

---

7 For useful surveys of these issues, see Masayoshi Honma, "Agricultural Issues in the Doha Development Agenda Negotiations", in Yasuhei Taniguchi, Alan Yanovich and Jan Bohanes (eds), *The WTO in the 21st Century: Dispute Settlement Negotiations and Regionalism in Asia* (Cambridge: Cambridge University Press, 2007) 328; Williams, supra note 5; Tracey D. Epps and Michael J. Trebilcock, "Special and Differential Treatment in Agricultural Trade: Breaking the Impasse", in Chantal Thomas and Joel P. Trachtman (eds), *Developing Countries in the WTO Legal System* (New York: Oxford University Press, 2009) 323; Robert Wolfe, "The Special Safeguard Fiasco in the WTO: the Perils of Inadequate Analysis and Negotiation", (2009) 8(4) *World Trade Review*, 517–44; Thomas Schoenbaum, "Fashioning a New Regime for Agricultural Trade: New Issues and the Global Food Crisis", (2011) 14(3) *Journal of International Economic Law*, 593–611.

8 WTO, "Bali Ministerial Declaration and Decisions: Agriculture", *WTO: 9th WTO Ministerial Conference, Bali* (2013). Accessed online <http://wto.org/english/thewto_e/minist_e/mc9_e/balipackage_e.htm#agriculture>. Accessed 12 September 2014.

9.4   The basic economics of agricultural supply management schemes

In understanding impediments to trade liberalization in the agricultural sector, it is important to understand the basic economics of agricultural supply management regimes that set minimum price floors and maximum production quotas for agricultural products (for example, eggs) and that are introduced ostensibly in order to enhance the welfare of small family farmers. The initial impact of the intervention can be graphed as shown in Figure 9.1.

At the competitive price (PC), quantity QC will be demanded and supplied. At the regulated price (PR), SR will be supplied but only DR will be demanded, yielding a surplus of SR – DR (the size of which depends on elasticities of demand and supply). The function of maximum production quotas is to ensure that producers only produce DR so that the market clears. On the demand side, an obvious prediction is that consumers will buy fewer eggs and those that continue to buy eggs

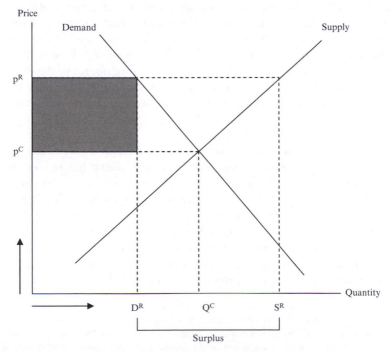

Figure 9.1   Agricultural supply management regime

will pay more for them, including people of modest means for whom eggs are a staple. On the supply side, assuming production quotas are initially allocated on an historical basis (producers with an established presence in the market), the initial quota recipients will obtain supra-competitive returns, measured by the shaded rectangle, at the expense of consumers who remain in the market. To the extent that some of these initial quota recipients are relatively less efficient egg producers, resources devoted to producing DR of eggs will be greater than necessary. Quotas might, on that account, be made tradeable to allow more efficient (lower cost) egg producers to produce the eggs demanded at PR. Prices paid for the quotas will tend to reflect the capitalized value of the future stream of supra-competitive prices (the shaded rectangle). Thus, after paying quota prices, the second generation of egg producers is likely to be making a normal competitive rate of return on its combined investment in egg production resources and quotas. The end result, it would be predicted, would be an allocatively inefficient industry (too few eggs – DR – are produced), but a productively efficient industry (the low-cost producers service the market after quota transfers), though arguably a distributively perverse outcome in that while small family farmers receive an initial wealth transfer, current egg producers gain nothing from the scheme, and current consumers, including poor consumers, pay more than they need to for eggs. Moreover, the scheme may be politically irreversible, as current egg producers who may have paid substantial sums for quotas to the initial recipients will strenuously resist any termination of the scheme without full compensation (often referred to as "the transitional gains trap" problem).[9]

This example can be readily extrapolated to explain the essential features of the EU Common Agricultural Policy, which has turned the EU from the world's largest importer of temperate zone agricultural products into the world's second largest exporter. Despite its byzantine complexity, the essential features of the CAP are straightforward. First, as a matter of history, EU agricultural producers were guaranteed minimum prices for many classes of agricultural products. However, standing alone, guaranteed price floors raised two problems. First, the floor would be undercut by imports. Hence, the EU imposed a variable

---

9 See Gordon Tullock, "The Transitional Gains Trap", (1975) 6:2 *Bell Journal of Economics* 671; Michael Trebilcock, *Dealing with Losers: The Political Economy of Policy Transitions* (New York: Oxford University Press, 2014), chapter 6: Agricultural Supply Management: Unravelling the Transitional Gains Trap.

import levy on imports to prevent price erosion from imports. Second, EU consumers would not choose to purchase all the products that would be produced at the guaranteed prices. Hence, the EU added to the CAP a commitment to purchase all goods produced at the guaranteed prices. With guaranteed prices and guaranteed purchase commitments, EU producers acted rationally and increased supply, creating growing surpluses which the EU was forced to stockpile. In order to dispose of these surpluses, the EU sold them into third country markets, depressing prices in these markets and squeezing out imports from often more efficient producers in other countries. The difference between export prices and guaranteed domestic prices was financed out of the EU budget, often accounting for more than half of its total budget. Hence from a domestic scheme designed to increase farmers' incomes within the EU, the scheme has affected agricultural markets world-wide as a result of export subsidies to surplus production and countervailing subsidies introduced by other countries and are a key and sharply divisive issue in the current Doha Round of multilateral trade negotiations.

9.5   Rationales for special protection of the agricultural sector

A number of rationales are conventionally advanced for special protection of the agricultural sector in many countries (often encompassed by the concept of "multifunctionality" of agriculture in trade negotiations).

9.5.1   Self-sufficiency/national security

It is often argued that a nation's survival, in a literal sense, depends upon access to food. In times of shortage, access to food from foreign imports may well dry up or, in any event, reduced dependency on foreigners for food imports may mitigate the risks associated with war or other disruptions of international trade.

9.5.2   Exceptional price instability

Some agricultural commodities are subject to much more extreme price fluctuations than those experienced by many other goods that are traded, in significant part because supply is susceptible to unpredictable factors such as weather and pestilence and hence, as a consequence, farmers' incomes are highly volatile even when they may have a long-term comparative advantage in producing food.

Moreover, food price volatility impacts consumers; high prices can leave the poor, in particular, food insecure. Connected with global climate change, rising food prices and concerns about a looming global food crisis have heightened concerns about food security, elevating its prominence on the international policy agenda in many areas, including global trade.[10] Food security engages, primarily, two issues pertaining to international trade: export restrictions and domestic supports (food stockpiling). First, states may wish to apply export restrictions on agricultural commodities in order to protect domestic consumers, particularly the poor, from spikes in international commodity prices. Some see this as an important policy tool for poverty reduction, as higher costs for consumers disproportionately impact poor families, who spend a larger proportion of their income on food. Others note that these policies further distort international food prices, inflating commodity prices overall. Under GATT Article XI:2(a), export restrictions can be temporarily imposed to relieve "critical shortages" of food or other essential products. However, those seeking to justify export restrictions on agricultural products under GATT Article XI:2(a) may find it more difficult in light of the Appellate Body's decision in *China – Raw Materials*.[11] In this ruling, the Appellate Body found that the term "critical shortage" refers only to situations or events that may be relieved or prevented through the application of measures on a temporary, rather than indefinite or permanent, basis. In other words, these measures cannot be imposed to address an ongoing crisis, such as the inevitable depletion of a finite resource.[12] Second, recent Doha Round discussions have revolved around the government-sponsored practice of food stockpiling, which may constitute a subsidy. Notably, India led 46 developing countries in proposing a reform in which poor countries would be exempt from limits on subsidies when stockpiling food to support low-income or resource-poor farmers. The "peace

---

10 See Thomas Schoenbaum, "Fashioning a New Regime for Agricultural Trade: New Issues and the Global Food Crisis", (2011) 14:3 *Journal of International Economic Law* 593–611.

11 *China – Measures Related to the Exportation of Various Raw Materials* (2012) WTO Docs WT/DS394/AB/R [*China – Raw Materials* 2012].

12 See Inside US Trade, "WTO Ruling on Raw Materials Could Strengthen Rules on Ag Export Curbs", Inside Washington Publishers (2012). Accessed Online <http://www.agritrade.org/pressroom/documents/AgritradeWTO RulingOnRawMaterials_IUST_11–12.pdf>. Accessed 12 September 2014; *International Food Policy Research Institute, 2012 Global Food Policy Report* (Washington, D.C.: IFPRI, 2013).

clause" on food stockpiling agreed to in the Bali Package constitutes a temporary solution on this issue, around which much disagreement remains.

9.5.3   Preservation of rural lifestyles and the environment

It is often argued that without special support or protection for small family farmers, food production would increasingly be dominated by large agri-businesses that are heavily mechanized and highly capitalized, and important community values associated with rural lifestyles and family farming would increasingly be undermined. Similarly, it is argued that with the continuing sharp contraction in the number of people engaged in agricultural activities and the continuing exodus of people from rural areas to cities, the rural environment is likely to be increasingly blighted by ugly, polluting industries or replaced by industrial or commercial towns, or simply be depopulated and largely abandoned.

While none of these arguments are bogus, important questions arise in each case as to whether trade protection or other forms of agricultural support are the most appropriate instruments for addressing these concerns. With respect to the self-sufficiency/national security concerns, few countries can realistically hope to be completely self-sufficient in their food production, and freer international trade enables them to diversify their sources of foreign supply and hence the risk of disruptions in the sources of these supplies. With respect to price instability, much of the agricultural industry in developed countries is now constituted by large commercial producers, and products such as beef, pork, lamb, milk, butter, eggs, and poultry are not subject to the same price fluctuations as crops, fruits and vegetables (although the latter are often an input into the production of the former). Moreover, policy instruments that seek to stabilize farmers' incomes directly, through income-averaging techniques or income insurance, or non-production related subsidies may be more cost-effective instruments than instruments designed to maintain artificially high domestic prices. With respect to concerns over the preservation of rural lifestyles and the environment, well-conceived regional development plans seem a more finely tuned instrument than agricultural protection to ensure balanced economic activity in rural areas. Much of the potential for reforming agricultural trade comes from the potential for "de-coupling" such policy goals from trade-distorting policy instruments.

9.5.4   Subsistence agriculture

In many developing countries traditional forms of agriculture are a critically important source of food sustenance and subsistence income generation, and may well be threatened by full agricultural trade liberalization. Traditional farmers in these sectors would face severe adjustment costs in the event of such liberalization due to low levels of education and literacy, poorly developed financial and insurance markets, weak social safety nets, and poor physical infrastructure. The normative case for providing exceptional forms of protection or support for these sectors is compelling.[13] Moreover, tariffs are a major source of government revenue in many developing countries.

9.5.5   Political economy factors

In developed countries, an obvious impediment to trade liberalization in agriculture is the transitional gains trap problem identified above where trade protection and other forms of support have been capitalized in land or quota values such that later generations of farmers who have acquired land or quotas at inflated values face severe out-of-pocket losses in the event of trade liberalization. Moreover, given the configuration of electoral boundaries in many countries, despite the continuing exodus of citizens from rural areas to cities, farmers and rural residents tend to be heavily overrepresented in national legislatures in many countries, conferring on them a disproportionate political influence. Both these factors suggest that trade liberalization in developed countries will be a slow and painful process, and counsel patience and modest expectations for the agricultural trade liberalization agenda.

9.6   Breaking the impasse

Moving forward, high priorities should be the complete prohibition of export subsidies and a major liberalization of border measures (tariffs and tariff rate quotas), with few dispensations except for developing countries with vulnerable traditional subsistence agricultural sectors where special ex ante safeguard measures may be warranted. With export subsidies prohibited, and import restric-

---

13 See Epps and Trebilcock, supra note 7.

tions substantially liberalized, more latitude should be accorded to domestic subsidies once a much greater proportion of the costs of these are internalized to the countries providing them, precipitating higher internal levels of political accountability for such expenditures.

10 Trade in services

10.1 Introduction

The GATT 1947 focused almost exclusively on international trade in goods. However, by the 1980s and 1990s, services accounted for 50 to 60 per cent of domestic GNP in many developed countries, and even higher in the USA, while international trade in services accounted for only about 20 per cent of total world trade. Hence, as comparative advantage in the production of many manufactured goods shifted to low-wage developing or newly industrializing countries, developed countries became increasingly concerned with enhancing their comparative advantage in many service sectors, such as financial services, telecommunications, transportation, computing, and professional services, by extending the ambit of the GATT to embrace the liberalization of international trade in services. In the Uruguay Round, beginning in 1986, negotiating a multilateral agreement on international trade in services became a priority for many developed countries and resulted in the General Agreement on Trade in Services (GATS) that came into force in 1995.

While the theory of comparative advantage, in principle, seems to apply equally to international trade in services as to international trade in goods, various assumptions that tended to view services markets as largely domestic increasingly came under challenge. First, as a result of technological advances, assumptions that most services required close physical proximity between service providers and consumers became increasingly questionable. Second, while in many countries through most of the post-war period, many important service sectors had been highly regulated, or maintained as state or private monopolies (for example, in the telecommunications or transportation sectors), regulatory reform movements in many countries during the 1970s and 1980s resulted in the privatization or deregulation of many service sectors, exposing all or large segments of them to domestic competition, and hence then raising further potential for international competition in these sectors. Third, many service sectors were viewed as performing functions integral to the production of goods and as not constituting separate markets in themselves. With the increasing out-sourcing by private enterprises of various inputs into the production of goods during this period, it became increasingly clear that service markets should be properly conceived of as separate from the markets for goods into which they might be inputs.

10.2   The General Agreement on Trade in Services (GATS)

The GATS is in many respects little more than a framework for an ongoing process of multilateral negotiations for liberalizing international trade in services.

10.2.1   Scope of the GATS

The Agreement applies to "measures by members affecting trade in services". Measures by members means measures taken by: i) central, regional or local governments or authorities; and ii) nongovernmental bodies in the exercise of powers delegated by central, regional or local governments or authorities. Article I of the Agreement defines four modes of supply of international trade in services:

a)   from the territory of one member into the territory of another member (cross-border supply);
b)   in the territory of one member to the service consumer of any other member (consumption abroad);
c)   by a service supplier of one member, through commercial presence in the territory of another member (commercial presence); and
d)   by a service supplier of one member, through the presence of natural persons of a member in the territory of any other member (presence of natural persons).

With respect to Mode 4 (presence of natural persons), an Annex to the GATS states that the Agreement does not apply to measures affecting natural persons seeking access to the employment market of a member, nor does it apply to measures regarding citizenship, residence, or employment on a permanent basis.

The Agreement also does not apply to services supplied in the exercise of governmental authority, which is defined as any service which is supplied neither on a commercial basis, nor in competition with one or more service suppliers. This exception has attracted criticism for its limited scope in that many predominantly government-provided services, for example health care, education and water distribution, are provided in competition with private providers and so may fall outside the exception.

10.2.2   Most Favoured Nation treatment

GATS Article II requires that Most Favoured Nation treatment be provided to all trading partners: "Each member shall accord immediately and unconditionally to services and service suppliers of any other member treatment no less favourable than it accords to like services and service suppliers of any other country". A member may maintain a measure inconsistent with Article II provided that such a measure is listed in and meets the conditions of an annex to the Agreement. Under this annex, the Council for Trade in Services shall review all exemptions in force for a period of more than five years to determine whether the conditions which created the need for the exemption still prevail; such exemptions should not exceed a period of ten years. In any event, they shall be subject to negotiation in subsequent trade liberalizing rounds.

10.2.3   Domestic regulation

Article VI of the GATS has proven controversial. Article VI: 4 provides:

> With a view to ensuring that measures relating to qualification requirements and procedures, technical standards and licensing requirements do not constitute unnecessary barriers to trade in services, the Council for Trade in Services shall, through appropriate bodies that it may establish, develop any necessary disciplines. Such disciplines shall aim to ensure that such requirements are, inter alia:
>
> a)   based on objective and transparent criteria, such as competence and the ability to supply the service;
> b)   not more burdensome than necessary to ensure the quality of the service;
> c)   in the case of licensing procedures, not in themselves a restriction on the supply of the service.

While these disciplines are still to be developed, critics of the GATS are concerned that they have the potential to constrain greatly the ability of members of the WTO to adopt domestic regulations with respect to services.

10.2.4   Specific commitments

Part III of the GATS covers specific commitments by members. There are two principal types of commitments: Market Access and National Treatment commitments. There is no requirement to make commitments, and commitments which are made may be qualified in any way in which a member chooses, for example by restricting the modes of supply to which the commitment applies. Market access commitments are dealt with in Article XVI, which provides that where market access commitments are undertaken, the measures which a member shall not maintain or adopt either on the basis of a regional sub-division or on the basis of its entire territory unless otherwise specified in its schedule, include limitations on the number of service suppliers; limitations on the total value of service transactions or assets; limitations on the total number of service operations or the total quantity of service outputs; limitations on the total number of natural persons that may be employed in a particular service sector or by a service supplier; measures which restrict or require specific types of legal entity or joint venture through which a service supplier may supply a service; and limitations on the participation of foreign capital in terms of maximum percentage limits on foreign shareholdings or the total value of individual or aggregate foreign investment.

Even though many of these kinds of restrictions may be non-discriminatory, and hence violate neither the MFN nor National Treatment Principles, member countries in the course of negotiations may be prepared to make full or qualified market access commitments designed to enhance market access for foreign service suppliers (in return for reciprocal commitment in these or other sectors).

The National Treatment commitments are dealt with in Article XVII, which provides that members may make either full or qualified National Treatment commitments with respect to the services and service suppliers of any other member in respect of all measures affecting the supply of services requiring treatment no less favourable than the member accords to its own like services and service suppliers.

Under Article XXI, either Market Access or National Treatment commitments that members have scheduled may be modified or withdrawn at any time after three years have elapsed from the date on which a commitment entered into force, but other members affected by the modification or withdrawal may enter into negotiations with a view to reaching agreement on any necessary compensatory adjustment with respect to other trade measures. If agreement cannot be reached, an affected member may refer the matter to arbitration to determine an appropriate compensatory adjustment. If the modifying member implements its proposed modification or withdrawal and does not comply with the findings of the arbitration, any affected member may modify or withdraw substantially equivalent benefits.

10.2.5 Exceptions

Part II of the GATS contains a number of exceptions including Article V relating to economic integration, which is a parallel provision to Article XXIV of the GATT; Article XII that deals with restrictions on trade in services to safeguard the balance of payments; Article XIV, which is a general exception provision that is a close counterpart to Article XX of the GATT but also permits measures of any member "necessary to protect public morals or to maintain public order" (the public order exception may be invoked only when a genuine and sufficiently serious threat is posed to one of the fundamental interests of society), the prevention of deceptive and fraudulent practices or to deal with the effects of a default on services contracts, and the protection of the privacy of individuals in relation to the processing and dissemination of personal data and the protection of confidentiality of individual records and accounts; and Article XIV bis, which provides for national security exceptions and is the counterpart to Article XXI of the GATT.

10.2.6 Mutual recognition agreements

Under Article VII members who are parties to such agreements may recognize the education or experience obtained, requirements met, or licenses or certifications granted in a particular country. But parties to such agreements shall afford adequate opportunity for other interested members to negotiate their accession to such an agreement or arrangement or to negotiate comparable agreements with it.

10.2.7   Anti-competitive practices

Article VIII provides that any monopoly supplier of a service in a member's territory shall not act in a manner inconsistent with a member's obligations under the Agreement and specific commitments that it has entered into. Where a member's monopoly supplier competes, either directly or through an affiliated company in the supply of a service outside the scope of its monopoly rights and which are subject to that member's specific commitments, the member shall ensure that such supplier does not abuse its monopoly position to act in a manner inconsistent with such commitments. Under Article IX members recognize that certain business practices of service suppliers may restrain competition and thereby restrict trade in services; each member, shall at the request of any other member, enter into consultations with a view to eliminating such practices.

10.2.8   Built-in negotiations

10.2.8.1   Emergency safeguard measures

Members of the WTO commit themselves to multilateral negotiations on the question of emergency safeguard measures based on the principle of non-discrimination (Art. X).

10.2.8.2   Government procurement

The Agreement does not apply to regulations or requirements governing the procurement by governmental agencies of services purchased for governmental purposes and not with a view to commercial resale or with a view to use in the supply of services for commercial sale, but members commit themselves to multilateral negotiations on government procurement in services under this Agreement within two years from the date of its entry into force (Art. XIII).

10.2.8.3   Subsidies

Members recognize that in certain circumstances subsidies may have distortive effects on trade in services and commit themselves to entering into negotiations with a view to developing the necessary multilateral disciplines to avoid such trade distortive effects and to address the appropriateness of countervailing procedures (Art. XV).

10.2.9   Dispute settlement

The general dispute settlement provisions of the Dispute Settlement Understanding apply to disputes relating to GATS. The Decision on Certain Dispute Settlement Procedures for the GATS provides that a special roster of panelists is to be established for purposes of settlement of disputes under GATS with expertise in issues relating to the service sectors to which the dispute relates.

10.2.10   The WTO Agreement on Financial Services

Negotiations over financial services commitments were incomplete at the time that GATS came into force, and led to further negotiations that concluded in December 1997 with an Agreement on Financial Services, where many countries made commitments designed to allow the commercial presence of foreign financial service suppliers by eliminating or relaxing limitations on foreign ownership of local financial institutions, limitations on the juridical form of commercial presence, and limitations on the expansion of existing operations. These improvements were made in all of the three major financial service sectors – banking, securities, and insurance.

10.2.11   The WTO Basic Telecommunications Agreement

As with negotiations for the liberalization of international trade in the financial services, negotiations over liberalizing trade in telecommunication services had made limited progress at the time that GATS was concluded, and negotiations were extended and reached a successful conclusion in February 1997, where many countries committed themselves to liberalized trade in international voice services, national long-distance services, local services, data transmission services, leased lines, cellular/mobile telephony services, mobile satellite services, and fixed satellite services, and relaxed restrictions on foreign ownership or control of telecommunication services and facilities. In addition to these commitments, most signatories made commitments to follow the regulatory principles in a Reference Paper negotiated simultaneously with the other commitments. The Reference Paper requires members to establish appropriate measures to prevent anti-competitive practices by major suppliers, which include cross-subsidization, using information obtained from competitors with anti-competitive results, and not making available to other service suppliers on a timely basis technical information about essential facilities and commercially relevant information which is necessary for them to provide services. Interconnection with a major supplier must be provided, inter alia, on a non-discriminatory basis. Other provisions in the Reference Paper relate to transparency and the existence of an independent regulatory regime to resolve disputes inter alia over interconnection issues.

10.3   WTO case law on the GATS

The GATS has attracted relatively little formal dispute settlement activity since it came into force. However, in two relatively early cases – *Canada – Periodicals* (1997)[1] and *EC – Bananas* (1997)[2] – the Appellate Body held that in a range of situations where services in question are directly related to trade in goods, both the GATS and the GATT may be applicable and require separate consideration and application.

The leading case on a number of GATS issues to date is *United States – Measures Affecting the Cross-Border Supply of Gambling and Betting Services* (Online Gambling).[3] In this case, Antigua challenged a variety of US federal and state laws and regulatory actions which it claimed amounted to a complete prohibition on the cross-border provision of gambling by Antiguan suppliers. Antigua argued that these prohibitions constituted a violation of US Market Access commitments under Article XVI of the GATS, given that the USA had made an unqualified market access commitment with respect to "other recreational services" which under the UN Central Product Classification Guidelines (CPC) included gambling and betting services. Both the WTO Panel and the Appellate Body held that, indeed, the USA was in violation of this commitment, but went on to consider whether the prohibitions were justified under the public morals and public order exception contained in Article XIV(a) of the GATS. The WTO Panel found that US concerns about money laundering, organized crime, protection of minors, and compulsive gambling fell within this exception, taking a reasonably liberal view of the ability of member countries to define the content of public morals and public order based on the beliefs of the nation or community in question as they relate to general or

---

1 *Canada – Certain Measures Concerning Periodicals* (1997) WT/DS27/ AB/R.

2 *EC – Regime for the Importation, Sale, and Distribution of Bananas*(1997) WT/DS27/AB/R.

3 *United States – Measures Affecting the Cross-Border Supply of Gambling and Betting Services*, 10 November 2004, WT/DS285/R and AB-2005–1, 7 April 2005 [*Online Gambling* 2005].

common interests. However, the Panel held that the US prohibition failed to meet the necessity test under Article XIV since it had made no efforts to resolve its concerns through exploring cooperation with the Antiguan authorities as to alternative, less trade-restrictive policies that would as effectively address these concerns.

On appeal, the Appellate Body overruled the Panel on this latter issue, holding that consultations with Antigua could not be considered a reasonably available alternative measure to achieve the US's public policy goals. Moreover, it held that the USA did not bear the burden of demonstrating that every conceivable alternative measure that might be less trade restrictive than the measures in place would be unable to vindicate the USA's public policy goals. Rather, Antigua bore the burden of identifying such a measure, at which point the burden of proof would shift back again to the USA to demonstrate that the particular measure identified would not satisfy its public policy goals. However, the Appellate Body went on to hold that, with respect to off-track betting on horse races, one of the US statutes in question, as administered, permitted this with respect to domestic suppliers of gambling services, but not off-shore suppliers, and in this respect violated the chapeau to Article XIV which prohibits the application of the measure in question in such a manner as to constitute arbitrary or unjustified discrimination. Antigua was authorized to impose retaliatory trade measures not exceeding $21 million per year, including through the suspension of its TRIPS commitments to the USA.

Most recently, the Appellate Body in *China – Audiovisual (Censorship)*[4] ruled against a number of trade restrictions introduced by China with respect to certain reading materials, audiovisual products, sound recordings and films. In this dispute, the Appellate Body considered the interpretation of the terms "sound recording distribution services" and "audiovisual services" in China's GATS Schedule, in particular whether it extends to the distribution of sound recordings in non-physical forms, especially through electronic means. The Appellate Body ruled that these terms refer both to tangible and intangible products.[5]

---

4 *China – Measures Affecting Trading Rights and Distribution Services for Certain Publications and Audiovisual Entertainment Products* (2009) WT/DS363/AB/R.

5 See Xiaohui Wu, "Case Note: China – Measures Affecting Trading Rights and Distribution Services for Certain Publications and Audiovisual Entertainment Products", (2010) 9(2) *Chinese Journal of International Law*, 415–32.

10.4   Critiques of the GATS

The GATS, and the more general agenda for ongoing negotiations to liberalize international trade in services, have attracted intense criticisms from many quarters. For commentators who support the liberalization agenda, the commitments made under the GATS are viewed as extremely modest and disappointing and as amounting to little more than "stand still" commitments, while progress on the built-in negotiating agenda relating to safeguard measures, government procurement, and subsidies, as well as further specific liberalization commitments, has been very limited. On the other hand, the GATS has attracted intense criticism from anti-globalization commentators, who see in the GATS and in ongoing liberalization negotiations with respect to services an implicit deregulation/privatization agenda which poses serious threats to the domestic political autonomy of member countries, especially with respect to essential services such as water, health care, and education, which have typically been provided in many countries exclusively or primarily by various levels of government and, if open to foreign competition through commitments made under the GATS, would leave governments with very limited future policy flexibility in terms of reversing or modifying policies so implemented. Defenders of the GATS respond by pointing out that member countries assume very few obligations under the GATS unless they choose to schedule Market Access or National Treatment commitments, and even then subject to whatever limitations they choose to impose and that commitments are further subject to modification or withdrawal under Article XXI (subject to negotiation of trade compensation).[6]

10.5   Alternative service liberalization modalities

While the theory of comparative advantage may, in principle, apply equally to international trade in services and international trade in goods, the negotiating challenges are much more formidable with respect to barriers to international trade in services than international trade in goods. In the case of goods, historically the challenge has been to negotiate down various border measures, in particular quantitative restrictions and tariffs. In the case of international trade in services,

---

6 For a critical review of these concerns, see booklet of WTO Secretariat, "GATS – Fact and Fiction" (2001).

the barriers to international trade are almost never border measures such as quantitative restrictions and tariffs, but internal domestic regulatory policies, and moreover often domestic regulatory policies enacted and administered by sub-national levels of government or delegated agencies of government including professional self-regulatory bodies. These regulatory measures obviously vary dramatically from one service sector to the other, precluding anything analogous to across-the-board tariff cuts and requiring highly transaction-cost-intensive negotiations service sector by service sector. In contemplating alternative negotiating modalities, it is useful to consider the following options.

10.5.1   Non-discrimination principles (MFN and National Treatment)

Just as these principles have been cornerstones of the GATT, one might argue that non-discrimination, rather than enhanced market access, should be the principal objective of the liberalization of international trade in services. However, in the case of MFN, this has proven problematic, both in the context of negotiations that led to the GATS and subsequent negotiations that led to the WTO Agreement on Financial Services and the WTO Agreement on Basic Telecommunication Services, where the USA insisted that it would not make MFN commitments without effective reciprocity from other member countries in order to foreclose the free-riding effect associated with the MFN Principle. With respect to the National Treatment Principle, GATS essentially operates on an opt-in principle, where National Treatment commitments must be affirmatively scheduled under Article XVII. An alternative approach is taken in Chapter 12 of the North American Free Trade Agreement (NAFTA), where the three countries make a general National Treatment commitment with respect to cross-border trade in services, with the right to enter reservations with respect to particular sectors – in effect, an opt-out rather than an opt-in regime. Sectors that are subject to reservations may then be the subject of periodic negotiation or renegotiation. However, as to what exactly the National Treatment Principle requires in particular contexts can be highly problematic. For example, in the case of the self-regulating professions, such as the legal profession, what would constitute conformity with the National Treatment Principle on the part of self-regulating bodies in evaluating and recognizing the credentials of foreign-trained lawyers?

10.5.2   Mutual Recognition agreements

Under the Mutual Recognition Principle, which has been extensively applied in the European Union, importing countries agree to recognize home country regulation with respect to service suppliers seeking to provide services in other countries. However, this principle, if unqualified, stands the National Treatment Principle on its head in that it may require importing countries to treat foreign suppliers better than their own suppliers and creates the risk that exporting countries may have incentives to adopt lax regulatory regimes that externalize the negative consequences of ineffective regulation to importing countries, for example with respect to prudential requirements for financial institutions, or licensing requirements for professionals, and may precipitate a race to the bottom. Hence, in practice, the Mutual Recognition Principle is typically accompanied, as it has been in the EU, with an ambitious agenda for setting minimum harmonized standards for cross-border trade in services. However, these harmonization initiatives crucially depend on an elaborate and sophisticated supranational institutional apparatus based in Brussels, which finds no ready counterpart in the World Trade Organization or other regional trade agreements.

10.5.3   Negotiated exchanges of specific commitments

This is essentially the strategy that has been adopted in the GATS, and finds its counterpart in negotiated product-by-product tariff concessions with respect to international trade in goods in the early rounds of the GATT. However, as has been noted above, these negotiations are likely to be highly transaction-cost-intensive (and not nearly as simple as exchanging tariff concessions) and make significant progress on liberalizing international trade in services a daunting challenge. While in specific sectors such as financial services and telecommunication services, significant progress has been made, the prospects for more general liberalization of international trade in services at the present time do not look strong.

11 Trade and investment

11.1 Introduction

Foreign direct investment (FDI) (which is the focus of this chapter) should be distinguished from portfolio investment. FDI typically involves some form of effective control and active management of assets in host countries, while portfolio investment typically involves passive investments in enterprises or government bonds in host countries. Over the last several decades, there has been a dramatic increase in FDI around the world, much of it between developed countries, but increasingly developing countries have been major recipients of FDI, including countries such as China, and in some cases have themselves become exporters of FDI (again, China is a prominent example).[1] More than 40 per cent of world FDI inflows are directed to developing countries. FDI flows to developing countries now exceed foreign aid flows by a factor of about 5 to 1.[2]

In their early post-independence years, many former colonies viewed FDI with skepticism, and in some cases outright hostility, as it was perceived to be a new form of economic imperialism (reflected in dependency theories of development that were influential in many developing countries in the 1950s and 1960s). More recently, many developing countries have come to see FDI as having at least the potential for making significant contributions to their economies – as a source of investment in infrastructure, as a source of technology transfers and spillovers, as a source of investment in human capital and skills upgrading, as a source of investment in major natural resource extraction projects, and as a major source of local employment in low-wage,

---

1 See generally, Americo B. Zampetti and Pierre Sauvé, "International Investment", in Andrew T. Guzman and Alan O. Sykes (eds), *Research Handbook in International Economic Law* (Cheltenham, UK: Edward Elgar, 2007).

2 UNCTAD, "Assessing the Impact of the Current Financial and Economic Crisis on Global FDI Flows", 19 January 2009.

low-skilled manufacturing activities.[3] Foreign direct investment can substitute for or complement trade, depending on context and application. In this respect, it is useful to distinguish between horizontal and vertical FDI.[4] If, for example, a manufacturer in North America wishes to access China's market to sell its products, it can export its products from North America to China or set up a replica manufacturing facility in China to service domestic customers in the Chinese market (horizontal FDI). Where host countries have large protected domestic markets, FDI may be the most effective way of accessing these markets behind prevailing tariff walls – particularly the case with host countries with large growing populations and hence significant potential demand for the goods or services that foreign investors can produce. In this case, FDI is a substitute for trade. In the case of vertical FDI, foreign investors are able to expand their opportunities for international trade in goods or services by accessing lower cost inputs (for example, natural resources or low-cost labour) in host countries and hence gain a comparative advantage in export markets. For example, a North American manufacturer may choose to set up foreign subsidiaries or affiliates to manufacture components for its products and export these components to its parent company in North America for incorporation in the final products. In this case, FDI and trade are complements.

In principle, the theory of comparative advantage should apply as much to international movements of FDI as to international trade in goods or services – capital is likely to gravitate to where its marginal productivity is greatest. If unqualified, this presumption would suggest the case for an international regime that facilitates the free movement of FDI, and constrains countries from adopting domestic policies designed either to encourage it – for example, through subsidies, tax breaks, or tax incentives – or to discourage it – for example,

---

3 See, for example, Theodore Moran, "Enhancing the Ability of Developing Countries to Attack and Harness FDI for Development", in Theodore Moran (ed.), *Harnessing Foreign Direct Investment: Policies for Developing Countries* (Washington, D.C.: Brookings Institute Press, 2006); Theodore Moran, Edward Graham and Magnus Blomstrom (eds), *Does Foreign Direct Investment Promote Development?* (Washington, D.C.: Peterson Institute, 2005); OECD Report, *Foreign Direct Investment for Development: Maximizing Benefits, Minimizing Costs* (Paris: OECD, 2002). For recent analysis of the benefits of FDI in developed and developing countries see Theodore Moran, *Foreign Direct Investment and Development: Launching a Second Generation of Policy Research: Avoiding the Mistakes of the First, Reevaluating Policies for Developed and Developing Countries* (Washington, D.C.: Peterson Institute, 2011).

4 See Elhanan Helpman, *Understanding Global Trade* (Cambridge, M.A.: Harvard University Press, 2011), chapter 6.

through regulations pertaining to local sourcing, minimum export requirements, restrictions on exports, trade balancing requirements that restrict the value or volume of imports to the value or volume of exports, technology transfer requirements, and so on. In fact, many countries have adopted a wide range of domestic policies that either encourage or restrict FDI either generally or, more commonly, in particular sectors.

Restrictions on FDI may be motivated by a range of concerns. First, there are likely to be concerns about foreign investors acquiring domestic firms where the nature of the activities in question raise national security issues – concerns that have been exacerbated by the rapid growth of Sovereign Wealth Funds.[5] Foreign investors who control these assets may have access to sensitive national security technology or information. Second, while there are few inherent legal constraints on the application of domestic jurisdiction to the activities that foreign investors engage in within a particular country, there may be significant practical constraints in the effective application of domestic laws where the bulk of the firm's assets, many of its senior personnel, and much of the information about its activities and decision-making are located abroad. Third, there may be concerns about attempts by home country governments to enforce their laws in foreign jurisdictions through foreign subsidiaries of home country parent corporations, that is, extra-territorial application of home countries' laws. Fourth, there may also be concerns that foreign subsidiaries will be managed in such a fashion as to reflect home country bias in business decisions, for example purchasing inputs from home country affiliates or using personnel from home country or other affiliates rather than local personnel, perhaps in some cases motivated by a desire to appear to be a "good corporate citizen" in the home country in order to maximize political influence in that jurisdiction. Fifth, there may be concerns that foreign investors will seek to protect their investments in specialized technology and know-how by restricting access to them by domestic firms or individuals in the host country, hence reducing the benefits of technological spillovers and human capital enhancements in the host country. Sixth, there may be cultural and political sovereignty concerns with permitting FDI in certain sectors, such as the print and electronic media.

---

5 See Jackie Van Der Meulen and Michael J. Trebilcock, "Canada's Policy Response to Foreign Sovereign Investment: Operationalizing National Security Exceptions", (2009) 47:3 *Canadian Business L.J.* 392.

Foreign direct investors, in turn, are likely to confront their own set of concerns in contemplating investments in a foreign country. These may include political and policy instability (including macroeconomic stability). Where investments are sunk, subsequent governments may have incentives to behave opportunistically towards foreign direct investors that lack direct political voice in host countries by unilateral *ex post facto* re-specification of the terms on which the initial investment was made. Other concerns include weak protection of private property rights (including intellectual property rights) and ineffective enforcement of contracts; law and order; and corruption in the administration of state functions (including legal functions).

11.2   Multilateral regulation of foreign direct investment

As has been noted in earlier chapters, historically the GATT was almost exclusively focused on international trade in goods, and not international trade in services or international movement of capital. However, a GATT panel decision in 1984,[6] in response to a complaint by the USA relating to various undertakings obtained from foreign investors pursuant to Canada's *Foreign Investment Review Act*, held that certain features of domestic foreign investment regulations may fall within the purview of the GATT where these affect international trade in goods. In this case, the USA challenged undertakings that required foreign investors to commit to certain local sourcing and minimum export requirements as a condition for approval of their investments in Canada. The Panel held that the local sourcing requirements violated the National Treatment Principle in Article III of the GATT by treating local suppliers of these inputs more favourably than foreign suppliers, although it held that minimum export requirements did not violate any provision in the GATT.

At the beginning of the Uruguay Round in 1986, the USA proposed that the multilateral negotiating agenda for this round should include a comprehensive agreement on foreign investment. The Agreement on Trade-Related Investment Measures (TRIMS) that emerged from the Round is, in fact, much more modest than the initial US proposals, and builds on the prior GATT Panel ruling in 1984 by prohibiting domestic regulations that would violate the National Treatment Principle in

---

6 *Canada: Administration of the Foreign Investment Review Act* (1984) BISD 305/140.

Article III.4 of the GATT, including local sourcing requirements, trade balancing requirements, and export restrictions. This illustrative list is non-exhaustive. The TRIMS Agreement has attracted very little subsequent formal dispute-settlement activity, in large part because it does little more than reaffirm the application of Article III.4 of the GATT to certain forms of regulation or FDI that may influence imports or exports of goods by foreign direct investors.

However, TRIMS was at issue in a recent case. In *Canada – Feed-in Tariffs*,[7] the Appellate Body considered the relationship between TRIMS Article 2.1 (which provides that no member shall apply any TRIMS that is inconsistent with Article III or Article IX of the GATT and is accompanied by an illustrative list of inconsistent measures in Article 2.2) and Article III.8(a) of the GATT (which provides an exception to the National Treatment Principle for government procurement). It upheld the Panel's finding that the illustrative list in TRIMS Article 2.2 does not remove the need to analyze whether a measure falls outside of the scope of the national treatment requirement by virtue of Article III.8(a). In this case, it was held that FIT contracts did not fall within the government procurement exception because the Government of Ontario's procurement under the FIT Programme was undertaken with a view to commercial resale.

Disaffected with the modest outcome from the Uruguay Round, the USA and other developed countries sought to shift the venue for multilateral negotiations on a comprehensive investment treaty from the WTO to the OECD. It was assumed that, due to the predominance of developed countries, the OECD would yield a readier consensus on liberalizing restrictions on FDI than the WTO where the preponderance of developing country members with more skeptical, or at least more cautious, views of the merits of FDI was likely to preclude achievement of a consensus on a more ambitious set of international disciplines. The expectation was that non-OECD members would be able to accede to any resulting treaty and that there would be strong inducements to do so in order to compete effectively for FDI. From 1996 through to 1998 negotiations on a multilateral agreement on investment (MAI) proceeded within the OECD, but negotiations were non-transparent, even clandestine, and the leaking of a draft of the agreement to various NGOs precipitated an international firestorm of criticism of the draft agreement and the process by which it was being negotiated. The

---

7 *Canada – Measures Relating to the Feed-in Tariff Program* (2013) WT/DS426/AB/R.

principal criticism was that it would confer extensive rights on foreign direct investors but with few, if any, concomitant obligations on their part to host countries or their citizens, for example, with respect to technology transfer, health and safety, the environment, labour standards, international human rights, and so on. In the face of these criticisms, the MAI negotiations were formally abandoned in December 1998. Proposals to include negotiations over FDI in the Doha Round of the WTO were also abandoned at the Cancun Ministerial in September 2003 in the face of opposition from developing countries.

11.3   Bilateral investment treaties

While attempts at negotiating a comprehensive multilateral treaty on FDI appear to have been abandoned, at least for the time being, a notable contrasting phenomenon has been the dramatic proliferation since 1990 in the number of bilateral investment treaties (BITS) or international investment agreements (IIAs) that have been negotiated – up from just over 400 in 1990 to more than 3000 today (paralleling the proliferation of Preferential Trade Agreements).[8] The primary impetus behind this proliferation of BITS appears to be that in the competition for FDI many countries, especially developing countries, feel obliged to provide investors with certain legally enforceable protections of their investment, although BITS are not limited to developed–developing country dyads (only about 40 per cent); about a quarter of all BITS are between pairs of developing countries.[9]

BITS typically include provisions on the scope and definition of FDI; admission of investment; national and Most Favoured Nation treatment; fair and equitable treatment; guarantees and compensation in respect of expropriation and compensation for war and civil disturbances; guarantees of free transfer of funds and repatriation of capital and profits; subrogation on insurance claims; and dispute settlement, both state-to-state and investor-to-state (typically by international arbitration, most often the International Centre for Settlement of Investment Disputes (ICSID) affiliated with the World Bank).

---

8 See Gus Van Harter, *Investing Treaty Arbitration and Public Law* (Oxford: Oxford University Press, 2008), chapter 2; Stephan Schill, *The Multilateralization of International Investment Law* (Cambridge: Cambridge University Press, 2009).

9 UNCTAD, "Recent Developments in International Investment Agreements", IIA Monitor No. 3 (2009).

The proliferation of BITS has raised a number of controversies. First, the "fair and equitable" standard of investment protection lacks precision and consistent interpretation or clearly articulated exceptions or qualifications for measures by host countries addressing health, safety, and environmental concerns or financial crises, which has led to criticisms of BITS as unduly constraining host countries' political sovereignty. Second, the expropriation provisions in most BITS also lack clear definition and may be interpreted as extending beyond outright transfer of title to foreign investors' assets or physical dispossession of those assets to various forms of regulatory "takings" that can be viewed as significantly impairing the value of these assets. This is criticized for constraining or "chilling" legitimate spheres of regulatory autonomy. Third, given that many countries have signed multiple BITS with various other countries, each of which typically contains a Most Favoured Nation clause, major disputes have arisen as to when foreign investors are able to invoke ("cherry pick") either substantive or procedural provisions in BITS other than the BIT to which their home country is a party (which are more favourable to their claims than their own BITS). Fourth, the National Treatment Principle, which is contained in most BITS, also gives rise to ambiguity as to when foreign investors have been treated less favourably than domestic investors in "like circumstances". Fifth, the international arbitral dispute resolution system has been criticized as lacking transparency, consistency, and scope for effective third-party (amicus) interventions, and in general for being biased towards the interests of foreign investors.[10] Finally, it is argued that BITS largely remove foreign investors as a political constituency for domestic legal reform in host countries by providing them with privileged supra-national legal protections.[11]

A new generation of BITS attempts to strike a finer balance between the interests of investors and the interests of host countries by adding interpretive provisions, general exceptions clauses, and new preambular language as to the purpose of the agreements,[12] but how arbitrators are likely to interpret such provisions and whether they are effectively justiciable in a consistent and credible manner remains to

---

10 For a review of many of the foregoing critiques, see David Schneiderman, *Constitutionalizing Economic Globalization: Investment Rules and Democracy's Promise* (Cambridge: Cambridge University Press, 2008).

11 Tom Ginsburg, "International Substitutes for Domestic Institutions: Bilateral Investment Treaties and Governance", (2005) 25:1 *International Review of Law and Economics* 107.

12 See Suzanne A. Spears, "The Quest for Policy Space in a New Generation of International Investment Agreements", (2010) 13:4 *Journal of International Economic Law* 1037–75.

be tested by experience. Evidence is mixed regarding whether BITS actually increase FDI flows to host countries that are signatories to them.[13] Perhaps the best reading of this evidence is that BITS have a modestly positive impact on attracting FDI – albeit a declining marginal impact as more BITS are signed – and are a weak substitute for well-functioning domestic legal institutions,[14] in part because arbitral awards still need to be enforced in host countries' domestic courts, and in part because purely private disputes may still need to be resolved in these courts unless the parties have contracted out of the jurisdiction through (increasingly common) choice of law and choice of forum clauses.[15]

Chapter 11 of NAFTA, while involving three parties, exemplifies many of the issues and controversies that have arisen with respect to BITS and has been a prominent lightning rod for critics of NAFTA. When Chapter 11 was initially negotiated, it was thought likely to apply in practice mostly to Mexican laws and regulations pertaining to FDI, given a long and somewhat tangled history in Mexico of cycles of nationalization and liberalization of FDI. However, Chapter 11 has provoked a number of formal complaints (in excess of 30 to date), including a number against measures adopted in Canada and the USA.

Chapter 11 of NAFTA contains a National Treatment provision in Article 1102 (subject to reservations that the three parties have entered in schedules to NAFTA) and a Most Favoured Nation Treatment provision (Article 1103). Article 1105 (Minimum Standard of Treatment) requires that each party shall accord to investments of investors of another party treatment in accordance with international law, including fair and equitable treatment and full protection and security. Article 1106 (Performance Requirements) prohibits a long list of performance requirements, including those contained in the TRIMS Agreement but extending to other performance requirements such as technology transfer requirements. Article 1110 (Expropriation and Compensation) provides that no party may directly or indirectly nationalize or expropriate an investment of an investor of another party in its territory or

---

13 See Amnon Lehavi and Amir N. Licht, "BITS and Pieces of Property", (2011) 36(1) *Yale Journal of International Law* at 11–13.

14 See Susan Rose-Ackerman and Jennifer Tobin, "When BITS Have Some Bite: The Political-Economic Environment of Bilateral Investment Treaties", (2011) 6(1) *Review of International Organizations* 1–32.

15 See Jans Damman and Henry Hansmann, "Globalizing Commercial Litigation", (2008) 94 *Cornell L. Rev.* 1.

take a measure tantamount to nationalization or expropriation of such an investment except: a) for a public purpose; b) on a nondiscriminatory basis; c) in accordance with due process of law and Article 1105; and d) on payment of compensation.

Chapter 11 then sets out a procedural regime for the resolution of disputes which permit private investors to file complaints with international arbitral panels, primarily the International Centre for Settlement of Investment Disputes (ICSID). Awards issued by such arbitral panels providing for monetary compensation for foreign investors who have been able to satisfy an arbitral panel that the host country's measures in question violate one of the substantive provisions of Chapter 11 are enforceable in the domestic courts of host countries.

The arbitral case law that has emerged under Chapter 11 has raised major uncertainties as to the interpretation and application of key substantive provisions in Chapter 11, especially the International Minimum Standard of Treatment requirement in Article 1105 and the Expropriation provisions in Article 1110, which different arbitral panels have interpreted both expansively and narrowly but without a system of appellate review or precedent to resolve inconsistencies. Critics of Chapter 11 argue that its provisions and the investor-driven complaints dispute-settlement process have undesirably constrained the domestic political autonomy of member countries and imposed a regulatory chill on legitimate environmental and health and safety measures that host countries have sought or might seek to adopt.[16] Moreover, the expropriation provisions of Chapter 11 risk standing the National Treatment Principle on its head by requiring compensation of foreign investors in circumstances where similarly situated domestic investors may lack any such entitlement.[17]

Other commentators take a more benign view of the operation of Chapter 11, and regard the few decisions that have led to liability as properly sanctioning protectionist or abusive behaviour by host coun-

---

16 See Chris Tollefson, "NAFTA's Chapter 11: The Case for Reform", in John Kirton and Peter Hajnal (eds), *Sustainability, Civil Society, and International Governance* (Aldershot: Ashgate Publishing Limited, 2006), chapter 10.

17 See David Schneiderman, "NAFTA's Takings Rule: American Constitutionalism comes to Canada", (1996) 46 *University of Toronto Law Journal* 499; Michael Trebilcock, "Trade Liberalization, Regulatory Diversity, and Political Sovereignty", in Kirton and Hajnal, *ibid* at 224, 225.

try governments.[18] While some of the procedural shortcomings of the dispute-settlement process under Chapter 11 have recently been mitigated by member countries in an Interpretive Statement and by reforms by arbitral panels themselves in authorizing the release of the written pleadings of the parties at the time they are filed with an arbitral panel, authorizing amicus curiae briefs, and making the oral hearings open to the public, concerns remain about the extent of the substantive constraints on host countries' jurisdiction to regulate FDI, particularly given the absence of any provision in Chapter 11 analogous to Article XX of the GATT.

11.4   Conclusion

The proliferation of BITS stands in stark contrast to successive failures to negotiate a multilateral agreement on investment. However, BITS entail a risk of collective action problems and a race to the bottom among host countries (especially developing countries). This argues for a further attempt at negotiating a multilateral agreement (where coalition bargaining is possible), probably under the aegis of the WTO, building on the new generation of BITS that attempt to strike a better balance between the interests of foreign investors and host countries.

---

18 See Julie Soloway, "NAFTA's Chapter 11: Investor Protection, Integration, and the Public Interest", in Kirton and Hajnal, *ibid.*

12 Trade-related intellectual property rights

12.1 Introduction

Prior to the launch of the Uruguay Round of multilateral trade negotiations in 1986, there were growing concerns in the USA and other developed countries over loss of export markets in various developing and newly industrializing countries due to weak protection of intellectual property rights. Some of these concerns related to counterfeit goods and the misappropriation of trademarks (for example, fake Rolex watches or Pierre Cardin garments). Other concerns related to unauthorized reproduction of sound recordings and videos and breach of copyright held in these recordings or videos by the original performers or their publishers. Further concerns related to substantively lower levels of patent protection and less effective procedural protection of patent rights in many countries, leading to a proliferation of imitation products, including generic pharmaceuticals. For developed countries, which were losing their comparative advantage in low-skilled, "smokestack" manufacturing industries to developing and newly industrializing countries, it became an important priority to seek better protection of their comparative advantage in scientific and technological innovation through stronger protection of intellectual property rights.

As to justifications for extending western-style protection of intellectual property rights to developing or newly industrializing countries, proponents relied in part on deontological natural rights (Lockean) theories of labour whereby all individuals can claim a proprietary right to all the fruits of their labour, and hence argued that appropriation by others of the fruits of the labour of innovators was tantamount to "stealing from the mind",[1] although such theories would seem to imply an infinite duration to intellectual property rights, which manifestly has never been the case. Proponents also in part relied on consequen-

---

1 See Peter Drahos and John Braithwaite, *Information Feudalism* (New York: New Press, 2003), chapter 4.

tialist or welfare theories, whereby attenuated returns to innovation as a result of free-riding on the innovations of others would reduce incentives to innovation, reducing long-run social welfare in both developed and developing countries.

On the other side of the debate, it was argued that the additional rents that intellectual property holders could realize in many developing countries were so modest that it was difficult to make the case that the loss of these rents would have a significant impact on incentives to innovate. Moreover, for many developing countries, particularly those at early stages of economic development, their comparative advantage would often lie in imitation rather than innovation, and global welfare requires an appropriate balance to be struck between technological or scientific innovation, on the one hand, and technical and scientific diffusion or dissemination, on the other.

12.2   The pre-Uruguay Round international legal framework

12.2.1   The GATT

The GATT was almost entirely silent on the relationship between international trade and intellectual property rights, except for Article XX(d) which exempted measures necessary to secure compliance with laws or regulations, including the protection of patents, trademarks, and copyrights, subject to the conditions in the chapeau to Article XX. A GATT panel decision in 1989[2] held that Article XX(d) did not justify the deployment of extraordinary remedies against potentially infringing imports of goods beyond those available against domestic infringers; such remedies were held to violate the conditions in the chapeau to Article XX relating to arbitrary or unjustifiable discrimination.

12.2.2   The Paris Convention (1883)

This Convention, which deals with patents and trademarks, contains a National Treatment Principle, but not an MFN Principle, and sets no minimum level of protection for patents. In the case of trademarks, signatories are obligated to accept trademarks once properly registered in the country of origin.

---

2 *United States – Section 337 of the Tariff Act of 1930* L 6439 (1989).

12.2.3   The Berne Convention (1885)

This Convention deals principally with copyrights, and contains a National Treatment and MFN Principle. It prescribes a minimum length of protection for copyrights – the author's life plus 50 years – with some limited exceptions. Both the Paris Convention and the Berne Convention were administered from 1967 onwards by a United Nations agency, the World Intellectual Property Organization (WIPO).

12.2.4   US unilateralism

Under Section 337 of the US Tariff Act of 1930 as amended, products imported into the USA that have been produced in such a way as to violate intellectual property rights that US individuals or firms hold may be subject to orders requiring the complete exclusion of the product from the USA unless the US holder of intellectual property rights and the foreign producer enter into a voluntary settlement (usually a licensing agreement). In addition, where a developing country insists on weak intellectual property protection, tariff concessions extended to it under the Generalized System of Preferences (GSP) can be withdrawn. Finally, under the so-called special 301 provision of the Omnibus Trade and Competitiveness Act of 1977, trade sanctions may be taken against countries engaging in "unfair trade practices", which may include failure to respect or enforce US intellectual property rights in foreign markets.

12.3   The Uruguay Round TRIPS Agreement

The WTO TRIPS Agreement was the result of extensive lobbying by high technology and pharmaceutical firms in the USA and other developed countries,[3] and essentially requires all members of the WTO to adopt domestic intellectual property laws that conform to the minimum standards set out in the TRIPS Agreement, which in turn, for the most part, reflect western standards of intellectual property protection.

12.3.1   General

The TRIPS Agreement contains a National Treatment Principle (Article 3) and an MFN Principle (Article 4). With respect to the doc-

---

3 See Drahos and Braithwaite, supra note 1.

trine of exhaustion, Article 6 provides that nothing in this agreement shall be used to address the issue of the exhaustion of intellectual property rights, leaving open divergences between countries that in some cases had adopted a doctrine of national exhaustion and others that had adopted a doctrine of international exhaustion. Under a doctrine of national exhaustion, once an intellectual property holder sells goods in a domestic market, it relinquishes all rights with respect to the goods in subsequent transactions within that market, but not in other markets where the intellectual property holder has enforceable intellectual property rights. Under the doctrine of international exhaustion the first sale by an intellectual property rights holder in any market extinguishes its rights in all markets, leaving open the possibility of parallel importation of goods from lower-priced markets into higher-priced markets. Article 7 of the Agreement provides that the protection and enforcement of intellectual property rights should contribute to the promotion of technological innovation and to the transfer and dissemination of technology, to the mutual advantage of producers and users of technological knowledge and in a manner conducive to social and economic welfare, and to a balance of rights and obligations. Article 8 provides that members may, in formulating or amending their laws and regulations, adopt measures necessary to protect public health and nutrition, and to promote the public interest in sectors of vital importance to their socio-economic and technological development, provided that such measures are consistent with the provisions of the Agreement.

12.3.2   Copyright and related rights

The basic obligations of the Berne Convention are incorporated into TRIPS. Computer programs and databases are included as literary works (Article 10). The minimum term of protection for copyrighted works is 50 years from the initial date of authorized publication or 50 years from the making of the work.

12.3.3   Trademarks

The Agreement requires that all signs with sufficient distinctiveness be accepted for registration by all members (Article 15). Registration may be cancelled only after an uninterrupted period of at least three years of non-use, unless there are valid reasons for non-use based on the existence of obstacles to such use (Article 19). Initial registration and each renewal of registration of a trademark shall be for a term of no less than seven years (Article 18).

12.3.4   Geographical indications

Members shall provide the legal means for interested parties to prevent the use of any means in the designation or presentation of a good that indicates or suggests that the good in question originates in a geographical area other than the true place of origin in a manner which misleads the public as to the geographical origin of the good (Article 22). Additional protection is required for geographical indications for wines and spirits (Article 23 and Article 24).[4]

12.3.5   Industrial designs

Members are required to provide for the protection of independently created industrial designs that are new or original. The duration of protection available shall amount to at least 10 years (Articles 25 and 26).

12.3.6   Patents

Patents shall be available for any invention, whether products or processes, in all fields of technology, provided that they are new, involve an inventive step and are capable of industrial application. Patents shall be available and patent rights enjoyable without discrimination as to the place of invention, the field of technology and whether the products are imported or locally produced (Article 27). Members may exclude from patentability inventions, the prevention within their territory of the commercial exploitation of which is necessary to protect the public order or morality, including to protect human, animal or plant life or health or to avoid serious prejudice to the environment. Members may also exclude from patentability diagnostic, therapeutic and surgical methods for the treatment of humans, and plants and animals other than micro-organisms. However, members must provide for the protection of plant varieties either by patents or by an effective *sui generis* system.

A patent shall confer on its owner exclusive rights to prevent third parties not having the owner's consent from the acts of making, using, offering for sale, or selling a product in which the owner holds a patent (Article 28).

---

4 See Tomer Broude. "Taking 'Trade and Culture' Seriously: Geographical Indications and Cultural Protection in WTO Law", (2004) 26:4 *University of Pennsylvania International Economic Law* 623–92.

Members may provide limited exceptions to the exclusive rights conferred by a patent, provided that such exceptions do not unreasonably conflict with the normal exploitation of the patent and do not unreasonably prejudice the legitimate interests of the patent owner, taking account of the legitimate interests of third parties (Article 30).

Under Article 31 compulsory licensing is permitted, subject to various conditions, including: i) the proposed user has made efforts to obtain authorization from the right holder on reasonable terms and conditions and that such efforts have not been successful within a reasonable period of time (this requirement may be waived by a member in the case of a national emergency or other circumstances of extreme urgency or in cases of public non-commercial use); ii) such use shall be non-exclusive; iii) such use shall be authorized predominantly for the supply of the domestic market of the member authorizing such use; iv) the right-holder shall be paid adequate remuneration in the circumstances of each case, taking into account the economic value of the authorization.

The term of protection for patents shall not end before the expiration of a period of 20 years counted from the filing date (Article 33).

Members are required to protect undisclosed information, including information provided to members as a condition of approving the marketing of a pharmaceutical or agricultural chemical product (Article 39).

Nothing in the Agreement shall prevent members from adopting appropriate measures to prevent anticompetitive practices with respect to intellectual property licenses, including exclusive grant-back conditions, conditions preventing challenges to validity, and coercive package licensing (Article 40).

12.3.7   Remedies

Every member is committed to ensuring that enforcement procedures with respect to the protection of intellectual property rights are in place that are not unnecessarily complicated, costly or protracted. Members must provide a right of judicial review of administrative decisions. Judicial authorities must have the power to award damages and injunctions and provide interim relief to intellectual property right holders against infringements (Articles 41 to 50). Members are also required to adopt procedures to enable an intellectual property rights holder to lodge an application with competent authorities for the suspension by the customs authorities of the release of infringing goods into free circulation of such goods (Articles 51 to 60). Members shall provide for criminal procedures and penalties in cases of wilful trademark counterfeiting or copyright piracy on a commercial scale (Article 61).

12.3.8 Dispute settlement

The general dispute settlement provisions of the GATT applies to disputes under the TRIPS Agreement, except that the non-violation nullification and impairment provisions of Article XXIII of the GATT did not apply to disputes under the TRIPS Agreement for a period of five years from its entry into force.

12.3.9 Transitional arrangements

Various transitional arrangements are provided for developing countries in terms of extended periods for ensuring compliance of the domestic intellectual property laws with the TRIPS Agreement, but these have all now expired (Article 65), except for certain limited exceptions for least-developed countries with respect to pharmaceutical patent protection, which were extended to 2016 by the Doha Declaration on Public Health, November 2001.

12.4 The essential medicines debate

The TRIPS Agreement, particularly as it applies to access to essential medicines, has been a lightning rod for vehement criticism by anti-globalists and civil society organizations around the world, who allege that developed country members of the WTO in effect have blood on their hands as a result of compelling all WTO members, including poor developing countries, to adopt domestic intellectual property regimes that conform to the minimum (western) standards prescribed by the TRIPS Agreement.[5] The criticisms focus on the fact that prices charged by proprietary pharmaceutical companies in developing countries for essential medicines, like HIV/AIDS antiretrovirals, deny access by most poor citizens of these countries to these lifesaving drugs and prevent, except under stringent conditions, access to

---

5 See Drahos and Braithwaite, supra note 1.

much cheaper generics. Moreover, it is argued that 90 per cent of global resources devoted to pharmaceutical research relates to 10 per cent of the world's disease burden, or conversely only 10 per cent of global pharmaceutical research is devoted to 90 per cent of the world's disease burden that is borne mostly by citizens in developing countries.

Critics of TRIPs are also critical of one of the leading WTO dispute-settlement decisions on the TRIPS Agreement: *EU – Canada-Patent Protection of Pharmaceuticals* (2000),[6] where under the Canadian Patent Act, exceptions from 20 year protection of patents were provided with respect to steps necessary to ensure regulatory approval of derivative (generic) products before the expiration of the patent on these products and with respect to stockpiling of derivative products for six months prior to the expiration of a patent on these products. A WTO Panel held that the regulatory review exception could be justified under Article 30 of TRIPS (because otherwise the interaction of regulatory review requirements and patent protection could lead to substantial de facto extension of patent terms), but not the stockpiling exception (because all patent protection precludes manufacture of derivative products until after patent expiration).

On the other side of the debate, it is argued that historically weak intellectual property protection in developing countries has provided few incentives for proprietary pharmaceutical industry to invest R&D resources in developing cures for tropical and related diseases that particularly afflict citizens of developing countries, and that the TRIPS Agreement, in principle, resolves a collective action problem among developing countries by committing them all to observe minimum standards of intellectual property protection. Moreover, it is argued that adoption of a doctrine of international exhaustion is likely to undermine efforts by proprietary pharmaceutical companies to practice geographic price discrimination (in other words, charging more to citizens with less elastic demand in richer countries and less to citizens with more elastic demand in poorer countries), in that parallel importation will undermine such efforts.[7]

While the compulsory licensing provisions in Article 31 of the TRIPS provide the potential for alleviating some of the concerns about access

---

6 *EU – Canada-Patent Protection of Pharmaceuticals* (2000) WT/ DS114/R.

7 See Alan O. Sykes, "TRIPS, Pharmaceuticals, Developing Countries and the Doha Solution", (2002) 3:1 *Chicago Journal of International Law* 47.

to essential medicines, key provisions in Article 31 lack clear definition. For example, prior to issuing a compulsory license efforts must
be made within a "reasonable period of time" to obtain authorization from the intellectual property holder on "reasonable commercial terms" (although this is not necessary for a "national emergency"
or circumstances of "extreme urgency"), but none of these terms are
defined, nor is the requirement that there be payment of "adequate
remuneration" where a compulsory license is issued. Moreover, compulsory licenses can only be issued predominantly for the supply of
the licensee's domestic market, which in the case of pharmaceuticals
is likely to preclude poor developing countries that lack a generic drug
manufacturing industry of their own from taking advantage of the
compulsory licensing provisions of Article 31.

Criticisms of the TRIPS Agreement as they relate to access to essential medicines led to the Declaration on the TRIPS Agreement and
Public Health at the Doha Ministerial Conference launching the new
Doha Round of multilateral trade negotiations in November 2001. In
this Declaration members reaffirm the right of WTO members to use,
to the full, the provisions in the TRIPS Agreement which provide flexibility in protecting public health and promoting access to medicines
for all. In particular, each member has the right to determine what
constitutes a national emergency or other circumstances of extreme
urgency; each member is free to establish its own regime for exhaustion of intellectual property rights without challenge; and the Council
for TRIPS was directed to find an expeditious solution to the problem
that WTO members with insufficient or no manufacturing capacities in the pharmaceutical sector could face difficulties in making
effective use of compulsory licensing under Article 31 of the TRIPS
Agreement.

Further to this direction, a Decision of the WTO General Council
of 30 August 2003 adopted a detailed set of provisions relating to
compulsory licensing of pharmaceuticals where in the case of WTO
members with insufficient or no manufacturing capacities in the pharmaceutical sector, compulsory licenses could be issued to generic drug
manufacturers in exporting countries and complementary compulsory
licenses also be issued by importing countries able to demonstrate the
lack of domestic manufacturing capacity. In order to prevent "leak-
age" of generic pharmaceuticals provided under this regime to other
countries, the Decision of the General Council requires that products
issued under compulsory licenses pursuant to these provisions should

distinguish such products through special packaging and/or special colouring or shaping of the products themselves.

While this Decision of the General Council was initially in the nature of a waiver of inconsistent provisions in the TRIPS Agreement, it is contemplated that it will eventually become a formal amendment to the TRIPS Agreement once two thirds of members have formally accepted it. Members originally set themselves a deadline of 1 December 2007 to do this, but have since extended the deadline to 31 December 2015.

Pursuant to these provisions, Canada in 2004 amended its *Patent Act* and *Food and Drugs Act* to permit the issuance of compulsory licenses under the conditions set out in the Decision of the WTO General Council. Both the Decision of the WTO General Council and the subsequent Canadian legislation have been widely criticized as being much too cumbersome to comply with, in that compulsory licenses in both exporting and importing countries must be issued for every shipment of the drugs in question, and in fact only one compulsory license has been issued to date under the Canadian legislation. Critics argue that an omnibus compulsory licensing regime would be more effective.

Two issues relating to the essential medicines debate warrant concluding comments. First, it is far from clear why proprietary pharmaceutical drug companies, even under the original TRIPS Agreement provisions, would not have found it rational (profit-maximizing) to have engaged in extreme forms of geographic price discrimination, pricing drugs down to close to marginal costs in poor developing countries and recovering their fixed investments in R&D in much richer developed country markets, provided they could be assured that drugs would not "leak" back from the former markets to the latter, thus undercutting their ability to recover their R&D costs in developed country markets. Part of the explanation for this puzzle may be that such extreme forms of geographic price discrimination would reveal to consumers in developed countries how low the marginal costs of production for propriety pharmaceuticals are, perhaps leading to pressures for price regulation in developed countries, although this assumes that consumers in developed countries could not be persuaded that somebody needs to bear the fixed costs of R&D.

Second, while this form of extreme geographic price discrimination has the potential for mitigating the access to essential medicines problems with respect to existing pharmaceuticals in wide use in both the

developed and developing world (facilitated by the now more credible threat of compulsory licensing), it is not nearly as clear that the
intellectual property regime, even as amended by the Decision of the
WTO General Council in August 2003, will ensure that there are adequate investments in pharmaceutical innovations for diseases that are
primarily prevalent in developing countries, where there may simply
be a lack of effective demand for these products, given poverty level
incomes on the part of many citizens and limited resources on the part
of their governments (and no demand in rich countries from which to
finance R&D costs). In order to address this problem, one might need
to look for solutions outside the intellectual property domain, such as
the Global Fund created by the former Secretary General of the United
Nations, Kofi Annan or investments by private foundations (such as
the Gates Foundation), with a view to entering into R&D contracts
with research institutions directed to finding cures for such diseases.[8]
In short, public or private foundation subsidies to investments in R&D
with respect to tropical and related diseases that particularly afflict
citizens in developing countries, are likely to be required if substantial
progress is to be made in addressing this problem, although effective design of the qualifications for, and incentive properties of, these
subsidy arrangements present their own set of challenges.[9]

---

8 See, for example, Institute for Health Metrics and Evaluation, *Financing Global Health 2013:
   Transition in an Age of Austerity* (Seattle: Institute for Health Metrics and Evaluation). Online:
   http://www.healthdata.org/sites/default/files/files/policy_report/2014/FGH2013/IHME_
   FGH2013_Full_Report.pdf. Accessed 14 July 2014; Faiz Kermani, "Maintaining the Focus for
   Neglected Diseases: Product Development Partnerships Seek to Bridge the Healthcare Gap",
   Contract Pharma (2011). Online: http://www.contractpharma.com/issues/2011-10/view_
   features/maintaining-the-focus-for-neglected-diseases/. Accessed 14 July 2014; Stephen M.
   Maurer, "Choosing the Right Incentive Strategy for Research and Development in Neglected
   Diseases", (2006) Bulletin of the World Health Organization. Online: http://www.who.int/bul-
   letin/volumes/84/5/376.pdf. Accessed 14 July 2014; M. Moran, G. Guzman, A.L. Ropars and
   A. Illmer, "The Role of Product Development Partnerships in Research and Development for
   Neglected Diseases", (2010) 2:2 *International Health* 114–22.
9 For a more general review of developing country responses to TRIPS, see Ruth Okediji, "Legal
   Innovation in International Intellectual Property Relations: Twenty One Years of the TRIPS
   Agreement", 36 (1) *University of Pennsylvania Journal of International Law* (2014).

13 Trade policy and domestic health and safety regulation

13.1 Introduction

With the progressive liberalization of border barriers to trade over the post-war period, internal or "beyond the border" regulatory divergences from one country to another, including domestic regulation of health and safety standards, have become an increasing source of tension in international trading relations. Exporting countries often complain that these regulations constitute a non-tariff barrier to trade, and even where they are not intended as a disguised form of protectionism, impose disproportionate burdens on small exporting countries, particularly developing countries, in facing multiple compliance costs in many of their export markets. Importing countries, in turn, complain of lax standards in exporting countries that create health and safety risks for their citizens, as well as constituting a form of unfair trade to the extent that firms in exporting countries face lower compliance costs than competing firms in importing countries.[1]

Free traders often propose international constraints on the use of domestic regulations as barriers to trade, while consumer and citizens groups favour constraints on the use of international trade agreements as barriers to regulation. These divergences in perspective have led to divisions between business interests and civil society groups, on the one hand, and between developed and developing countries on the other. Those favouring international constraints on domestic health and safety regulation to address concerns of regulatory discrimination or disguised protectionism often assign pre-eminence to compliance with international standards or scientific justifications, arguing that regulatory protectionism typically entails higher welfare losses than

---

1 See Cary Coglianese, Adam Finkel and David Zaring (eds), *Import Safety: Regulatory Governance in the Global Economy* (Philadelphia: University of Pennsylvania Press, 2009).

other forms of protectionism (such as tariffs or subsidies).[2] Those favouring fewer constraints on domestic political autonomy in regulating health and safety risks facing a country's citizens emphasize the importance of democratic accountability and responsiveness to public sentiments and concerns of citizens (whether based on science or not),[3] recognizing that public attitudes to risk often do not reflect the tenets of scientific or economic rationality (as the growing body of literature on behavioural law and economics demonstrates).[4]

13.2   The GATT framework

13.2.1   The evolution of the GATT/WTO[5]

The original GATT did not contain separate provisions constraining the regulation of domestic environmental health and safety standards. However, bans on imports might violate Article XI, and discriminatory treatment of imports from different foreign countries might violate Article I (MFN), and discriminatory regulation of imports generally relative to domestic like products might violate Article III.4 (National Treatment). In such an event, the regulating country might seek to justify its regulations under Articles XX(b) or XX(g), which provides exceptions from the disciplines of the GATT for trade measures necessary to protect human, animal, or plant life or health, or relating to the conservation of natural resources. However, during the Tokyo Round, the Agreement on Technical Barriers to Trade (often referred to as the Standards Code) was adopted. This was a plurilateral agreement signed by 46 members and while it covered both agricultural and industrial products, it was widely thought deficient in failing to distinguish adequately between "necessary" and "unnecessary" restrictions on trade. Thus, during the Uruguay Round two new agreements were negotiated: the Agreement on Sanitary and Phyto-sanitary Measures (SPS Agreement) and the Technical Barriers to Trade Agreement (TBT Agreement), which are binding on all members. Before reviewing these

---

2 Alan O. Sykes, "Regulatory Protectionism and the Law of International Trade", (1999) 66 *University of Chicago L. Rev.* 1.

3 See Tracey D. Epps, "Reconciling Public Opinion and WTO Rules Under the SPS Agreement", (2008) 7:2 *World Trade Review* 359.

4 See Daniel Kahneman, *Thinking, Fast and Slow* (Toronto: Doubleday Canada, 2011).

5 See Tracey D. Epps and Michael J. Trebilcock, "Import Safety Regulation and International Trade", in Coglianese, Finkel, and Zaring (eds), *Import Safety, supra* note 1.

Agreements, a brief discussion of GATT case-law relating to health and safety regulation is in order.

13.2.2   The GATT case law

In the *Thai – Cigarette* case (1990),[6] the USA challenged a ban on imports of cigarettes into Thailand as a violation of Article XI of the GATT. Thailand defended the ban under Article XX(b) as necessary for the protection of public health. While no comparable ban existed on domestic Thai cigarettes, the Thai government claimed that American imports were more likely to induce women and young persons to take up smoking, because of sophisticated advertising directed at these groups. The panel ruled that an import ban would only be "necessary" for public health reasons, within the meaning of Article XX(b), if alternative non-trade restricting measures were not available to achieve the public health objectives in question. The panel considered that restrictions or bans on advertising, and labelling and content requirements that applied in a non-discriminatory basis to both domestic cigarettes and imports would be satisfactory alternatives to an import ban, and therefore the ban could not be justified under Article XX(b).

The *EC – Asbestos* case (2000),[7] while post the creation of the WTO, was resolved under the general GATT provisions, after a WTO panel had held (perversely) that a product ban could not be a technical regulation or standard requiring review under the TBT Agreement. In this case, a French prohibition on the sale or importation of asbestos or products (such as cement) containing asbestos was challenged by Canada. The WTO Panel found that asbestos and PCG fibres (for example, cellulose and glass fibres, which were not banned) were like products and hence the ban on the former was a breach of Article III.4 (the National Treatment Principle), although the Panel went on to hold that the measure was justified under Article XX(b). The Appellate Body was critical of the Panel for looking exclusively at overlapping end-uses under Article III(4), and even then not the extent of these overlaps. According to the Appellate Body the Panel should have examined all four factors enumerated in the Border Tax Adjustment Working Group Report in 1970: a) physical properties; b) end uses; c)

---

6 *Thailand – Restrictions on Importation of and Internal Taxes on Cigarettes* (1990) DS10/R – 37S/200.

7 *European Communities – Measures Affecting Asbestos and Asbestos-Containing Products* (2000) WT/DS135/R.

consumer preferences; and d) tariff classification. All four factors bear on the competitive relationship in the marketplace between allegedly like products. In this case, differences in the physical properties of asbestos and PCG fibres were critical – one was carcinogenic and the others not. This raised a strong presumption against the two classes of products being like products.

Like the Panel, the Appellate Body also held that the measure was justified under Article XX(b) and was not satisfied that any alternative measure, such as "controlled use" requirements, were available which France could reasonably be expected to employ to achieve its health and safety policy objectives, which in this case was zero health risk from exposure to asbestos. The Appellate Body in interpreting and applying Article XX(b) suggested that there may be different levels of scrutiny applicable to the analysis of whether a measure is "necessary" depending on the importance of the objectives or interests it serves. In a case such as the present, where the objective pursued by the measure is the preservation of human life and health, and the country's objective is to reduce the health risks in question to zero, the measure is entitled to a "margin of appreciation", and the availability of alternative, less trade-restrictive measures that may not achieve this objective as fully would not disqualify the measure from exemption under Article XX(b).

The recent *Brazil – Tyres* (2007)[8] case reaffirms and extends the analysis in Article XX(b) by the Appellate body in *Asbestos. Brazil – Tyres* can be alternatively thought of as implicating health and safety or environmental issues. In this case, the EU challenged a Brazilian import ban on used and retreaded tyres. The justification offered by Brazil for this ban was that, along with other policies, it was designed to reduce the volume of waste tyres, which were a breeding ground for mosquitoes that carried malaria and dengue fever, and moreover that large quantities of waste tyres raised health risks from tyre fires that generated toxic fumes and residue.

Brazil conceded that the ban was a violation of Article XI but sought to justify the ban under Article XX(b). The Appellate Body, upholding the decision of the Panel in these proceedings, interpreted the "necessity" test under Article XX(b) as requiring that the measure in question

---

8 *Brazil – Measures Affecting Imports of Retreaded Tyres*, 3 December (2007) WT/DS332/AB/R (07–5290).

make a "material contribution" to the achievement of the health and safety objectives in question. A contribution to the achievement of health and safety objectives under Article XX(b) exists when there is a genuine relationship of ends and means between the objective pursued and the measure at issue. To be characterized as necessary, a measure does not have to be indispensable. However, its

> contribution to the achievement of the objective must be material, not merely marginal or insignificant, especially if the measure at issue is as trade-restrictive as an import ban. Thus, the contribution of the measure has to be weighed against its trade restrictiveness, taking into account the importance of the interests or the values underlying the objective pursued by it.

This is, in effect, a proportionality test or qualitative cost-benefit test.[9]

With respect to the issue of whether less trade-restrictive alternatives might have been available to achieve these objectives, the Appellate Body, again affirming the Panel, held that the EU bore the burden of identifying such alternatives, and that the alternatives the EU had identified, such as stockpiling and incineration, on the evidence before the Panel, were not as likely to achieve Brazil's health, safety and environmental objectives as the measures it had adopted.

However, turning to the conditions in the chapeau, the Appellate Body overturned two determinations of the Panel in these proceedings. By virtue of a ruling by a MERCOSUR tribunal, following a complaint initiated by Uruguay, the Brazilian ban was held to violate its Mercosur obligations to other Mercosur members, and hence Brazil had begun permitting imports of retreaded tyres from other Mercosur countries, including retreaded tyres originating outside of the Mercosur countries. The Appellate Body held that this was unjustifiably discriminatory towards imports of retreaded tyres from the complainant (the EU). In addition, by virtue of injunctions issued by Brazilian courts at the instance of Brazilian tyre retreaders, imports of used tyres by Brazilian retreaders were being permitted by the Brazilian authorities, again in the Appellate Body's view discriminating unjustifiably against imports of retreaded tyres from the EU.

---

9 See Alan O. Sykes, "The Least Restrictive Means", (2003) 70:1 *University of Chicago L. Rev.* 403.

13.3   The SPS and TBT Agreements

13.3.1   The SPS Agreement[10]

SPS measures include measures applied to protect animal or plant life or health within a territory of a member from risks arising from the entry, establishment or spread of pests, diseases, disease-carrying organisms or disease-causing organisms; and to protect human or animal life or health within the territory of the member from risks arising from additives, contaminants, toxins or disease-causing organisms in foods, beverages or feedstuffs.

Members shall ensure that any SPS measure is applied only to the extent necessary to protect human, animal or plant life or health, is based on scientific principles and is not maintained without sufficient scientific evidence, except as provided for in Article 5.7 (Article 2.2). Members shall ensure that their SPS measures do not arbitrarily or unjustifiably discriminate between members where identical or similar conditions prevail, including between their own territory and that of other members. SPS measures shall not be applied in a manner which would constitute a disguised restriction on international trade (Article 2.3).

SPS measures which conform to international standards, guidelines or recommendations shall be presumed to be consistent with the provisions of this Agreement (Article 3.2). Members may introduce or maintain SPS measures which result in a higher level of SPS protection than would be achieved by measures based on the relevant international standards, guidelines or recommendations, if there is a scientific justification, or as a consequence of the level of SPS protection a member determines to be appropriate in accordance with Article 5.1 to 5.8 (Article 3.3). In such cases, members shall ensure that their SPS measures are based on an assessment, as appropriate to the circumstances, of the risks to human, animal or plant life or health, taking into account risk assessment techniques developed by the relevant international organizations (Article 5.1). Each member shall avoid arbitrary or unjustifiable distinctions in the levels of SPS protection it considers to be appropriate in different situations, if such

---

10 See generally, Tracey D. Epps, *International Trade and Health Protection: A Critical Assessment of the WTO's SPS Agreement* (Cheltenham, UK: Edward Elgar, 2008).

distinctions result in discrimination or a disguised restriction on international trade (Article 5.5). When establishing or maintaining SPS measures to achieve the appropriate level of SPS protection, members shall ensure that such measures are not more trade-restrictive than required to achieve their appropriate level of SPS protection, taking into account technical and economic feasibility (Article 5.6). For purposes of this article, a footnote to the Agreement provides that a measure is not more trade-restrictive than required unless there is another measure, reasonably available taking into account technical and economic feasibility, that achieves the appropriate level of SPS protection and is significantly less restrictive to trade. When a member has reason to believe that a specific SPS measure introduced or maintained by another member constrains or has the potential to constrain its exports and the measure is not based on relevant international standards, an explanation of the reasons for such an SPS measure may be requested and shall be provided by the member maintaining the measure (Article 5.8).

In cases where relevant scientific evidence is insufficient, a member may provisionally adopt SPS measures on the basis of available pertinent information. In such circumstances, members shall seek to obtain the additional information necessary for a more objective assessment of risk and review the SPS measure accordingly within a reasonable period of time (Article 5.7).

Members shall accept the SPS measures of other members as equivalent if the exporting member objectively demonstrates to the importing member that its measures achieve the importing member's appropriate level of SPS protection. For this purpose, reasonable access shall be given, upon request, to the importing member for inspection, testing and other relevant procedures. Members shall, upon request, enter into consultations with the aim of achieving bilateral and multilateral agreements on recognition of the equivalence of specified SPS measures (Article 4).

The provisions of the SPS Agreement (as with the TBT Agreement) are subject to the general WTO dispute-settlement regime.

13.3.2   TBT Agreement

The TBT Agreement covers all technical product regulations and standards not covered by the SPS Agreement.[11]

Technical regulations may pursue the objectives listed in the 6th per-ambulatory recital to the TBT Agreement, provided that they are not applied in a manner that would constitute a means of arbitrary or unjustifiable discrimination between countries where the same conditions prevail, or a disguised restriction on international trade, and are otherwise in accordance with the TBT Agreement. Article 2.1 obliges Members, with regard to technical regulations, to accord products originating from any other Member country, treatment no less favourable than like products produced domestically. Article 2.2 places an obligation on members to ensure that technical regulations are not more trade-restrictive than necessary to fulfill a legitimate objective. The burden of proof is on the complainant to show that a less trade-restricting alternative measure is available. Article 2.2 also states that this obligation not to make technical regulations more trade-restrictive than necessary must take into account the risks that non-fulfillment of the regulatory goal would create. This implies that the length to which a member should be expected to go in exhausting all regulatory alternatives to find the least trade-restricting one is connected to the kind of risk that is being regulated.

Article 2.4 stipulates that, where they exist, members shall use relevant international technical standards as the basis for their own technical regulations, except where such international standards would be an ineffective or inappropriate means for the fulfillment of the legitimate objectives pursued, due to factors such as climate, geography, or technological inability. Unlike the SPS Agreement, "international standards" is not a defined term in the TBT Agreement and there is no list of international standard-setting bodies whose standards are recognized for the purposes of Article 2.4.

Other important provisions under the TBT Agreement include: Article 2.7, which states that members shall give consideration to accepting the technical regulations of other countries as equivalent to their own, provided that the foreign regulations accomplish the

---

11 On the TBT Agreement generally, see Tracey Epps and Michael Trebilcock, *Research Handbook on the WTO and Technical Barriers to Trade* (Cheltenham, UK: Edward Elgar, 2013).

same objectives as their own regulations; Article 2.8, which instructs members to design regulations based on product requirements in terms of performance rather than design or descriptive elements; and Articles 2.5, 2.9, and 2.11, which together impose notification and publication requirements on members enacting new technical regulations, and also require publication in accessible format of existing technical regulations. An Annex to the Agreement contains a Code of Good Practice for the Preparation, Adoption, and Application of Standards to which domestic standardizing bodies are expected to adhere.

13.3.3   SPS case law

The leading case on key provisions in the SPS Agreement is *Beef Hormones* (1998)[12] which concerned a European ban on the sale of beef from animals that had been treated with growth hormones, a practice which was widespread in the United States (and Canada) but not in Europe. Thus, the ban had a significant effect on US beef producers, who either could not sell their beef in Europe or had to take expensive measures to ensure that it was hormone-free, while having little effect on European producers. The United States argued that the ban was disguised protectionism, whereas the European Union maintained that the ban was a legitimate public health measure designed to protect its citizens from possible health risks associated with the presence of hormones in beef. The Appellate Body upheld the US complaint, holding that the EU's regulatory measures did not conform to international standards and were not based on a risk assessment consistent with its WTO obligations.

However, the Appellate Body held that non-conformity with international standards does not create a reverse onus of proof on the respondent to prove compliance with the alternative risk assessment procedures contemplated in Article 5. The burden of proof of non-compliance rests on the complainant. The Appellate Body endorsed an approach of examining whether the scientific evidence was "reasonably sufficient" to justify the SPS measure in question.[13] Also, the Appellate Body rejected the existence of any minimum procedural requirements

---

12 *EC Measures Concerning Meat and Meat Products* (1998) WT/DS26/ AB/R, WT/DS48/AB/R [*Beef Hormones* 1998].

13 *Ibid.* at para. 198.

for domestic risk assessment.[14] Thus, it is not necessary for a member who enacts an SPS measure to conduct an investigation, engage in formal fact-finding, or publish a report justifying the SPS measure, and may rely, by way of justification, on risk assessments conducted by other countries or organizations. The Appellate Body held that in the presence of scientific controversy or disagreement, a member may base an SPS measure upon minority, as opposed to mainstream, scientific opinion, provided that the minority opinion comes from "qualified and respected sources".[15] The Appellate Body declined to take a position on whether the precautionary principle has evolved into a principle of customary international law (as the EU urged). However, it noted that Article 5.7 permits countries to adopt provisional measures where there is insufficient scientific evidence to conduct risk assessments, and that Article 3.3, which recognizes the right of countries to establish their own appropriate level of sanitary protection, permits governments to act from perspectives of prudence and caution where risks of irreversible damage to human health are concerned. With respect to the consistency requirement under Article 5.5, the Appellate Body held that closely comparable risks were required in order to evaluate regulatory consistency and that independent proof of discrimination or a disguised restriction on international trade was required (a form of "aims-and-effects" test).

Thus, in the *Beef Hormones* case the Appellate Body adopted a relatively deferential approach to its review of domestic evidence relied on by the respondent to support contested measures. However, the EU was unable to satisfy even this standard of review in this case, being unable to point to any scientific risk assessment that supported its position.

In the *Japan – Apples*[16] case the Appellate Body struck a less deferential posture, holding that an assessment of the "rational connection" between scientific evidence and the impugned SPS measure did not require deference to the authorities of the regulating member. However, more recently again, the Appellate Body in further dispute-settlement proceedings in *Beef Hormones* (2008), after the EU had undertaken a new risk assessment, sharply criticized the Panel in these proceedings for "somewhat peremptorily" deciding what it

---

14 *Ibid.* at para. 189.
15 *Ibid.* at para. 194.
16 *Japan – Measures Affecting the Importation of Apples*, (2003) WT/ DS245/AB/R, paras 160–67.

considered the best science from its review of expert scientific opinion, rather than the more limited exercise of determining whether the member's risk assessment "is supported by coherent reasoning and respectable scientific evidence and is, in this sense, objectively justifiable".[17]

In another recent case, *Australia – Measures Affecting the Importation of Apples from New Zealand*,[18] the Appellate Body upheld a complaint by New Zealand that various measures adopted by Australia that essentially banned the importation of New Zealand apples failed to satisfy the requirements under Articles 5.1 and 5.2 of the SPS Agreement that such measures be based on a scientific risk assessment. The Appellate Body concluded that the Panel in the case was correct in requiring that the risk assessment base its conclusions, including those reached through expert judgment, on the available scientific evidence and also agreed with the Panel that the risk assessment's use of expert judgment had not been sufficiently documented or transparent and therefore did not constitute a proper risk assessment within the meaning of Articles 5.1 and 5.2. With respect to New Zealand's claim that alternative measures would achieve Australia's appropriate level of protection under Article 5.6 (for example, the restriction of imports to mature, symptomless apples or sampling requirements for each import lot), the Appellate Body held that the Panel erred in importing the reasoning and findings relating to the deficiencies in the risk assessment from its analysis of New Zealand's Article 5.1 claim to its Article 5.6 claim. Assessing an Article 5.6 claim requires that a Panel undertake an independent analysis of whether the alternative measure proposed by the complainant would achieve the importing Member's appropriate level of protection. The Appellate Body concluded that there were insufficient uncontested facts or factual findings to enable it to make a finding on the level of risk associated with New Zealand's alternative measures and therefore could not complete the legal analysis with respect to Article 5.6.

Article 5.7 allows a member to maintain a provisional SPS measure, notwithstanding the requirements of Article 2.2. The Appellate Body has set out four criteria that must be met for a provisional measure

---

17 *US – Continued Retaliation in the Hormones Dispute* (2008) WT/ DS320/R [*US – Continued Suspension*].

18 *Australia – Measures Affecting the Importation of Apples from New Zealand* (2010) WT/DS367/AB/R.

to be maintained under Article 5.7: a) the relevant scientific information is insufficient; b) the measure is adopted on the basis of pertinent available information; c) the member adopting the measure is seeking to obtain the additional information necessary for a more objective assessment of the risk; and d) the member adopting the measure will review it within a reasonable period of time.[19]

A ruling by a WTO Panel in *EC – Biotech* appears to shed some additional light on Article 5.7.[20] In this dispute, the complainants (the United States, Canada, and Argentina) challenged the EC's regulatory scheme for the approval of genetically modified organisms (GMO). Among other things,[21] the Panel found that specific EC country bans on certain GMO crops did not meet the requirements of Article 5.7 of the SPS. Although Article 5.7 does permit members to adopt provisional measures where there is insufficient scientific evidence to assess the risk, the Panel found that studies carried out on the banned GMO crops by the EC scientific committee and by other competent national authorities, which concluded that the GMO crops were safe, constituted sufficient risk assessments under the SPS Agreement. Therefore, the first branch of the test set out for Article 5.7, that there be insufficient scientific information, was not met. Consequently, the Panel recommended that the ban on certain GMO crops be removed. In *Beef Hormones II*, the Appellate Body held that the adoption of provisional measures under Article 5.7 need not be based on a paradigm shift in scientific information on which previous measures had been based, but merely a significant evolution in scientific understanding.

13.3.4   TBT case law

The first Appellate Body decision on the TBT Agreement is *European Community – Trade Description of Sardines*.[22] In this case Peru challenged a regulation adopted by the European Communities that provided that only products prepared from a certain sub-species of sardines found around the coasts of the eastern North Atlantic, the

---

19 *Japan – Measures Affecting Agricultural Products* (1999) WT/DS76/ AB/R, paras 86–9.

20 *EC – Measures Affecting the Approval and Marketing of Biotech Products* (2006) WT/DS291, 292, 293/INTERIM.

21 The Panel also found that the EC, by applying a de facto moratorium on the approval of new GMO products and failing to consider specific GMOs for approval, had acted inconsistently with Annex C(1)(a) of the SPS Agreement, which requires members to complete testing and approval procedures without undue delay.

22 *European Community – Trade Description of Sardines* (2002) WT/ DS231/AB/R.

Mediterranean, and the Black Sea may be marketed as preserved sardines. Only products of this species were permitted to have the word "sardines" as part of the name on the container. Peru argued that this regulation violated Article 2.4 of the TBT Agreement, which requires that relevant international standards shall be used as a basis for technical regulations except when such international standards or relevant parts would be an ineffective or inappropriate means for the fulfillment of the legitimate objectives pursued. In this case, a standard adopted by the Codex Alimentarius Commission provided that canned sardines could be marketed in accordance with specific labelling provisions using the name "sardines" and including sub-species of sardines other than that to which the EC regulation was restricted and which were found mainly in the eastern Pacific along the coasts of Peru and Chile. The Appellate Body held that the EC regulation was not based on relevant international standards and that Peru had met the burden of proof of demonstrating that the international standard would be effective in accomplishing all three of the objectives advanced for the EC measure – market transparency, consumer protection, and fair competition.

Four recent cases have addressed the TBT Agreement: *US – Clove Cigarettes*, *US – Tuna (II)*, *US – COOL*, and *EC – Seal Products*.

In *US – Clove Cigarettes*,[23] Indonesia argued that the US ban on clove cigarettes and most other flavoured cigarettes except for menthol cigarettes (on the grounds that they encourage smoking, especially by youth), violated the National Treatment obligation in Article 2.1 of the TBT Agreement because it resulted in treatment less favourable to imported clove cigarettes than to menthol cigarettes, which are primarily made in the USA and which Indonesia argued was a like domestic product. The Appellate Body upheld the Panel's findings that the US measures were inconsistent with Article 2.1 and that the USA had acted inconsistently with Article 2.12 (which obliges states to allow a reasonable interval between publication and entry into force of technical regulations). It also considered the interpretation of "like products" and "treatment no less favorable" in the context of the TBT Agreement. The Appellate Body held that whether products are "like" in the context of the TBT Agreement is a determination about the competitive relationship between the products, based on the analy-

---

23 *United States – Measures Affecting the Production and Sale of Clove Cigarettes* (2012) WT/
DS406/AB/R.

sis of the criteria traditionally used to determine likeness under the GATT – physical characteristics, end uses, consumer tastes and habits, and tariff classification. It further considered how to interpret the obligation to accord "treatment no less favorable" in Article 2.1, finding that it does not prohibit a detrimental impact on imports that stems exclusively from a legitimate regulatory distinction, as recognized in the preamble to the TBT Agreement. Nonetheless, the Appellate Body found that the design, architecture, revealing structure, operation, and application of the ban on clove cigarettes reflected discrimination against the group of like products from Indonesia.

In *US – Tuna Labeling (II)*,[24] Mexico challenged a US labeling scheme that established conditions for the use of a "dolphin-safe" label on tuna products. The TBT Agreement only applies to technical regulations; to be a technical regulation, a measure must identify a group of products, prescribe either characteristics for those products or for their related processes and production methods, and compliance with the measure must be mandatory. A key issue was whether the US measure fell within the definition of a technical regulation, given that it was not a mandatory labeling scheme. The Panel found that the measure was a technical regulation because it had some mandatory features (unusually, one Panelist dissented with regard to the finding that the measure was mandatory, noting that this was a voluntary and not mandatory labeling scheme, despite the fact that the labeling measures regulated the characteristics of the product it applied to). This controversial finding was upheld by the Appellate Body, rejecting the US contention that producers of tuna retained the option of not using the "dolphin safe" label while still being able to place their products on the market. To be mandatory, the Appellate Body held that a technical regulation must regulate the "characteristics" of products in a binding or compulsory fashion, as was the case of requirements for use of the "dolphin safe" label. The Appellate Body reversed the Panel's ruling on Article 2.1 of the TBT Agreement, finding that the US labeling provisions are inconsistent with Article 2.1 of the TBT Agreement. It reasoned that, by excluding most Mexican tuna products from access to the "dolphin-safe" label while granting access to most tuna products from the USA and most other countries, the measure modified conditions of market competition to the detriment of Mexican tuna products, thus according "less favorable treatment" to them. Next, the Appellate Body found that this

---

24 *United States – Measures Concerning the Importation, Market and Sale of Tuna and Tuna Products* (2012) WT/ DS381/AB/R.

impact did not stem exclusively from a legitimate regulatory distinction because the USA had failed to demonstrate that its different treatment of Mexican tuna was caused by the different levels of risks faced by dolphins inside and outside the ETP (Eastern Pacific) region, which could justify its more stringent treatment of ETP tuna.[25] The Appellate Body also reversed the Panel's finding that Mexico had demonstrated that the US "dolphin-safe" labeling provisions were more restrictive than necessary to fulfill the US's legitimate objectives. It found that the alternative measure identified by Mexico (the co-existence of two labels) would contribute to a lesser degree than the US measure on both objectives – consumer information and dolphin protection – because it would allow more tuna harvested in the ETP region in conditions that adversely affect dolphins to be labeled "dolphin safe". Finally, the Appellate Body considered what level of participation is required for an international organization to constitute an "international standardizing body" in its determination of whether the measure was based on an international standard, as is called for in Article 2.4 of the TBT Agreement. The Appellate Body found that the international body in question, the Agreement on International Dolphin Conservation Program (AIDCP), which would have permitted the alternative label proposed by Mexico, failed to meet the definition of an international standardizing body since WTO members can only accede by way of invitation, which implies that membership is not open.

US – COOL (Country of Origin Labeling)[26] concerned US statutory provisions and implementing regulations that set out a mandatory country of origin labeling regime for beef and pork and that were challenged by Canada and Mexico. The Appellate Body addressed three issues: whether the US measure pursued a legitimate objective; if so, whether the measure was necessary to achieve that objective; and whether the measure was non-discriminatory in nature. It agreed with the Panel that the COOL measure has a detrimental impact on imported livestock, but found that the Panel's analysis was incomplete as it did not consider whether this de facto detrimental impact stems exclusively from a legitimate regulatory distinction (in which case it would not violate Article 2.1 of the TBT Agreement). It upheld, although for different reasons, the Panel's finding that the COOL measure is

---

25 See Lukasz Gruszczynski, "Re-tuning Tuna? Appellate Body Report in US – Tuna II", (2012) 3:3 *European Journal of Risk Regulation*, 430–36.

26 *United States – Certain Country of Origin Labelling (COOL) Requirements* (2012) WT/ DS384/ AB/R.

inconsistent with Article 2.1 of the TBT Agreement. It found that the recordkeeping and verification requirements of the COOL measure are such that a large amount of information must be tracked and submitted by upstream producers and processors but much of this is not communicated to consumers and, as such, the detrimental impact on imported livestock does not exclusively derive from a legitimate regulatory distinction and instead constitutes discrimination in violation of Article 2.1. The Appellate Body reversed the Panel's finding that the COOL measure did not fulfill a legitimate objective and, therefore, was inconsistent with Article 2.2 of the TBT Agreement. The Appellate body found that the Panel did not err in concluding that the USA had identified a legitimate objective for the COOL measure. However, as the Panel specified and the Appellate Body confirmed, a regulating state must define its objectives and pursue them in a coherent – not self-contradictory – manner. The objective identified by the USA was to provide consumer information on origin (a legitimate objective as recognized in Article IX of the GATT). The Appellate Body found that the Panel erred in considering that a measure must fulfill its objective completely, or surpass some minimum level of fulfillment, in order to be consistent with Article 2.2, and therefore reversed the Panel's finding that the COOL measure was inconsistent with Article 2.2. However, it was unable to complete the analysis of whether the US measure was more trade restrictive than necessary to fulfill its objective.[27]

Finally, in *EC – Seal Products*,[28] which will be considered in greater detail in the following chapter, Norway and Canada argued that the EC seal regulatory regime, which prohibits the importation and sale of processed and unprocessed seal products, affords privileged access to seal products originating in the EC and certain third countries. Norway argued that the EC seal regime is inconsistent with various articles of the TBT Agreement, in addition to provisions in the GATT 1994 and the Agreement on Agriculture. The Panel concluded that the EU seal regime is a technical regulation and is inconsistent with Article 2.1 of the TBT Agreement, but rejected the claim under Article 2.2 because it fulfilled a legitimate objective – addressing EU public moral concerns

---

27 See Petros Mavroidis and Kamal Saggi, "What is not so Cool about US – COOL Regulations? A Critical Analysis of the Appellate Body's ruling on US – COOL", (2014) 13:2 *World Trade Review*, 299–320; WTO, "United States – Certain Country of Origin Labelling Requirements", *WTO Dispute Settlement*. Accessed online <http://www.wto. org/english/tratop_e/dispu_e/cases_e/ds384_e.htm>. Accessed 17 September 2014.

28 *European Communities – Measures Prohibiting the Importation and Marketing of Seal Products* (2014) WT/ DS401/AB/R.

over seal welfare flowing from cruelty in harvesting methods – and no alternative measure was demonstrated to make an equivalent or greater contribution to meeting this objective. The Appellate Body, however, reversed the Panel's finding that the EU seal regime was a technical regulation, thereby rendering the Panel's conclusions on Articles 2.1, 2.2, 5.1.2, and 5.2.1 of the TBT Agreement moot. As noted above, a technical regulation must prescribe either characteristics for a group of products or for their related processes and production methods. The Appellate Body's conclusion was based on a reversal of the Panel's finding that the EU seal regime lays down product characteristics. It held that whether a particular seal product can be imported in the EU turns on factors such as the identity of the hunter or purpose of the hunt, which are not characteristics of the product itself. This decision narrows the scope of the TBT Agreement by making clear that not all product-related rules constitute a technical regulation, although the scope of the term technical regulation remains unclear. Notably, the Appellate Body did not rule on whether the EU seal regime lays down "related processes and production methods" within the meaning of Annex 1.1, because this question had not been sufficiently explored by the Panel and the participants.[29]

Finally, a Panel has been composed in response to complaints by Ukraine, the Dominican Republic, Cuba, Indonesia, and Honduras against Australia with regards to its imposition of trademark restrictions and other plain packaging requirements on tobacco products and packaging, intended to make the packaging of cigarettes less appealing to consumers.[30] Complainants argue that Australia's measures are inconsistent with Article 2.1 and 2.2 of the TBT Agreement, as well as Article III:4 of the GATT 1994 and several Articles of the TRIPS Agreement. With regards to Articles 2.1 and 2.2 of the TBT Agreement, complainants argue that the measures are more trade restrictive than necessary to achieve Australia's stated public health objective and that they violate national treatment requirements set out in the TBT Agreement.

---

29 See Rob Howse, Joanna Langille, and Katie Sykes, "Sealing the Deal: the WTO's Appellate Body Report in EC – Seal Products", (2014) 18:2 *American Society of International Law*. Accessed online   <http://www.asil.org/insights/volume/18/issue/12/sealing-deal-wto%E2%80%99s-appell ate-body-report-ec-%E2%80%93-seal-products>. Accessed 17 September 2014.

30 *Australia – Certain Measures Concerning Trademarks and Other Plain Packaging Requirements Applicable to Tobacco Products and Packaging* (Panel composed 5 May 2014) WT/DS434, 435, 441, 458, 467/INTERIM.

13.4 Conclusion

The Appellate Body of the WTO has generally steered a prudent middle course between complete deference to domestic regulatory authorities in setting health and safety standards that may have adverse impacts on international trade and encouraging panels to engage in a complete, *de novo* review of the scientific evidence relied on to justify such standards (acting as a de facto World Science Court).[31] However, with the dramatic growth in imported consumer products, including food products, in many countries over recent years, the fault-lines between consumer and producer (domestic and foreign) interests, and between developing and developed countries are likely to yield a continuing stream of high-profile disputes for resolution by the WTO's Dispute Settlement Body.[32]

---

31 See Michael J. Trebilcock and Julie A. Soloway, "International Trade Policy and Domestic Food Safety Regulation: The Case for Substantial Deference", in Daniel Kennedy and James Southwick (eds), *The Political Economy of International Trade: Essays in Honor of Robert E. Hudec* (Cambridge: Cambridge University Press, 2002).

32 See Coglianese, Finkel, and Zaring, *supra* note 1.

14 Trade policy and the environment

14.1 Introduction

The relationship between trade policy and the environment is one of the most controversial issues on the current trade policy agenda.[1] These issues have been brought into particularly sharp relief by climate change policies currently under consideration in some developed countries that would impose on imports at the border similar burdens, in terms of carbon taxes or emission trading allowances, to those imposed on domestic industries. Two very different classes of claims are made for linking trade policy and environmental concerns.

One class of claim emphasizes the cross-border nature of many environmental problems that entail negative externalities beyond any given jurisdiction. In some cases these concerns implicate the global environmental commons, including the impact of greenhouse gas emissions on climate change; in other cases, shared natural resources or common water or air bodies that straddle the boundaries of more than one jurisdiction. In all these cases, effective environmental regulation ideally requires cooperation amongst all member countries affected by the environmental concern in question. In some cases, trade sanctions, such as a ban on imports, can be seen as a way of enforcing compliance with multilateral environmental agreements (MEAs); in other cases, as inducing non-members to become signatories to such agreements; and in yet other cases, as providing the impetus for the negotiation of such an agreement in the first place.

With this class of claim, it is important to evaluate the likely efficacy of trade sanctions in achieving their intended objective: the empirical evidence suggests that trade sanctions are effective in about one-third of

---

1 See generally, Richard H. Steinberg, "Power and Cooperation in International Environmental Law", in Andrew T. Guzman and Alan O. Sykes (eds), *Research Handbook in International Economic Law* (Cheltenham, UK: Edward Elgar, 2007).

all cases and are likely to be more effective where large countries invoke them against small countries; where policy modifications required are reasonably modest and do not entail full-scale political regime change; and where countries imposing such sanctions and countries targeted by such sanctions generally enjoy workable relationships.[2]

The second class of claim for linking trade policy and environmental concerns is not directly concerned with enhancing environmental protection per se, but levelling the competitive playing field. Here it is argued that it is unfair that firms and workers in countries that have imposed stringent environmental standards should have to bear the burden of these standards through loss of market share to foreign producers who face less stringent standards in their home jurisdictions. In turn, it is argued that it is unfair for countries with lax environmental standards to exert downward pressure, through trade, on the more stringent environmental standards in other countries, hence risking a race to the bottom. This kind of claim often leads to arguments for equalizing regulatory compliance costs through the imposition of restrictions or duties on imports, whether or not these lead to more stringent environmental standards in exporting countries. Since all kinds of costs vary amongst countries, it is not clear why differences in environmental regulatory compliance costs per se, at least in the absence of jurisdictional environmental externalities, warrant special treatment.

While none of the GATT/WTO agreements contain detailed provisions on the relationship between trade policy and the environment, Article XX of the GATT permits countries to adopt measures "necessary to protect human, animal or plant life or health" (Article XX(b)), or "relating to the conservation of exhaustible natural resources if such measures are made effective in conjunction with restrictions on domestic production or consumption" (Article XX(g)), provided that these measures are not applied in a manner which would constitute a means of arbitrary or unjustifiable discrimination, or a disguised restriction on international trade. The Preamble to the Agreement establishing the World Trade Organization refers to "allowing for the optimal use of the world's resources in accordance with the objective of sustainable development, seeking both to protect and preserve

---

2 See Gary C. Hufbauer, Jeffrey J. Schott and Kimberly A. Elliott, *Economic Sanctions Reconsidered: History and Current Policy* (Washington, D.C.: Institute for International Economics, 2nd edn, 1990).

the environment and to enhance the means for doing so in a manner consistent with [members'] respective needs and concerns at different levels of economic development". A number of high profile trade and environment disputes have engaged the formal dispute settlement regime of the GATT/WTO over recent years.

14.2   Overview of GATT/WTO case law

In one of the first cases involving the relationship between trade policy and the environment to come before a GATT Panel, was the *Tuna – Dolphin* case (1991),[3] the USA had imposed an embargo on imports of tuna caught by fishing methods that endangered dolphins. The USA had banned the use of such fishing techniques in the case of its own fishing fleet. Mexico complained that this embargo violated Article XI of the GATT. The GATT Panel upheld Mexico's complaint, finding a violation of Article XI, and rejecting the application of either Article XX(b) or (g), on the grounds that these two exceptions only applied to health, safety or conservation concerns arising within the territorial jurisdiction of the country seeking to justify trade restrictions and could not be invoked with respect to environmental concerns lying outside such jurisdiction. A second *Tuna – Dolphin* case (1994)[4] involved an EU challenge to a secondary embargo in the US legislation aimed at the trans-shipment of dolphin-unfriendly tuna through a third country that had not adopted a primary embargo of its own. In this case, the GATT Panel accepted that a state could justify trade restrictions under Article XX with respect to environmental concerns beyond its territorial limits, but not if the sole environmental impact of such restrictions sought to be achieved would be through inducing other countries to change their policies. According to the Panel, if Article XX were interpreted to permit members to take trade measures so as to force other members to change their policies within their own jurisdictions, including their environmental policies, rights of access to markets would be seriously impaired, as exporting countries may face multiple and conflicting pre-conditions to such access.

In the first post-1995 WTO case implicating trade and environment issues, *Reformulated Gasoline* (1996),[5] Brazil and Venezuela

---

3 *United States – Restrictions on Imports of Tuna* (1991) DS21/R – 39S/155.

4 *United States – Restrictions on Imports of Tuna* (1994) DS29/R.

5 *United States – Standards for Reformulated and Conventional Gasoline* (1996) WT/DS2/R.

challenged requirements in regulations under the US Clean Air Act to reduce pollutants in gasoline on a specified time schedule with a 1990 baseline set on a refinery-specific basis for US refiners, but in the case of foreign refiners set on the basis of the constructed average 1990 US quality baseline. In this case, the Appellate Body emphasized that the appropriate approach to interpreting and applying Article XX was a two-tiered approach pursuant to which, firstly, the measure in question was evaluated for consistency with one or more of the exceptions enumerated in Article XX, and then second, to evaluate whether the measure in question was being applied in such a way as to violate one or more of the conditions in the chapeau. In this case, the Appellate Body found that the measures in question fell within Article XX(g) and XX(b) but were being applied in a way that was unjustifiably discriminatory towards foreign refiners, and rejected arguments by the USA that verification and compliance in the case of foreign refineries with an individual refinery baseline could be administratively burdensome, pointing out that the USA had apparently made no attempt to enter into cooperative arrangements with foreign authorities.

However, the leading WTO Appellate Body decision on the relationship between trade and the environment to date is undoubtedly the *Shrimp – Turtles* case,[6] initially decided in 1998 by the Appellate Body and then subsequently revisited in Article 21.5 Compliance Proceedings in 2002.[7] In this case, several Asian countries complained against a US ban on imports of shrimp from countries that had not adopted a comparable regulatory regime to that in place in the USA, which required shrimp trawlers to install and employ turtle excluder devices (TEDs) when fishing for shrimp in waters where certain rare species of sea turtles, listed on a Schedule to the Convention Against International Trade in Endangered Species (CITES), were known to be present. The USA conceded that the ban was a violation of Article XI but sought to justify it under Article XX(g). In this case, the WTO Panel, contrary to the approach adopted by the Appellate Body in *Reformulated Gasoline*, started with the chapeau to Article XX and found that the kind of measures in question were inconsistent with the purposes of the GATT and WTO Agreements and were likely to destabilize the multilateral trading system by confronting exporters

---

6 *United States – Import Prohibition of Certain Shrimp and Shrimp Products* (1998) WT/DS58/ AB/R.

7 *United States – Import Prohibition of Certain Shrimp and Shrimp Products: Recourse to Article 21.5 of the DSU by Malaysia* (2001) WT/DS58/ AB/RW.

with multiple compliance preconditions for accessing foreign markets. Given this approach, the Panel never reached the exceptions to Article XX.

The Appellate Body overruled the Panel in this respect and re-emphasized the importance of the two-tiered approach that it had adopted in *Reformulated Gasoline*, in which the first line of inquiry is whether the measure in question fits within one of the enumerated exceptions to Article XX. The Appellate Body emphasized that there was no inherent territorial limitation on the scope of the exceptions enumerated in Article XX. The Appellate Body also held that the concept of "exhaustible natural resources" in Article XX(g) was not restricted to minerals and non-reproducible things, but extended to living things, citing various environmental and conservation treaties to this effect. As to the meaning of "relating to" in Article XX(g), the Appellate Body held that the means adopted in the measure in question should be reasonably related to the ends sought to be achieved, hence implying a kind of proportionality test. In addition, Article XX(g) requires that the measures be made effective in conjunction with restrictions on domestic production or consumption, which in this case was a requirement that the USA had clearly satisfied by imposing similar measures on its own fishing fleet.

The Appellate Body then turned to the conditions in the chapeau, whereby measures that are provisionally justified under one of the exceptions to Article XX must not be applied in a manner that would constitute a means of arbitrary or unjustifiable discrimination between countries where the same conditions prevail or a disguised restriction on international trade. The Appellate Body held that these conditions reflected a need to maintain a balance of rights and obligations amongst members so that exceptions did not overwhelm more general obligations, or the reverse. The Appellate Body viewed the conditions in the chapeau as implying a principle of good faith or abuse of rights and the drawing of an "equilibrium line" between when a member may invoke exceptions and when other members may insist on enforcement of obligations owed to them.

In this case, the Appellate Body held that the US measures were being applied in a manner that was unjustifiably discriminatory in that all exporting countries were required to adopt essentially the same policy applied by the USA to its own shrimp trawlers and took no account of the circumstances of members who might be differently situated and might be able to achieve comparable levels of effectiveness to the US requirements through other policies. The Appellate Body was also critical of the USA for failing to engage in serious across-the-board bilateral or multilateral negotiations with all affected countries, despite directions to this effect in the US statute in question. The Appellate Body emphasized that for cross-border environmental issues, a number of recent environmental treaties and declarations had emphasized the importance of avoiding unilateral measures, if possible, and noted that the USA had indeed signed a convention with five countries in Latin America with respect to shrimp exports that provided them with more latitude in various respects as to how to meet US objectives than in the case of the Asian country complainants. Finally, the Appellate Body was also critical of the lack of transparency in the certification processes employed by the US agencies in question where there were no formal opportunities for countries to be heard during the certification process or to be appraised of potential objections to their certification, nor were reasons given for decisions denying certification.

Subsequent to this decision, the USA amended its Guidelines, substituting a requirement for a comparably effective regulatory programme in order to qualify for certification and rendering more transparent the certification process by providing for notification of potential concerns to countries seeking certification and providing them with an opportunity of reply. Despite these changes, Malaysia argued in Article 21.5 compliance proceedings that the USA was still not non-compliant with its GATT/WTO obligations. While the USA had embarked on a series of steps designed to yield consensus on an international agreement with respect to shrimp fishing in the South East Asian region, Malaysia argued that the USA was not only under a duty to negotiate but in fact to conclude an international agreement. The Appellate Body rejected this argument, pointing out that this would give exporting countries a veto over a right of an importing country to invoke trade restrictions that would otherwise fall within one of the Article XX exceptions, and thus negate such exceptions. The Appellate Body accepted that there was evidence of recent good faith efforts by the USA to negotiate an agreement with Southeast Asian countries and that the revised Guidelines were sufficiently flexible to accommodate different policies that would achieve comparable levels of effectiveness with the policies that the USA had imposed on its own fishing trawlers.

In many respects the cumulative effect of the two Appellate Body decisions in *Shrimp – Turtles* (along with its recent decision in *Brazil –*

Tyres,[8] discussed in the previous chapter) is largely to overturn the two earlier GATT Panel decisions in the *Tuna – Dolphin* cases and to establish a more sensitive balance between trade and environmental concerns.

Finally, a recent case, *EC – Seal Products*,[9] concerned a complaint by Norway and Canada that the EU seal regime, which prohibits the importation and sale of processed and unprocessed seal products, while containing certain exceptions for seal products hunted by Inuit or indigenous communities (the IC exception) and seal products hunted for marine resource management (the MRM exception) that, Norway and Canada argued, afford privileged access to seal products originating from the EC and certain third countries (especially Greenland). As discussed in the previous chapter, the Appellate Body determined that the EU seal regime does not constitute a technical regulation within the context of the TBT Agreement. It then upheld the Panel's findings that the EC seal regime is inconsistent with GATT Articles I.1 (Most Favored Nation) and III.4 (National Treatment). These provisions were violated by the EU measures because they impaired the competitive relationship between imports from some countries relative to others, and between foreign and domestically produced like products, thus requiring justification under Article XX.

The Appellate Body considered the Panel's finding that the measure was not justified under GATT Article XX(a) (public morals). Assessing a claim of justification on the basis of Article XX involves a two-tiered analysis.

First, the challenged measure must be determined to address a particular interest specified in a subparagraph of Article XX, with a sufficient nexus between the measure and the protected interest. The Panel identified two objectives of the EC seal regime – addressing public morals concerns relating to the EU public's participation as consumers in the market for products derived from inhumanely killed seals and

---

8 *Brazil – Measures Affecting Imports of Retreaded Tyres*, 3 December (2007) WT/DS332/AB/R (07–5290).

9 See "Appellate Body Reports – *European Communities – Measures Prohibiting the Importation and Marketing of Seal Products*", (June 2014) *WorldTradeLaw.net Dispute Settlement Commentary*; for a detailed review of the issues raised in this case, see Robert Howse and Joanna Langille, "Permitting Pluralism: The Seal Products Dispute and Why the WTO Should Permit Trade Restrictions Justified by Noninstrumental Moral Values", (2012) 37 *Yale Journal of International Law* 367.

addressing public morals concerns relating to the number of inhumanely killed seals – and found these to be necessary to protect public morals, and therefore provisionally justified under Article XX(a).

Moving to the second tier of analysis, an appraisal of the measure under the chapeau of Article XX, the Panel had concluded that the discriminatory impact of the IC and MRM exceptions constituted "arbitrary" or "unjustifiable" discrimination within the meaning of the chapeau. In the appeals and cross-appeals that resulted, Canada and Norway argued that the Panel erred in applying the same test to determine the existence of arbitrary or unjustifiable discrimination under the chapeau of Article XX as it had applied in determining whether the measure was inconsistent with TBT Article 2.1. While the Appellate Body acknowledged that there are important parallels between TBT Article 2.1 and the chapeau of GATT Article XX, it also emphasized significant differences between the two, such as the applicable standards as well as their main function and scope. One of the most important factors in determining arbitrary or unjustifiable discrimination under the chapeau to Article XX is examining whether discrimination can be reconciled with, or is rationally related to, the policy objective. The Appellate Body found that the EU had failed to demonstrate how the discrimination resulting from the manner in which the EU seal regime treats IC hunts, as compared to commercial hunts, is related to the policy objective of addressing EU public moral concerns regarding seal welfare. Moreover, the ambiguities and vagueness of requirements for the IC exception, as well as the broad discretion in applying IC requirements, could allow for instances of abuse. Thus, the Appellate Body held that the EU had not justified the EU seal regime under the chapeau to GATT Article XX(a).

14.3   Trade policy and climate change[10]

As noted at the outset of this chapter, a number of developed countries, including the USA and the EU, are actively considering imposing, on imports of goods, carbon tariffs or emission allowance requirements comparable to those imposed on their own domestic producers of like products. These proposals have already begun to generate intense controversy in international trade circles and are seen by some

---

10 See generally, Andrew Green and Tracey D. Epps, *Reconciling Trade and Climate Change* (Cheltenham: Edward Elgar, 2010).

developing countries, on the one hand, as an attempt to force on them greenhouse gas abatement policies comparable to those in place in developed countries, notwithstanding the fact that developed countries are historically responsible for most of the effects of greenhouse gas emissions on climate change that have occurred to date. Developed countries, on the other hand, are concerned that in the absence of such measures, their domestic measures designed to reduce CO_2 emissions will be negated if this means a loss of market share and jobs to firms in developing countries, such as China and India, who might face less stringent requirements and who are now major CO_2 emitters. Moreover, developed countries' governments are concerned that their own firms may simply relocate to countries with less stringent regimes, not only negating the abatement objectives of the climate change policies adopted by developed countries (carbon migration), but sacrificing domestic jobs and investment in the process.[11]

While assessing the compatibility of carbon tariffs and like measures with members' GATT/WTO obligations, a number of complex issues are raised, which are in part a function of the particular design features of the measures in question, certain provisions in the GATT are likely to assume central importance.[12] First, Article II:2 provides that "Members are free to impose at any time on the importation of any product a charge equivalent to an internal tax imposed consistently with provisions of paragraph 2 of Article III in respect of the like domestic product or in respect of an article from which the imported product has been manufactured or produced in whole or in part". A report of the GATT Working Party on Border Tax Adjustments in 1970 sought to clarify the scope of this provision, pointing out that it was largely limited to indirect taxes such as excise taxes, sales taxes, value-added taxes, and not direct taxes, such as income taxes or payroll taxes. In general, Article II:2 has been applied to various kinds of

---

11 See Michael Trebilcock, *Dealing with Losers: The Political Economy of Policy Transitions* (Oxford: Oxford University Press, 2014), chapter 8.

12 See Paul-Erik Veel, "Carbon Tariffs and the WTO: An Evaluation of Feasible Policies", (2009) 12:3 *Journal of International Economic Law* 749; Zhong Xiang Zhang, "The US Proposed Carbon Tariffs, WTO Scrutiny and China's Responses", in Raimund Bleischwitz, Paul Welfens and Zhong Xiang Zhang (eds), *International Economics of Resource Efficiency* (Heidelberg: Physica-Verlag HD, 2011), chapter 7; Steven Nathaniel Zane, "Leveling the Playing Field: the International Legality of Carbon Tariffs in the EU", (2011) 34 *B.C. International and Competition Law Review*, 199; Warren Maruyama, "Climate Change and the WTO: Cap and Trade versus Carbon Tax", (2011) 45:4 *Journal of World Trade*, 679–726; Henrik Horn and Petros Mavroidis, "To B(TA) or Not to B(TA)? On the Legality and Desirability of Border Tax Adjustments from a Trade Perspective", (2011) *The World Economy*, 1911–37.

consumption taxes, which are often waived or rebated by exporting countries, and imposed by importing countries, thus avoiding double taxation of imports. As to whether measures equivalent to carbon tariffs would also fall within the scope of Article II:2, in part, turns on whether the tariff or other charge can be viewed as imposed in respect of either the imported product or an article from which the imported product was manufactured, rather than CO_2 emissions generated in the course of its production. Even if permitted, Article II:2 requires that the requirements of Article III.2 of the GATT be satisfied, which embodies the National Treatment Principle as applied to internal taxes, and prohibits charging taxes on imported products in excess of, or dissimilar to, taxes imposed on domestic like products. This non-discrimination requirement implies that any attempt to impose carbon tariffs or similar charges at the border is likely to be closely scrutinized in dispute-settlement proceedings in terms of whether, as designed and applied, it has a differential impact on imports.

Even if carbon tariffs or similar measures are unable to satisfy the terms of Article II.2, or violate other provisions of the GATT, for example Article I (Most Favoured Nation) or Article XI (Quantitative Restrictions), the country imposing such measures is likely to seek to justify these measures under Article XX, especially Articles XX(b) and XX(g). It seems likely that such measures can be justified as falling within the scope of one or both of these exceptions, but ensuring that such measures satisfy all the conditions in the chapeau may be more challenging, particularly if some foreign exporting countries are exempted from the measures, while attempts are made to differentiate the burdens imposed on remaining exporting countries reflecting relative abatement efforts undertaken in these countries. These differentiated burdens presumably will require justification so as to avoid characterization as arbitrary or unjustifiable forms of discrimination or disguised restrictions on trade.

Government subsidies to promote renewable energy production or to offset costs of retooling conventional production processes to reduce carbon emissions may fall within the ambit of the SCM Agreement (reviewed in Chapter 7), which notably does not contain any equivalent provision to Article XX of the GATT. This was a key issue in a recent case, *Canada – Feed-in Tariffs*,[13] which dealt with an Ontario feed-in tariff (FIT) programme. The *Green Energy and Economy Act*

---

13 *Canada – Measures Relating to the Feed-in Tariff Program* (2013) WT/DS426/AB/R.

established a FIT programme that allowed certain renewable energy producers to lock into fixed-price, long-term electricity purchase contracts at premium rates in exchange for feeding into the grid, with the aim of encouraging renewable energy production and investment. However, the FIT programme conditioned eligibility on the use of locally produced materials; Japan, the USA and the EU argued that, due to these local content requirements, the FIT programme constituted a subsidy that was inconsistent with the SCM Agreement (the complainants also argued that the measure was inconsistent with GATT Article III and Article 2.1 of the TRIMs Agreement). The Appellate Body was unable to complete the analysis of whether the challenged measure constitutes a subsidy under the SCM Agreement and whether Canada acted inconsistently with Articles 3.1(b) and 3.2 of that Agreement due to incomplete evidence before the Panel, while finding a violation of the TRIMS Agreement and the National Treatment provisions of the GATT. Government procurement policies relating to the construction of renewable energy facilities, especially local sourcing requirements, are also likely to be reviewable under the Government Procurement Agreement for member states that are signatories to this Agreement (or regional agreements, such as the government procurement provisions of NAFTA).

Plurilateral negotiations on the liberalization of trade in green goods have been launched at the WTO, based on an agreement between a subset of WTO members, with the aim of making access to clean energy technologies cheaper and easier. Negotiations will draw from a concrete list of green products devised by Asia-Pacific Economic Cooperation (APEC), a 21-country economic and trade group including Canada and the USA, as a starting point. Significant challenges will need to be overcome in order to reach a deal – for example, addressing non-tariff barriers such as standards and configuring an approach to "dual use" products (those that can be used for green and non-green purposes).[14]

---

14 Robert Howse, "Obama's Free-Trade Green Plan has a Chance of Breaking WTO Inertia", (27 June 2013) *The Globe and Mail*. Online: http://www.theglobeandmail.com/report-on-business/economy/economy-lab/obamas-free-trade-green-plan-has-a-chance-of-breaking-wto-inertia/article12870243/. Accessed 14 July 2014; Robert Howse, "Launching the WTO Plurilateral Green Goods Negotiations Next Week", (5 July 2014), *International Economic Law and Policy Blog*, Online: http://worldtradelaw.typepad.com/ielpblog/2014/07/launching-the-wto-plurilateral-green-goods-negotiations-next-week.html?utm_source=feedburner&utm_medium=feed&utm_campaign=Feed%3A +ielpblog+(International+Economic+Law+and+Policy+Blog). Accessed 14 July 2014.

15 Trade policy, labour standards and human rights

15.1 Introduction

The idea of using international labour standards to protect workers from economic exploitation was first promoted by individual social reformers in the first half of the nineteenth century in the early stages of the Industrial Revolution. The work of these reformers was taken over by various non-governmental organizations, including various international organizations (in particular, international associations of trade unions) in the second half of the nineteenth century. Inter-governmental actions to promote international labour standards began to be reflected in international conferences beginning in 1890 and culminated in the establishment of the International Labour Organization (ILO) by the Treaty of Versailles in 1919. The ILO, a tripartite organization of government, employer and worker representatives, has mostly pursued its mandate by setting minimum international standards through Conventions and Recommendations, subject in the former case to ratification by member states and promoted by investigation, public reporting and technical assistance, but not formal sanctions. In 1998, the ILO adopted the Declaration of Fundamental Principles and Rights at Work providing that all members have an obligation to respect and promote certain core labour standards (CLS): 1) freedom of association and the right to engage in collective bargaining; 2) the elimination of forced labour; 3) the elimination of child labour; and 4) the elimination of discrimination in employment. This Declaration parallels, in many respects, references to core international labour standards in the UN Universal Declaration of Human Rights (1948), the UN Covenant on Civil and Political Rights, and the UN Covenant on Economic, Social and Cultural Rights that came into force in 1976.[1]

---

[1] See more generally, Michael J. Trebilcock and Robert Howse, "Trade Policy and Labour Standards", (2005) 14:2 *Minnesota J. of Global Trade* 261; Christian Barry and Sanjay G. Reddy, *International Trade and Labor Standards: A Proposal for Linkage* (New York: Columbia University Press, 2008).

The 1948 Havana Charter that was intended to embody the framework for a new world trading system also declared that "members recognize that unfair labour conditions, particularly in production for export, create difficulties in international trade and accordingly each member shall take whatever action may be appropriate and feasible to eliminate such conditions within its territory". However, the Havana Charter was never adopted because of opposition in the US Congress, so that the GATT that emerged in 1947 contains few references to labour standards. The Ministerial Declaration following the first WTO Ministerial Conference in Singapore in 1996 appears to have removed labour issues from the WTO agenda and remitted them to the ILO. The 2001 Doha Ministerial Declaration reaffirms this position.

As noted in Chapter 4, over the past 20 years there has been a dramatic increase in the number of preferential trade agreements in force. An increasing percentage of these (currently around 30 per cent) contain explicit provisions on labour standards – typically commitments by signatories to enforce effectively their current labour laws or, more expansively, to respect core labour standards of the kind articulated by the ILO in its 1998 Declaration of Fundamental Principles and Rights at Work.[2] Regional and bilateral trade agreements such as NAFTA, the US – Jordan Free Trade Agreement, and the US – Cambodia Free Trade Agreement require signatories to effectively enforce their own labour standards and to strive towards improving and enhancing their existing labour standards. In the case of NAFTA, failure to enforce existing labour standards may lead to formal complaints and determinations by dispute-settlement panels of violations resulting in fines against the offending country which, in the case of the USA and Mexico, can be enforced by trade sanctions and in the case of Canada by direct enforcement of the penalty in Canadian courts. These fines are payable to the offending country on condition that they be devoted to enhancing labour standards. Beyond these regional trade agreements, a number of developed countries, most notably the USA and the EU membership, have often conditioned the granting of preferences to developing countries under their Generalized System of Preference (GSP) programmes on conformity with international

---

2 See Christian Ebert and Anne Posthuma, *Labour Provisions and Agreements: Current Trends and Perspectives* (Geneva, Switzerland: International Labour Organization, 2010); Michael Trebilcock, Robert Howse, and Antonia Eliason, *The Regulation of International Trade*, 4th edition (London: Routledge, 2013), pp. 740–42.

labour standards. In the case of the EU, accession negotiations with prospective member states have often entailed insistence on adherence to core labour standards and basic human rights more generally.[3]

15.2   Rationales for a trade policy–labour standards– human rights linkage

Several rationales for such a linkage have often been advanced. First, it is argued that it is unfair for firms and workers in developed countries to have to compete with firms and workers in developing countries where labour standards and labour costs are much lower, and hence risk losing market share and jobs to these countries. Second, it is argued that this form of competition may lead to a race to the bottom, where countries will be induced to ratchet down their labour standards to the lowest common denominator, but at the end of this process of destructive competition, end up with similar market shares (a form of Prisoner's Dilemma or collective action problem). Third, it is often argued that core labour standards should be conceived of as basic human rights as reflected in the UN Universal Declaration of Human Rights and the UN Covenants on Civil and Political Rights and Economic, Social and Cultural Rights.

The first two rationales for a trade policy–labour standards linkage are problematic, in that they focus on social welfare in importing countries, rather than on social welfare in exporting countries where the allegedly low labour standards prevail. Moreover, objecting to this form of competition carries a serious risk of depriving developing countries of one of their major sources of comparative advantage, that is, low labour costs. However, in this respect, it is important to note that labour costs and labour productivity are closely correlated and, in the case of developing countries, reflect the absence or low quality of many complementary factors of production, such as infrastructure, education and training, managerial expertise, and health care policies. Thus, it would be a mistake to assume that international trade, or foreign direct investment, is mostly driven by differences in labour costs and standards – indeed, international trade and foreign direct investment flows have typically been dominated by North–North rather than North–South relationships.

---

3 See Michael J. Trebilcock and Ronald Daniels, *Rule of Law Reform and Development: Charting the Fragile Path of Progress* (Cheltenham: Edward Elgar, 2008), chapter 10.

With respect to the third rationale for a trade policy–labour standards linkage, the focus is squarely on social welfare considerations in exporting countries, rather than importing countries, and seems an entirely cogent basis for collective global action to ensure that core labour standards in all countries, conceived of as universal human rights, and other international human rights are respected. Basic universal human rights, while defying precise definition, have increasingly come to be viewed as a fundamental element of customary international law (*Jus Cogens*), and to the extent that they extend beyond particular treaty obligations, are viewed as obligations *Erga Omnes* which are owed to the international community at large and hence are enforceable by all members of that community.

This said, the precise content of several of the core labour standards (and indeed the scope of international human rights more generally) is subject to debate. In the case of labour standards, what forms of child labour are unacceptable; what limits on collective bargaining and the right to strike are acceptable? In addition, adopting a human rights perspective on core labour standards, the trade policy–labour standards linkage is problematic to the extent that it is triggered by the importation of goods from countries where these goods are produced in violation of core labour standards. Many violations of core labour standards occur in non-traded goods sectors (for example, the use of child labour) and hence are likely to escape the reach of trade sanctions by importing countries. Also, conditioning the imposition of such sanctions on the importation of goods produced in circumstances that reflect non-compliance with core labour standards risks protectionist abuse of such sanctions by importing countries, rather than an exclusive focus on the effect of inadequate labour standards on the welfare of citizens in exporting countries. Finally, there is no defensible case for privileging core labour standards over other basic international human rights such as freedom from genocide, torture, arbitrary arrest or detention without trial, or racial or gender discrimination – to do so risks eliding protectionist rationales for a trade policy–labour rights linkage with human rights rationales that are much more congruent with normative conceptions of development.[4]

---

4 See generally Amartya Sen, *Development as Freedom* (New York: Knopf, 1999).

15.3   Choice of instrument

15.3.1   The enforceability of ILO conventions

As noted above, the ILO has not historically invoked formal sanctions for violations of its Conventions, although Article 33 of the ILO Constitution can be interpreted as embracing trade sanctions in some circumstances. Critics of the ILO argue that it has been largely ineffective in ensuring adherence to its Conventions, although defenders of the ILO point out that, as a tripartite organization, attaching trade sanctions to violations of its Conventions may destabilize the organization and induce some countries to withdraw from membership or, alternatively, decline to ratify Conventions that may attract trade sanctions for breach.

15.3.2   Soft law options

A prominent class of soft instruments that has emerged in recent years entails a range of certification, labelling and voluntary code-of-conduct mechanisms that purport to identify firms or products that conform to core international labour standards and to promote corporate social responsibility. The efficacy of these mechanisms turns largely on market reactions to the signals that they entail, principally by consumers in importing countries, and to a lesser extent by investors. "Soft" or voluntary approaches suffer from a number of limitations. Currently, they apply to a small percentage of exports in a number of sectors where non-compliance with core labour standards is thought to be common, and they vary widely in various dimensions, including: 1) which core labour standards are recognized; 2) how these core labour standards are defined, if at all; and 3) how effectively adherence to these standards is monitored, if at all. Moreover, their efficacy largely turns on how consumers, and possibly investors, are likely to react to the information conveyed by these mechanisms. In this respect, the voluntary and decentralized nature of the soft law mechanisms currently employed in this context does little to mitigate the information problems faced by consumers (and investors) in importing countries. Moreover, these mechanisms do not address collective action problems confronting consumers in importing countries who may be prepared to pay a premium for goods produced in conditions that meet core labour standards but will be concerned that other consumers who share their concerns may opportunistically purchase lower-priced goods, relying on other consumers to bear the financial costs of vin-

dicating their collective preferences. However, if every consumer sus-
pects every other consumer of being likely to behave opportunistically,
that is, to free-ride on their sacrifices, an effective voluntary collective
response may not emerge. Finally, because these mechanisms largely
turn on potential consumer responses in importing countries, they are
not responsive to abuses of core labour standards or other violations of
basic human rights in non-traded goods sectors.

15.3.3   Carrots

As noted above, various developed countries have often conditioned
GSP preferences, or additional margins of preference, on adherence
by developing countries with core labour standards, or other human
rights, and there appears to be some evidence that these inducements,
at least in some cases, have had positive effects on labour standards
and their enforcement in developing countries, although carrots
sometimes have the perverse effect of rewarding non-compliance.[5]
Differentiation amongst recipient countries must, however, satisfy
the somewhat ambiguous constraints enunciated in the WTO's *EC –
Tariff Preferences* case (2004), discussed in the next chapter.[6]

15.3.4   Sticks

Trade sanctions, for example in the form of bans on imports of goods
produced in circumstances that violate core labour standards or other
international human rights, have sometimes been invoked. While
the efficacy of trade sanctions in changing offending behaviour has a
mixed record, this record must be compared to other responses, from
diplomatic protest notes, on the one hand, to military intervention on
the other, which also exhibit mixed records of efficacy. Trade sanctions
raise difficult questions under the GATT/WTO system as it currently
exists. For example, conditioning MFN treatment on adherence to core
labour standards is likely to raise questions as to whether this form of
conditionality violates the requirement of "unconditional" extension
of MFN treatment to all GATT/WTO members under Article I of the
GATT. Existing case law would appear to rule out conditionality tied

---

5 Lance Compa and Jeffrey Vogt, "Labour Regulation and Trade: Labour Rights and the Generalized
System of Preferences: A 20-Year Review", (2001) 22 *Comparative Labour Law and Policy Journal*
199; Howard Chang, "Carrots, Sticks, and International Externalities", (1997) 17 *International
Review of Law and Economics* 309.

6 *European Communities – Conditions for Granting of Preferences to Developing Countries*, 20
September 2004, WT/DS246/R [EC – Tariff Preferences 2004]; (2004) WT/DS246/AB/R.

to country of origin, but perhaps not other forms of conditionality that are not country-of-origin specific. Similarly, under Article III of the GATT (National Treatment), complex issues are likely to arise as to whether goods produced in exporting countries in circumstances that do not conform to core labour standards are "like" products produced in importing countries that conform to these standards. Moreover, a ban on offending imports may well trigger Article XI of the GATT (Quantitative Restrictions).

In the event that trade sanctions in these circumstances are held to violate Article I, Article III or Article XI, an importing country would be required to justify these measures under Article XX, which for the most part is silent on labour standards, although a cogent argument can be made that the "public morals" exception under Article XX(a), interpreted in a dynamic way, should be viewed as embracing the body of core international labour standards and universal human rights more generally that has evolved in the post-war period. A recent decision by a WTO panel and the Appellate Body in the *Online Gambling* case (2004),[7] in interpreting the public morals–public order exception in Article XIV of GATS, which is analogous to the "public morals" exception in Article XX(a) of the GATT, lends some support for this view.

15.3.5   Choice of institutional regime

It is far from clear that the WTO, as an international trade organization, can credibly and legitimately serve as the central international institutional locus for resolving concerns over core labour standards or universal human rights more generally. In the case of gross violations of universal human rights, such as genocide, apartheid, torture, and detention without trial, specialized UN organs, including the Security Council in the most egregious cases, and UN Committees on Human Rights, are a more credible locus of institutional responsibility. Similarly, in the case of violations of core labour standards, the ILO clearly has much more expertise and legitimacy than the WTO. These issues of institutional competence and legitimacy would appear to require creative forms of horizontal coordination or linkage between the WTO and other international organizations, particularly in the WTO's dispute-settlement role. For example, where trade sanctions

7 *United States – Measures Affecting the Cross-Border Supply of Gambling and Betting Services* (2004) WT/DS285/R; US – Gambling (2005) WT/DS285/AB/R.

have been invoked against imports from foreign countries for failure to observe core labour standards or other universal human rights, and these sanctions have been challenged before the WTO Dispute Settlement Body by exporting countries, it would seem appropriate that the WTO Dispute Settlement Body seek opinions from other international organizations whose mandates squarely embrace these issues about whether systematic violations of core labour standards or universal human rights have occurred or are occurring, leaving the WTO dispute-settlement system to address the proportionality of the proposed sanctions relative to the severity and persistence of the abuses in question and to screen out arbitrary or unjustifiable forms of discrimination or disguised restrictions on trade under the conditions in the chapeau to Article XX.

16 Trade policy and developing countries

16.1 Introduction

There are four main sources of external revenue for developing countries: exports, FDI, foreign aid, and remittances. Developing country merchandise exports have risen from $599 billion in 1980 to almost $5 trillion in 2009. Over this period, developing countries' share of world merchandise exports rose from about 29 per cent to 39 per cent (however, this increased relative share of world merchandise exports was largely attributable to China).[1] In 2008, foreign direct investment flows to developing countries reached almost $520 billion,[2] and official development assistance flows (foreign aid) about US $130 billion[3] (with about another $30 billion from NGOs).[4] Remittances from emigrants from developing countries to relatives and friends in their home countries are currently running at about $400 billion per year. Thus, export earnings are by far the most important source of external revenues for developing countries, followed by FDI and remittances; in comparison, the volume of foreign aid is much smaller. International trade is therefore of critical importance to developing countries. However, many developing countries face special challenges in competing in an increasingly global economy, leading to early recognition by GATT members that various dispensations were justified in accommodating their needs within the multilateral trading system. These dispensations permit greater scope for restricting imports to

---

1 United Nations Conference on Trade and Development, UNCTAD *Handbook of Statistics* (Geneva, Switzerland: United Nations, 2010).

2 UNCTAD, "Assessing the impact of the current financial and economic crisis on global FDI flows", 19 January 2009, available at http://unctad.org/en/Docs/webdiaeia20091_en.pdf. Accessed 21 September 2014.

3 Jennifer Paul and Marcus Pistor, "Official Development Assistance Spending", 13 May 2009, Parliamentary Information and Research Service Library of Parliament. Available at http://www.parl.gc.ca/Content/LOP/researchpublications/prb0710-e.htm. Accessed 21 September 2014.

4 Roger C. Riddell, *Does Foreign Aid Really Work?* (Oxford: Oxford University Press, 2007) at 259, 317.

promote infant industries or to address balance of payments problems and as a necessary corollary contemplate non-reciprocal trade concessions by developed countries with respect to products of actual or potential export interest to developing countries (often referred to as "special and differential treatment").

16.1.1   Special and differential treatment

Developing countries played a peripheral role in the formation of the GATT. However, they now dominate numerically the membership of the WTO. A key challenge facing the WTO is how to better integrate developing countries into the multilateral trading system.[5]

Article XVIII of the GATT (in the form that emerged after a review of the Agreement in 1954–55) contains detailed provisions regarding developing country members. In large part, these provisions granted developing country members exemptions from their GATT commitments in order to "grant the tariff protection required for the establishment of a particular industry", that is, to promote specific domestic industries through import substitution policies, and to restrict imports in order to address balance of payment difficulties. In 1965, Part IV of the GATT, entitled "Trade and Development" was added. Unlike Article XVIII, which focuses on permitting developing country protectionism, Part IV focuses on expanding developing country access to developed country export markets. The key principle of Part IV was "special and differential treatment", under which developed countries were urged to make tariff concessions to developing countries on a non-reciprocal basis. However, most of the commitments in Part IV are merely hortatory and non-binding on developed country members.

The most substantive measures taken in the GATT to address the plight of developing countries were two waivers adopted in 1971. One waiver provided an exception to the MFN obligation in order to allow developed countries to grant preferential tariff treatment to developing countries (known as the Generalized System of Preferences (GSP)). The second waiver to the MFN principle permitted developing countries to exchange such preferences amongst themselves. These waivers were formalized as a permanent part of the GATT in 1979 through an

---

5 For a history of developing countries in the GATT system, see Robert E. Hudec, *Developing Countries in the GATT Legal System* (London: Gower, 1987).

instrument known as the Enabling Clause.[6] Article 1 authorizes preferential tariff reductions toward developing countries on a "generalized, non-reciprocal and non-discriminatory" basis, providing that notwithstanding the MFN obligation, "contracting parties may accord differential and more favorable treatment to developing countries, without according such treatment to other contracting parties". Under Article 5, such preferential treatment is non-reciprocal: "The developed countries do not expect reciprocity for commitments made by them in trade negotiations to reduce or remove tariffs and other barriers to the trade of developing countries . . .". Article 5 is also authority for "special and differential treatment" for developing countries, providing that in the course of multilateral trade negotiations, developing countries shall not be required to make "concessions that are inconsistent with [their] development, financial, and trade needs". Article 7 is known as the "graduation clause", which envisions that as developing countries' "capacity to make contributions or negotiated concessions" increases along with their economic development, they are expected to "participate more fully in the framework of rights and obligations under the [GATT]".

Many developed countries have adopted GSP programmes which extend preferential terms of trade to developing countries.[7] However, these GSP tariffs usually entail escape clause provisions in the event of import surges, and have often not been extended to politically sensitive items such as textiles, clothing, and footwear, even though such items are often of major export interest to many developing countries. Furthermore, as MFN tariff rates have continued to decline since the inception of the GSP in the 1970s, the margin of preference between MFN rates and GSP rates has contracted.

Major issues pertaining to the administration of the GSP system arose in the *EC – Tariff Preferences* (2004),[8] where India complained that additional tariff preferences were being offered by the EC, beyond base-

---

6 GATT Contracting Parties Decision of November 28, 1979 on Differential and More Favourable Treatment, Reciprocity and Fuller Participation on Developing Countries (Enabling Clause).

7 Some examples of US legislation include the Caribbean Basin Trade Partnership Act, the Africa Growth and Opportunity Act, the Andean Trade Preferences Act. The EU's Cotonou Agreement extends tariff preferences to a wide range of developing countries. See Mitsuo Matsushita, Thomas Schoenbaum and Petros Mavroidis, *The World Trade Organization: Law, Practice and Policy* (Oxford: Oxford University Press, 2003) at 384.

8 *European Communities – Conditions for Granting of Preferences to Developing Countries*, 20 September 2004, WT/DS246/R [EC – Tariff Preferences 2004]; (2004) WT/DS246/AB/R.

line GSP preferences, to a sub-set of developing countries that agreed to certain conditions pertaining to labour standards, environmental standards, and the war on drugs. In the event, India chose to focus only on the last of these three conditions (drug trafficking), where additional preferences were extended to a closed list of 12 countries, without any articulated criteria or any opportunity for other countries to qualify, short of a change in the relevant EC regulation. India argued that this violated both the unconditionality requirement of Article I of the GATT, and the non-discrimination requirement in the 1979 Enabling Clause. The WTO Panel upheld India's complaints on both grounds. On appeal, the Appellate Body focused only on the terms of the Enabling Clause and held that nondiscriminatory treatment did not require extension of GSP preferences to all developing countries without differentiation, but only to developing countries similarly situated in terms of stages of development and financial and economic needs. Thus, developed countries could discriminate amongst developing countries on this basis, although the Appellate Body held that the European Communities' programme of additional preferences for some developing countries with particular drug trafficking problems, by virtue of its closed list nature and the absence of articulated qualifying criteria, violated this condition.

Most GATT/WTO agreements contain other forms of "special and differential treatment", entailing less onerous obligations and longer phase-in periods for developing countries. The following is a brief overview of the provisions for special and differential treatment in some GATT/WTO agreements.

16.1.2   SCM Agreement

Under Article 27.1 of the SCM Agreement, members recognize that subsidies may play an important role in the economic development programmes of developing country members. Thus, Article 27 provides certain exemptions from the SCM Agreement for developing countries. Under Articles 27.2 and 27.3, the prohibitions in Article 3 on export subsidies and subsidies contingent on the use of domestic inputs do not apply to least-developed countries, and other developing countries are given a grace period of five to eight years to comply with this prohibition. A further series of provisions appear to be designed to raise the legal standard that must be met in order to bring a successful subsidies complaint against developing countries, thus reducing the possibility of "trade harassment". With respect to actionable subsidies, the dispute resolution process may not be invoked unless the subsidy entails nullification or impairment of GATT concessions or injury to the complaining party's domestic industry (Article 27.9). Countervailing duty actions may not proceed if a domestic agency determines that the overall level of a subsidy granted by a developing country is less than 2 per cent of the per-unit value, or the subsidizing country has less than 4 per cent market share with respect to the subsidized product in the complaining country (Article 27.10).[9]

Despite the special and differential treatment provided for in the SCM Agreement, developed countries are by far the most frequent initiators of countervailing duty claims, and developing countries are the most frequent targets. Out of the 335 countervailing duty initiations filed with the WTO from its inception in 1996 to 31 December 2013, 247 of those were filed by the European Union, United States, and Canada alone. Developing countries and economies in transition were the target of 237 of these initiations.[10]

16.1.3   Government Procurement Agreement

Article V of the GPA provides for special and differential treatment for developing countries. In particular, developing countries may negotiate exclusions from rules on national treatment under the GPA. Developed countries are under an obligation to facilitate increased imports from developing countries, provide government procurement-related technical assistance to developing countries, and respond to reasonable information requests from developing countries in the context of a tendering process.[11]

16.1.4   SPS and TBT Agreements

Both the TBT and SPS Agreements contain provisions regarding technical assistance and longer phase-in periods for developing countries. Article 9 of the SPS Agreement provides that technical assistance, for example assistance in developing national regulatory

---

9   The comparable *de minimis* rule for developed countries is 1 per cent of per-unit value. (SCM Article 11.9).

10   Data source: WTO – CV Initiations: By Reporting Member – 01/01/95 – 31/12/13. Online: http://www.wto.org/english/tratop_e/scm_e/scm_e.htm. Accessed 14 July 2014.

11   Vinod Rege, "Transparency in Government Procurement: Issues of Concern and Interest to Developing Countries", (2001) 35:4 *Journal of World Trade* at 497.

agencies, will be given to developing countries in order to allow them to achieve the appropriate level of sanitary or phytosanitary protection in their export markets. Article 10.2 of the SPS Agreement states that where developed countries introduce new SPS regulations and there is a phase-in period, longer compliance time-frames should be accorded to products of export interest to developing countries. Developing country members are also accorded the possibility of time-limited exceptions in whole or in part from obligations under this Agreement, taking into account their financial, trade, and development needs.

Article 11.8 of the TBT Agreement gives priority to the technical assistance needs of developing countries. Article 12.3 states that technical regulations, standards, and conformity assessment procedures of developed country members should take account of the needs of developing country members, with a view to ensuring that such technical regulations, standards, and conformity assessment procedures do not create unnecessary obstacles to exports from developing country members.

16.1.5   TRIPS Agreement

Developing countries are entitled to a one year delay in implementing the Agreement and a further four year delay upon application to the TRIPS Council. A further five year delay applies where a particular area of technology is currently unprotectable under the domestic law of a developing country. Least-developed countries are exempted entirely from the Agreement for ten years (extended to 2016 in the case of pharmaceutical patent protection by the Doha Declaration on Public Health, November 2001).

16.1.6   The Agreement on Textiles and Clothing

The Multi-Fiber Arrangement (MFA), governing trade in textiles and clothing was formally established in 1974, between nine importing developed countries and 31 exporting developing countries. It limits exports by the developing countries to developed countries, through a variety of special safeguard measures, quotas, and voluntary restrictions. The effect of the MFA on developing countries has been severe. It has been estimated that if all trade restrictions on LDC textile and clothing imports were lifted by the EU, Japan and the United States, the gains to LDCs would be no less than 50.8 per cent of total possible gains related to trade.[12] The Uruguay Round Agreement on Textiles and Clothing provides for the gradual removal of the quantitative restrictions provided for under the MFA, but still leaves high tariffs in place on many products and is subject to a special safeguards regime.

16.1.7   Dispute Settlement Understanding

The Dispute Settlement Understanding (DSU) contains various procedural safeguards designed for the benefit of developing country members. Among them are Article 12.10, which grants developing country members additional time in answering a complaint brought against them, and Article 12.11, which requires panels, where one or more of the parties to a dispute is a developing country, to explicitly indicate the form in which account has been taken of relevant provisions on special and differential treatment for developing country members which have been raised by the developing country member in the course of dispute-settlement procedures. Article 8.10 provides that in disputes involving a developing country member and a developed country member, if the developing country member requests, at least one of the panelists must be from a developing country member. Finally, Article 24 requires developed country members to exercise "due restraint" in initiating trade disputes and claims for trade compensation against least-developed country members, and provides for an enhanced mediation process for disputes involving a developing country member before the dispute is referred to a panel.

16.2   Special and differential treatment: an assessment

The two limbs of special and differential treatment (SDT) that are sketched above need to be seen as inherently interrelated. The much greater policy flexibility extended to developing countries on the import side necessarily implies that in securing better access to developed countries' markets for their exports, they cannot be expected to offer reciprocal trade concessions (without undermining their policy flexibility on the import side). Hence the second limb of SDT contemplates non-reciprocal and preferential treatment of exports from developing countries by developed countries. While it was assumed

---

12 Marcelo de Paiva Abreu and Winston Fritsch, "Market Access for Manufactured Exports from Developing Countries: Trends and Prospects", in J. Whalley (ed.), *Developing Countries and the Global Trading System*, vol I. (London: Macmillan, 1989) at 117.

that this combination of policies would substantially enhance the economic prospects of developing countries, this assumption has come under increasingly searching scrutiny in academic research.

16.2.1 Import substitution policies

Extensive dispensations from GATT disciplines (that can be compendiously characterized as infant industry or import substitution rationales for protectionism) were justified on various grounds. First, it was widely argued by many developing countries, and indeed by many mainstream development economists in developed countries and international agencies in the early years of the GATT, that developing countries had often inherited truncated economies from their colonial overseers, where they had been largely restricted economically to the role of "hewers of wood and drawers of water", leaving them with large, traditional and inefficient agricultural sectors where the marginal product of labour was often thought to be negligible or even zero. As with most developed countries earlier in their histories, a major transformation in developing country economies was called for in reallocating resources from traditional agricultural sectors to industrial or manufacturing sectors. To facilitate and encourage this, it was argued that at least temporary protectionism was required for these fledgling manufacturing industries, in order to enable them to achieve minimum efficient scale and become competitive in both domestic and export markets. Second, it was widely argued that infant industry protectionism had been aggressively pursued by many developed countries early in the process of their economic development, including the United States, Canada, Germany, and many other currently developed countries, and that developing countries that found themselves at similar stages of development in their early post-independence histories should not be denied similar policy flexibility. Third, it was often argued that because of low levels of education, poor physical infrastructure, weakly developed financial, credit and insurance markets, and inadequate or nonexistent social safety nets, adjustment costs faced by many developing countries in moving to a fully open international trading regime were likely to prove much more severe than those facing developed countries embarking upon a similar strategy of trade liberalization. Fourth, it was also often argued that, at least for smaller and poorer developing countries, their share of world trade, and in particular imports, was typically so small that protectionist policies on their part were likely to have negligible adverse impacts on world prices in the commodities affected by these policies and hence any terms-of-trade externalities from the pursuit of such policies were likely to be small to nonexistent.

However, much research beginning in the 1960s and increasing through the 1970s has found that import-substitution policies were not achieving their goals and were actually hindering the growth of developing countries.[13] For example, research by Balassa found that protectionist policies had hurt developing countries by encouraging industrialization at the expense of agriculture, worsened income distribution, reduced domestic savings, increased unemployment, and led to a very low rate of capital utilization. Little et al. demonstrated the high and indiscriminate levels of protectionism in many developing countries, and research by Krueger revealed the rise of rent-seeking behaviour and corruption that accompanied highly discretionary protectionist trade policies and related policies such as foreign exchange controls. More recent scholarship has provided further evidence of the positive relationship between trade openness and growth, stemming from gains from improved resource allocation, greater potential to realize economies of scale, improved access to technology, greater domestic competition, and increased domestic savings and foreign direct investment. While measuring trade openness is not unproblematic, these findings are reflected in Table 16.1 from Williamson.[14]

These findings are often reinforced by reference to the trade policies pursued by the so-called East Asian high-growth economies, beginning with Japan in the early post-war years and followed by Hong Kong, Singapore, Taiwan, Korea, Malaysia, Thailand and more recently by Vietnam, Indonesia, China and India, or African countries like Botswana and Mauritius or Latin American countries like Chile. In one respect or another, all these countries have pursued policies of export-led growth, although it must be acknowledged that there is ongoing, and to some extent unresolved, controversy as to the extent

---

13 Writing in 2001, Jeffrey Williamson reports that the World Bank has conducted over 41 studies of developing countries and contrasted the performance of relatively open and relatively closed economies and concluded that trade openness and growth are positively correlated. See Jeffrey G. Williamson, "Winners and Losers over Two Centuries of Globalization", (2002) World Institute for Development Economics Research Annual Lecture (WIDER) at p. 9. Also see Jeffrey D. Sachs and Andrew Warner, "Economic Reform and the Process of Global Integration", (1995) 26:1 Brookings Papers on Economic Activity 1; and David Dollar, "Outward-Oriented Developing Economies Really Do Grow More Rapidly: Evidence from 95 LDCs, 1976–1985", (1992) 40:3 *Economic Development and Cultural Change* 523.

14 Williamson, supra note 13.

Table 16.1 Trade-policy orientation and growth rates in the Third World, 1963–1992

Trade policy orientation	Average annual rates growth of GDP per capita (%)		
	1963–1973	1973–1985	1985–1992
Strongly open to trade	6.9	5.9	6.4
Moderately open	4.9	1.6	2.3
Moderately anti-trade	4.0	1.7	−0.2
Strongly anti-trade	1.6	−0.1	−0.4

Source: Jeffrey G. Williamson, "Winners and Losers over Two Centuries of Globalization", (2002) World Institute for Development Economics Research Annual Lecture (WIDER).

which this export-led growth has been managed by interventionist trade and related policies designed to protect infant industries in their early stages and to support selective export-oriented industries (various versions of so-called strategic trade theory). At the very least, it is true that most of these countries have pursued somewhat idiosyncratic paths to integration with the global economy.[15]

16.2.2 Non-reciprocal market access

As to the second limb of SDT – non-reciprocal trade preferences – much recent research suggests that these preferences have not proved as valuable to developing countries as they had hoped. First, the benefits of the preferences seem to be concentrated on the more advanced developing countries that needed them least. For example, under the US African Growth and Opportunity Act of 2003 just three of the 33 eligible sub-Saharan countries (Nigeria, South Africa, and Gabon) account for 86 per cent for preferential imports under this scheme. Second, GSP market access preferences have tended to become less valuable as margins of preference have been eroded through successive negotiating rounds which reduced MFN tariff levels. Third, preferences are also not durable, since they have often been tied to the level of a country's economic development; countries that are successful

---

15 See Dani Rodrik, "How to Save Globalization from its Cheerleaders", (September 2007) Working Paper 07–038, Kennedy School of Government, Harvard University; see more generally, Rodrik, *One Economy, Many Recipes: Globalization, Institutions and Economic Growth: Democracy and the Future of the World Economy* (Princeton: Princeton University Press, 2007); Rodrik, *The Globalization Paradox* (New York: W.W. Norton & Co., 2011).

in increasing per capita incomes are often graduated out of the programmes. Fourth, donor countries often reserve the right to withdraw preferences if imports became too competitive with domestic products. Fifth, many import-sensitive products of major export interest to developing countries have been excluded from GSP schemes. Sixth, preferences have increasingly been subject to various forms of conditionality such as human and labour rights and environmental standards, and ideological or geo-political factors (such as countries' perceived efforts to combat terrorism). Seventh, complex rules of origin also have often diluted the value of GSP preferences, preventing developing countries from producing goods most efficiently. Eighth, preferences cause trade diversion from non-preference recipient developing countries to the preference recipients. Thus, while preferences may benefit some developing countries in the short term, they are unlikely to benefit developing countries overall and they create inducements to distort comparative advantage, which puts the preference recipients at risk in the long term if and when preferences are withdrawn.[16] Finally, and most importantly, because these preferences are non-reciprocal, developing countries have forsaken significant bargaining leverage in negotiations with developed countries – without a quid there is often a very meager quo. This is simply to acknowledge the *réal politique* of trade negotiations – one has to give in order to get.

Despite these reservations about the past and prospective efficacy of SDT, some prominent and respected commentators continue to defend its continuing vitality and indeed argue for its strengthening and expansion. For example, Nobel laureate Joseph Stiglitz in two recent books[17] argues that the empirical evidence demonstrating the economic benefits of a liberal trading regime for most developing countries is much more ambiguous than conventional academic thinking acknowledges, pointing to the gradualist and sometimes strategic approach to trade liberalization adopted by most of the high-growth

---

16 Gene M. Grossman and Alan O. Sykes, "A Preference for Development: The Law and Economics of GSP", (2005) 4:1 *World Trade Review* 41.

17 Joseph E. Stiglitz and Andrew Charlton, *Fair Trade for All: How Trade Can Promote Development* (Oxford: Oxford University Press, 2005) and Joseph E. Stiglitz, *Making Globalization Work* (New York: W.W. Norton & Co., 2006), chapter 3 (Making Trade Fair). For more radical critiques of conventional economic rationales for free trade, see Roberto M. Unger, *Free Trade Reimagined* (Princeton: Princeton University Press, 2007); Ha-Joon Chang, *Bad Samaritans: the Myth of Free Trade and the Secret History of Capitalism* (New York: Bloomsbury Press, 2008); Eric Reinert, *How Rich Countries Got Rich and Why Poor Countries Stay Poor* (New York: Public Affairs, 2008).

East Asian economies, the relative failure of the so-called Washington consensus to stimulate high and sustainable growth in much of Latin America, and the devastating short-run economic consequences of "shock therapy" in Russia. He argues that even if in the long run an open trading regime is to the benefit of developing countries, the absence of most of the adjustment cushions that exist in developed countries means that many developing countries face relatively more severe adjustment costs from trade liberalization. From these premises, he argues for a radically expanded form of SDT, where countries would be divided into various per capita income tranches and countries in higher income tranches would be required to liberalize all trade with countries in lower income tranches and among themselves, while countries in lower income tranches would only be required to liberalize trade with countries in even lower income tranches and among themselves but not with respect to trade with countries in higher income tranches.

The future scope of special and differential treatment for developing countries has become a major fault line between developing and developed countries in the current Doha Round of multilateral trade negotiations, and in part explains the dramatic proliferation of PTAs in recent years, in many cases between or among developing countries. However, such agreements do not enhance access by developing counties to the economies of large developed countries, while bilateral PTAs between poor developing countries and large developed countries may entail burdensome additional commitments that reflect unequal bargaining power. In the case of large, rapidly growing and highly competitive developing countries, such as China, India, and Brazil, it is difficult to imagine major developed countries, especially in today's global economic environment, being prepared to expand SDT treatment to them, hence implying a need (going forward) to differentiate among developing countries.

In future multilateral negotiations, there is much merit in the position that member countries should agree to provide immediate, unconditional and non-reciprocal duty-free access to their markets for all exports (without exceptions) from the least-developed countries. Developing countries in higher income tranches, in contrast, should follow a different path. It is likely to be in their long-term interests to phase out reliance on SDT and bargain reciprocally for enhanced access to developed countries' markets, albeit with longer transition periods. There is also a need for more gradual reductions in trade barriers, more expansive safeguard protections, and cross-issue bargaining where reductions in developed country trade barriers can be exchanged for not only reductions in developing country trade barriers but also a relaxation of restrictions on foreign direct investment and services. In addition, specialized agreements like TRIPS and TRIMS should in future generally be plurilateral rather than multilateral in nature (as they were prior to the Uruguay Round), leaving more policy flexibility for developing countries on the scope and timing of commitments beyond the general GATT principles.[18]

---

18 See Paul Collier, "Why the WTO is Deadlocked: And What Can Be Done About It", (2006) *The World Economy*, 1423–49; Bernard Hoekman and David Vines, "Multilateral Trade Cooperation: What Next?", (2007) 23:3 *Oxford Review of Economic Policy*, 311–34; Michael Trebilcock, "Between Trade and Development: The Future of the World Trading System", *Journal of World Investment and Trade Law*, (forthcoming).

17 Future challenges for the world trading system

Drawing together a number of the issues that have been discussed in earlier chapters in this book, several themes emerge that pose major challenges to the future of the world trading system.

17.1 Governance of the World Trade Organization

While the one-country one-vote and consensus principles have served the World Trading System well for much of its history, principles that worked well when the GATT/WTO system had a relatively small number of members do not work nearly as well today with a WTO membership of 160 countries in widely varying stages of economic, social, and political development, as reflected in the gridlock in the current Doha Round of multilateral trade negotiations. However, reforming the current decision-making processes of the WTO presents formidable challenges. Moving to a regime of majoritarian or representative decision-making puts large members (such as the USA or the EU) at risk of being out-voted by smaller member countries on important issues and may threaten their commitment to the organization. Conversely, moving to some form of trade-weighted majoritarian decision-making (as in the EU) is likely to marginalize small members and threaten their commitment to the organization. An alternative strategy is to provide much greater scope for plurilateral agreements amongst subsets of members within the WTO ("coalitions of the willing"), with subsequent accession open to other members prepared to make similar commitments (a form of conditional MFN).[1]

---

1 See Michael Trebilcock, "Between Theories of Trade and Development: The Future of the World Trading System", *Journal of World Investment and Trade Law* (forthcoming).

17.2   Multilateralism versus preferential trade agreements

The proliferation of preferential trade agreements (PTAs) while in part, no doubt, reflecting paralysis within the multilateral system, also, in turn, undermines the centrality and vitality of the latter. One general line of response is to blur the boundaries between multilateralism and bilateralism, by providing much greater flexibility within the WTO for plurilateral agreements among sub-sets of members (as noted above), along with an amendment to Article XXIV of the GATT that would permit signatories to preferential trade agreements to designate the WTO dispute settlement body as the dispute settlement body under a PTA, thus promoting coherence and integration of international trade law on similar issues.[2]

17.3   Developing countries in the world trading system

While special and differential treatment for developing countries in the GATT/WTO system has long been a feature of this system, it is far from clear that this special treatment has served many developing countries well, and tends, for the most part, to treat all developing countries – from the least developed to the large and rapidly growing – in much the same way. Compelling arguments can be made for unqualified dispensations to least-developed countries, both with respect to non-reciprocal access for their exports to other countries' markets and for very broad policy flexibility on the import side. However, with respect to other developing countries, their long-term interests are likely to be better served by fuller integration into the GATT/WTO system with relatively few dispensations on either the export or import sides, beyond the case for recognizing special ex ante or ex post safeguard regimes for highly vulnerable, subsistence agricultural sectors.

17.4   Trade and cognate areas of international law

The increasing interface between international trade policy and a variety of cognate areas of international law, such as environmental law, labour law, and human rights law, suggests continuing to cabin

---

2 See Trebilcock, *ibid.*

international trade law as a self-contained body of international law is likely to compromise its credibility and legitimacy with a wide variety of constituencies in the future, and calls for more efforts than have hitherto occurred both at the dispute settlement and negotiating level to integrate international trade law more fully into the general corpus of public international law.

17.5   Contingent protection regimes

Antidumping duties are promiscuously applied by many countries without any coherent economic or other policy rationale, while the safeguard regime (as interpreted by the Appellate Body) is almost impossible to comply with, despite having a more coherent rationale. A major rebalancing of these two regimes is required.

17.6   Trade and agriculture

In breaking the impasse in negotiations over liberalizing international trade in agriculture products, high priority should be assigned to the complete elimination of export subsidies and major liberalization of tariffs and tariff rate quotas with few dispensations except for developing countries with vulnerable traditional subsistence agricultural sectors. Conversely, fewer constraints should be imposed on domestic subsidies once a higher proportion of the costs of these are internalized to the countries providing them (precipitating higher internal levels of political accountability for these expenditures).

17.7   Trade policy and exchange rates

While the rules of international trade law have a fair degree of stability and predictability to them, this stability and predictability is increasingly threatened by misvalued currencies and highly volatile exchange rates (and the risk of currency wars) that impact substantially on trade flows and opportunities. Better management and coordination of exchange rates, through bodies such as the G20 or the IMF, has emerged, in the wake of the recent global financial crisis, as an important complement to an open global trading system, but this challenge is only beginning to be addressed seriously.

17.8   Trade policy and foreign direct investment

International trade and foreign direct investment are in important respects both complements to and substitutes for each other and require some over-arching multilateral framework for their regulation. This is largely non-existent in the case of foreign direct investment, which (rather like the proliferation of PTAs) is increasingly governed by a proliferation of bilateral investment treaties (BITs) containing divergent substantive provisions and forms of dispute settlement. A balanced multilateral agreement on foreign direct investment reflecting the interests and concerns of both capital-exporting and capital-importing countries and developed and developing countries would be an important complement to the GATT/WTO system, which at present largely regulates only international trade in goods and services, and has only peripheral relevance to international movements of foreign direct investment.

Index